SURPRISE

Dawn had not yet come. Th[...]
Colonel Ballard and some o[...]
lines to wait for the prelimi[...]
out of sight of the enemy, the tank gunners loaded their
weapons. Three minutes to go . . .

Somewhere there was the bassoon piping of frogs.

Two minutes . . .

A light scattering of rifle fire rippled along the lines.

One minute . . .

The men who were going to attack waited, their hearts
pounding, their lips dry. Here and there was the click of
a canteen.

Fire!

FOUR STARS OF HELL

Laurence Critchell

"It is fitting that the story of the 501st Parachute Regiment
of the famed 101st Airborne Division should be told by a
parachute captain."
—*The New York Times*

"A personalized record, told in terms of the men of all
ranks, of how they trained and fought and died . . . the
story has an authentic ring."
—*U.S. Quarterly*

"The greatest airborne operation of this or any other war."
—Lewis H. Brereton,
Former Lt. General, First Allied Airborne Army,
World War II

Other War Books from Jove

FOUR STARS OF HELL

LAURENCE CRITCHELL
Captain, Infantry

with a foreword by
LIEUTENANT GENERAL LEWIS BRERETON, U.S.A.

A JOVE BOOK

This Jove book contains the complete
text of the original edition.
It has been completely reset in a typeface
designed for easy reading and was printed
from new film.

FOUR STARS OF HELL

A Jove Book / published by arrangement with
The Battery Press, Inc.

PRINTING HISTORY
Originally published by the Declan X. McMullen Company
Ballantine Books edition / February 1968
Battery Press edition / 1982
Jove edition / February 1987

ISBN: 0-515-08913-3

Jove Books are published by The Berkley Publishing Group,
200 Madison Avenue, New York, NY 10016.
The words ''A JOVE BOOK'' and the stylized ''J'' with sunburst
are trademarks belonging to Jove Publications, Inc.

PRINTED IN THE UNITED STATES OF AMERICA

For those who died

"They died and others lived and nobody knows why it is so.
They died and thereby the rest of us can go on and on."

—ERNIE PYLE

Author's Note

The individual accounts in this narrative were based on interviews with the soldiers and officers concerned. Tom Rice, Val Suarez and Davis Hart were chosen at random from among the regimental personnel, but the remainder were selected because they were best able to tell a clear story of what had happened. In some cases only the last names were available; in other cases the soldier's name was deliberately omitted.

Although I had to use my own judgment in deciding which actions to minimize and which to give in detail, I did my best to maintain historical accuracy. Whenever the individual stories differ from the official War Department records, as in the case of Colonel Johnson's seizure of the La Barquette locks, there is a weight of eyewitness testimony to support the account.

There is really only one way to look at war, and that is through the eyes of the men who fought it. You gain little by going to the high peaks where the plans are made, where regiments of men are only blocks of fire power; you gain little except that sense of absolute power which, as Lord Acton said, absolutely corrupts. It is better to stay down where your fellow men stayed, close to the earth and the terror. For the truth of war is there, among solitary human beings who have no possessions except their lives.

LAURENCE CRITCHELL

France—Germany—Austria—United States
1945–1947

Acknowledgments

Acknowledgment is gratefully made to the following:

Colonel S. L. A. Marshall, Historian of the European Theater of Operations, for allowing the writer access to the European Theater records while they were at St. Germaine, France

Historical Division of the War Department Special Staff, for access to yet unpublished historical studies of the European operations

Corporal John Robins, for the preparation of the maps

The Atlantic Monthly Company, for permission to reprint "Come You Home a Hero" by Laurence Critchell, copyright 1945 by The Atlantic Monthly Company

Lieutenant General Lewis H. Brereton, for permission to use passages from *The Brereton Diaries,* published 1946 by William Morrow and Company, Inc.

Kenneth S. Davis, for permission to use passages from *Soldier of Democracy*, published 1945 by Doubleday Doran & Company, Inc.

Henry Holt and Company, for permission to quote from *Here is Your War* by Ernie Pyle, copyright 1943 by Henry Holt and Company, Inc.

The Infantry Journal Press, for permission to quote from *Bastogne—The First Eight Days* by Colonel S. L. A. Marshall

Time, Inc., for permission to reprint from LIFE "The Incredible Patrol" by Corporal Russ Engel of the 101st Airborne Division

Foreword

When I took command of the 1st Allied Airborne Army, I did so reluctantly. General Eisenhower's personal request came at a time when the effects of the long-range strategic bombing of German industrial resources and lines of communication were being felt for the first time by the ground forces. The close cooperation of the tactical air forces and the armies had welded a weapon that had breached the wall of *Festung Europa*. My old organization was the 9th Air Force; the big break-through was on and, needless to say, I was eager to see it through. We were all sure, in the midsummer of 1944, that Germany would soon collapse.

When I assumed my new command I knew what every airborne trooper knew: that airborne strategy still was in the experimental stage. What had been exploited first by the Germans at Eben Emael and Cyprus had been developed by the Allies on an unprecedented scale and was being field-tested in the brutal laboratory of war itself. There was no other way to test it. With the formation of the 1st Allied Airborne Army, the supreme commander possessed a weapon for which there were no textbooks and no classroom strategy. Its use was a matter of judgment. There was nothing to go on except the just-past experiences in the Normandy invasion, Africa, Sicily and the Pacific.

My new command was at once a serious responsibility and a unique adventure. In a very short time I was deeply involved. While the Germans were still in disorganized retreat to the north and east after the break-through at Avranches, we worked to devise a plan that would force them into a rout and bring a quick end to the war. This was the purpose of the Holland campaign. Later, at Wessels, our units formed the assault wave of what became the north salient of the Ruhr encirclement, and our earliest hopes were realized.

The credit for our success as an organization belongs to the divisions, regiments and battalions that did the actual fighting. Their soldiers were the ones who ate dirt, slept in the snow and sweat blood; and they are the ones who have a story to tell. This particular account is one of them. It begins in the earliest days of worry and uncertainty in America; goes on to the confusion of the first week on the Cotentin peninsula in Normandy, where our invasion began; and then to the gigantic airborne assault of Holland, which was the greatest airborne operation of this or any other war. The succeeding story of the famous siege of Bastogne is not strictly part of the airborne history, for it was a ground operation by one of our units. But it illustrates one very important factor that contributed to all our previous success—the fighting qualities of the airborne trooper.

By far the greater majority of the airborne men were volunteers. In my opinion they had no equal among fighting troops. It was in their nature to be tenacious, stubborn, proud, tough, and hard to put down. They had more vitality than the average man. They were unable to do anything by halfmeasures. What they sometimes lacked in military courtesy (I have not forgotten, though I have forgiven, the 501st man who stole my cap for a souvenir!) they made up for in military discipline at the front. They were well trained troops. Their commanders were as tough as the men themselves, and it was no coincidence that of the three commanders of this particular regiment, one, Colonel Howard R. Johnson, was killed in action on the front lines of Holland, and the second, Colonel Julian J. Ewell, was seriously wounded in action at Bastogne.

This story of the 501st Parachute Infantry Regiment singles out only one unit among the many that comprised the 1st Allied Airborne Army. Thus it is only a sampling of the airborne war. But if it makes the reader remember that some very brave, very daring, very willing young American soldiers fought their hearts out on a strange soil in order to go home in peace to a country they loved—and that many of them died trying—then it will have spoken for every one of the Allied airborne soldiers who were our comrades.

LEWIS H. BRERETON
Lieutenant General, U.S.A.
Wartime Commander of the
1st Allied Airborne Army

Contents

Prologue

"The whisper of a distant drum. . . ."

1
The Distant Drum

In the early winter of 1942 the Germans had reached a high-water mark in Europe. The reinforced *Afrika Korps* had retaken Italian Cyrenaica and overrun the British army as far west as El Alamein. In Russia the *Wehrmacht* had almost reached the suburbs of Moscow. In the Caucausus the oil fields of Baku had been threatened, and British Tommies were digging tank traps in the Khyber Pass. The American invasion of Africa had almost begun, under the command of a comparatively unknown general named Eisenhower, but in the early winter of that year only a few people knew anything about it. All that we could read in the newspapers, in late October, was that General Montgomery had somehow managed to counter-attack at El Alamein.

Two years were to pass before the invasion of Normandy. Yet, even then, plans for the cross-channel assault were taking shape. And when, in November of that gloomy year, a young lieutenant colonel named Howard Johnson was sent from Washington to the parachute school at Fort Benning to qualify as a parachutist, one more small segment of the spearhead into Europe was fitted into place.

Colonel Johnson was a singular personality. He was not at home with the commonplace. The energy stored up in his slight, wiry frame was so intense that his occasional rages made most men tremble. He had light blond hair and a leathery, sunburned skin in which the eyes seemed extraordinarily direct. He had no patience for delay of any kind, nor for human weakness in any form, and, if he was an idealist, it was because he believed that men could be raised to that pitch of fury where the impossible could be accomplished. When he was ordered to activate a new parachute regiment in

Georgia, his friends had an idea in advance of what kind of regiment it would be.

He set up the skeleton framework of his new unit in a makeshift area, called Camp Toccoa, in the north Georgia hills. Toccoa was like a score of other army camps in those days—Camp Mackall and Hondo Field and North Camp Hood—built for the expediencies of war and not for comfort. The one-story frame huts were roofed with tar paper. The walls were thin and the wind blew through the knotholes in the doors. Around the roads the mud was thick, and around the mud the disconsolate moth-eaten pine forests of Georgia climbed hills that had Indian names like Currahee, or were nameless and anonymous like the forests themselves.

A small group of qualified parachutists, officers and enlisted men, were sent to Colonel Johnson to become the nucleus of his new regiment. He interviewed them all. Those who satisfied him (and the basis of choice was chiefly aggressiveness) he retained. The others went back to that catch-all of the airborne infantry, the parachute school, to await a regimental commander with fewer battle stars in his eyes.

Meanwhile, the remainder of the equation was being established at the induction centers. At Camp Perry, Ohio, a small young man named Val Suarez, who came from South Bend, Indiana, turned to the man behind him in the line.

"They ask you about the paratroops?"

The other man nodded.

"What'd you say?" asked Suarez.

"What the hell d'you think I said? What do I want to jump out of airplanes for?"

Suarez shrugged. The line moved up slowly towards the desk ahead. "What'd *you* say?" asked the second man.

"I volunteered."

"Why?"

Suarez shrugged again.

That was how many of them came to the paratroops. Unrealized even by the men who had devised the induction center systems, a subtle screening of character was taking place. The greater majority of those who volunteered had no clear idea of why they were doing so. They were too new to the army to be sure about the extra pay. A few volunteered because the word had glamor. A few volunteered because it seemed a way to get overseas in a hurry—over where they could raise hell with universal approval. And a few volunteered because they had been called timid or self-effacing all their lives, and in the paratroops they saw an opportunity to demonstrate the lion behind the lamb.

But in all of them, bank clerks who were timid and steel workers who were not, was one common trait. They were men who were impatient with the commonplace.

Of the fifty men who comprised Suarez' group at the reception center, forty-nine were shipped out. Suarez remained. When the second group came through, one more man volunteered. His name was Donald Roswurn. He was almost six feet in height. He came from Altoona, Pennsylvania, and except for the directness of his eyes he looked a little like Donald Crisp. He volunteered for the paratroops because the situation that Suarez had found himself in looked like a "good deal."

The screening process was under way. When Suarez and Roswurn were sent by train to a place that sounded to them like Coca-Cola, Georgia, they were joined along the way by eight more men. Ten men out of several hundred—and not even the army realized how subtle the selection had been.

2

The officers under Colonel Johnson who screened these mothball-smelling recruits were a mixed lot. Many things were afterwards said about them by the soldiers in private, but nobody could deny that they had color.

The most feared of them all was a disciplinarian named Bottomly. Raymond Bottomly was a first lieutenant when he went to Toccoa. An old-time parachutist, he had been a commissioned officer before Pearl Harbor. Prior to that, with a reserve commission, he had majored in forestry at Montana State University. As he once confided to his adjutant, "After the war, Allworth, I'm going to get a plaid shirt and a Stetson hat and live so far up in the mountains they'll call me Bottomly the Queer."

But he was not a misanthropist; he was a disciplinarian. Most disciplinarians, who see perfection as a reasonable goal for everybody, are idealists, and, if the junior officers and most of the men despised Bottomly for his acrimony, this was largely because he insisted upon their taking the trouble to improve themselves. He was the kind of young officer in those days who, when he happened to be talking, told other officers of the same grade not to interrupt him. As time passed, the influence of Captain Ballard, his battalion commander, smoothed him off and tempered his irritability. But he never quite lost his acidity and even much later, when he had become a lieutenant colonel, he retained the conviction that nobody was as good as he could try to be.

The notable thing about Bottomly's commander, Captain Robert A. Ballard, was not only the difference between the two men, but also the difference between Ballard and most of the other officers in the regiment. Captain Ballard, a Floridian, was quiet. Where others stormed, he sometimes dozed. Like many men whose opinions about things were his own business, he seldom made a positive statement. When he did suggest something to a man, he gave the impression of nudging him with his elbow. His men loved him. In some way difficult to understand, he aroused a personal feeling between them. When he attended the enlisted men's beer parties he sat with them and drank beer and talked about hunting alligators in Florida, or some other topic close to his interests, and little by little the men fell silent, listening to him.

Among his junior officers was a company commander named Richard Allen, who came from Atlanta, Georgia. He was only twenty-four and looked younger. He combined the intolerance of youth with the intelligence of an older man, and from the start he fell into that indefinite but unmistakable category of "outstanding." Like Bottomly, he was a disciplinarian. He drove his men and drove his officers, holding meetings on Sundays to find out if the latter had prepared their forthcoming classes. He had very little patience, but he had one of the best companies in the regiment, and his men—almost in spite of themselves—liked him. He was making them into something better than they had expected to be. And Allen had by nature that characteristic which makes men forgive even a tyrant—a real appreciation of a job well done.

For his regimental staff Colonel Johnson chose two of the most able officers in the airborne infantry. Both were his opposites in temperament. Captain Kinnard, the operations officer, was a small man who looked like the miniature of someone much bigger. He was remarkable for his universal kindness. He remembered men's names and was genuinely interested in what was happening to them. He had great patience, a quiet diffidence of manner and a humility that would have aroused derision among the ignorant had it not been for his personal dignity. He wore his dignity like a higher rank. Somehow remaining in harmony with an environment that offered no encouragement to moderation, Captain Kinnard was like Goethe's portrait of the Prince of Orange—his thoughts were far-reaching, he was reserved, appeared to accede to everything, never contradicted, and while maintaining the show of reverence, with clear foresight accomplished his own designs.

Both Kinnard and Major Ewell shared a penetrating skill for tactics. Ewell, who came from Washington, D. C., was Colonel Johnson's executive officer, the second in command of the regiment. Like Kinnard, he was a West Pointer. He was not interested in making people better; he expected them to be better. Because the officers valued his opinion about them, he usually got what he wanted. He was tall and had a pronounced drawl, an ironic sense of humor and a standard of appreciation so high that he seemed bored with the scramblings of average human beings. Men and officers respected him. His drawling humor was much imitated, and years later men could still repeat the opening lines of his classic lecture on the military message book:

"It's a very simple little form, gentlemen . . ." drawling, "the simplest form the army ever devised. But every dumb son of a bitch always screws it up—and nobody keeps a copy. . . .

Dominating the regiment, however, was Colonel Johnson.

3

Johnson's brilliance as a tactician remained to be seen. But nobody denied his extraordinary influence on the men. They were reporting to him by the hundreds, all volunteers, fresh from civilian life. He and his officers interviewed them all, rejecting three for each one they accepted. Were they physically fit? Were they mentally alert? Were they aggressive? Could they kill? Johnson wanted killers; he wanted to fight force with greater force; he wanted a regiment that could be fused into a single weapon.

He himself led the men on the morning runs. He could run farther and faster than most of the youngest of them. He was the friend of anyone who could bite his teeth and go on until he was blind. The utmost, the impossible—those were his goals. So violent was his hatred of cowardice that his voice rose to a scream whenever he encountered it, as he did sometimes at the training towers. He asked his men to do nothing that he was not ready to do himself, but he demanded of them an extreme of endurance that made those who failed hate him. To those who succeeded, he was the symbol of their success.

Bookkeepers, iron workers, bank clerks, farmers, bricklayers, plumbers, dishwashers, college graduates, ex-criminals— these were his raw materials. And he was hammering them into shape to the whisper of a distant drum.

2

"A Helluva Way to Die"

In mid-March of 1943 spring touched the bleak dolefulness of Georgia. The men of the 501st Parachute Infantry, as the new organization had been called, moved to Fort Benning for parachute school. They were more excited than they were later to be at the prospect of going overseas.

The bitter clamor of the public for an American invasion somewhere, anywhere, had been stilled that winter by the arrival of General Eisenhower's forces in French Northwest Africa. Algiers had been taken; Matruh had surrendered; the green troops from Little Rock and Pasadena and Abilene had captured Oran and advanced through Tunisia to Hill 209 and the Kasserine Pass. In March the British Eighth Army was close to the main defenses of the Mareth Line; Bizerte and Cape Bon were in sight. The opinionative American public, accustomed to speaking its mind on subjects of which it was in the profoundest ignorance, was silent for a while; the clamor for an invasion of France was yet to begin.

But at the parachute school in Fort Benning the preparations for that invasion had been under way for quite some time.

When the men of the 501st Parachute Infantry arrived at the school, they were quartered in an area called the "Frying Pan." This was a shoddy, second-rate encampment that gave the impression of having been overlooked by the inspector general's department. While the faculty members of the infantry school had their daily eleven o'clock coffee in the breakfast room of the officers' club on the main area of the post, the men who were later to be the assault troops of the alumni lived in a broken-down and dirty collection of shanties on a hill above Lawson Field—where nothing except mosquitoes ever made an inspection.

The regular line soldiers were not always on the best of terms with the parachutists. When the regular infantrymen visited that area of the parachute school, near the dispensary, called "Malfunction Junction," and saw the scores of would-be paratroopers with legs or bodies in casts, hobbling along the street on crutches, they were confirmed in their opinion that parachuting was only for the insane. They resented the lordly private soldiers who wore the boots and the wings and who walked the streets of Columbus with an air. Paratroopers, it seemed, were too noisy. They threw their weight around too much. The officers were too loud and sometimes they looked like ex-prizefighters; one of them, at a formal dance at the club, had even demonstrated a parachute jump from the balcony over the dance floor. And worst of all, the girls of Columbus somehow had the notion that no man was a man unless he wore wings.

This resentment was to disappear later in the blood of combat. When the 101st Airborne Division entered Bastogne on December 19, 1944, it was the 28th Infantry Division, scattered but still fighting, that had slowed von Rundstedt long enough for them to get there.

The parachute school was, perhaps, the only army school that was tougher than legend reputed it to be. Physically, it was the American equivalent of the British commando school—differing in that it was more concentrated: it lasted only four weeks. Discipline was severe. The treatment, both for officers and men alike, was snarling in its animality. An unofficial policy of pushing men until they broke—and qualifying those who didn't—made the parachute school something that most graduates remembered afterwards with mixed feelings of pride and revulsion.

Colonel Johnson's men skipped the first week, known as "A" stage. Physically they were tough enough. As a matter of fact, they were so accustomed to pushing themselves beyond the limit of endurance that for the next two weeks of school they had (to the annoyance of the instructors) a good rest. They learned for the hundredth time how to tumble, how to jump off the forty-foot towers, how to make a good exit from the dummy planes. It was old stuff. The 250-foot "free towers," certainly the largest army teaching aid in existence (and a showplace—unlike the Frying Pan—for visiting dignitaries) were a new experience. But the men were mostly waiting, marking time, for the pay-off: the jump from a flying plane.

2

Monday morning of the last week was a clear day with a fair breeze. Those whose legs still were unbroken after the previous training sat in rows at the edge of the flying field, waiting to take off for their first jump. Frank Lasik of East Orange, New Jersey, had sprained his ankle so badly the week before that it was hard for him to walk. He sat with the others, hoping his name was still on the roster. Suarez, whose slight form looked ungainly with its huge parachute, tried to hide the trembling of his hands. They were all nervous. This—as they were to say twice again in the next fifteen months—was it.

The men had packed their own parachutes. Contrary to popular belief, a man was more confident of a 'chute he had packed himself than of those packed by a regular rigger. A man took greater care with his own than did the soldier who had to pack fifteen or twenty parachutes a day—and when he was finished he could be sure that no one had accidentally left the folding irons inside. Besides, it was general knowledge at the parachute school, supported by the experience of more than 300,000 jumps, that most parachutes opened satisfactorily no matter how clumsily they were packed. The remark, "I'll jump that 'chute if you stuff it in a barracks bag," was a common exaggeration of this understanding. There *were* a few critical stages—storing the suspension lines, and the way the break-cord was tied—that sometimes spelled the difference between life and death. But if a man took his time and used his head, he had nothing to worry about. Nothing at all. . . .

Sitting among the group that spring morning was a young soldier named Thomas Rice. Tom Rice was twenty-three years old. He was a good-looking person with a firm jaw, serious eyes and a steady expression on his face. He came from the small island of Coronado off the coast of Southern California, where he, his mother and his sister had lived since his father, a warrant officer in the navy, had been killed in a plane crash in the Canal Zone in 1933. Rice had been majoring in mechanical engineering at San Diego State College when the war came. He had had two and a half years of study ahead of him. So he chucked his classes and enlisted. At Oxnard, California, where he was processed, he learned that a new parachute regiment was being formed on the east coast. Rice had read that the paratroops were rugged boys. He had done track and cross-country work at college, and he thought he could stand the gaff; besides, it sounded exciting. So he volunteered.

Now he leaned against the wood bench in the sunlight of Georgia and waited to make his first jump.

He felt no different from the others. He would not have turned back. He would have been disappointed if the jump had been cancelled. One man, a lanky, dark-haired fellow named Byron Moser, who came from Bay Shore, Long Island, was called from the waiting line to go to A.S.T.P. He begged to be allowed to jump. One jump—just one. But he had to stand aside and watch while the rest of them climbed into the C-47s.

The tension mounted a little when they were inside the plane. The light was green in the cabin and the air was hot. They buckled the thick safety straps, checked their steel helmets and then rested their arms on the emergency 'chutes and tried to remember what they had learned. Rice could feel the blood beginning to pound a little in his temples. His skin was unnaturally hot. He was glad of the forty-pound weight of parachute silk strapped to his body. "Remember to count," he reminded himself. It was important to count, they had said. Otherwise, if the parachute failed to open, you could fall all the way to the ground without realizing it.

"Count . . . and keep your feet eight inches apart. . . . Keep your head down. Check your canopy when it opens. . . . If the panels are blown, look at the men around you—if you're dropping too fast, pull your reserve. . . . Prepare for a landing a hundred feet above the ground. . . . Make a body turn if you have to, get the wind at your back. . . . Don't double up your knees. . . . Keep mentally alert. . . ."

The men were joking among themselves. They kidded each other about their nervousness. The jumpmaster, a thin, wiry, blond lieutenant named Ed Jansen, who came from Osceola, Illinois, and who was their platoon leader, stood with the crew chief and the school instructor at the open door. This was Jansen's first jump, too. His last would be in Belgium, from a flaming plane, with one leg torn open by flak.

When the plane taxied across the runways, the men stopped play-acting and fell silent. The air grew cooler in the cabin. They looked out of the celluloid windows, above the round rubber gun-ports. For many of them, who could later claim that they had made four takeoffs but never made a landing, this was their first plane ride. When the plane took off they held to the edges of the windows, staring out. "Remember to count. . . ." The coffee-colored Chattahoochee River swished under the plane. The wings rocked, steadied, rocked again. Through the open door they saw forests and clearings, unfamiliar from two hundred feet.

"Unbuckle your safety belts!" shouted the sergeant-instructor. "Light up!"

Almost as one man—except Rice, who did not smoke—they lighted cigarettes. There was no more joking. The tension had mounted. Around Rice on the seat and on the row across from him were the familiar faces of the men who had come through the training at Toccoa with him. They looked different. The steel helmets were strapped tight around their chins, fixed in place by a leather cup. Their faces were pale. Rice could feel the coldness of his own hands. He looked out of the window and saw that the plane was over the main area of Fort Benning. He could see the empty aquamarine rectangle of the swimming pool behind the officers' club, the motion picture theater, the soda shop near the ball diamond. He remembered the quiet evenings when he and the others had stopped there for a soda before the show. All that was in the remote past—now there was no way down except through that open door.

3

The plane was approaching the parachute school. The men put out their cigarettes. Rice's heart pounded.

Lieutenant Jansen had been leaning out of the open door. Now he came back into the plane.

"STAND UP!" he shouted, his voice so hoarse it was unrecognizable.

That was the worst moment. It was the moment when the steady pound-pound-pound of heartbeat leaped up, the moment when the tension in the plane was suffocating. The first "stick,"* Rice among them, shuffled to their feet; the second group watched them from across the aisle. Rice felt a shakiness in his legs. "Feet eight inches apart. . . ." The wind roared through the open door. No wonder they paid paratroopers fifty dollars extra a month!

"HOOK UP!" came the hoarse roar.

With the others, Rice hooked his anchor-line snap-fastener to a steel cable extending head-high, the length of the cabin. "Snap towards the body"—that was it. The fastener was attached to a static line, a heavy canvas tape fifteen feet long, the other end of which was fixed to the back-flap of the parachute. When a man went out of the open door, the static line unwound to its full length and ripped the parachute open.

"If it doesn't open take it back and get a new one." Rice thought of all the grim old jokes they had made. *"Circle the field three times and go in for a crash landing."* Or the man who fell past his comrades with an unopened 'chute, shouting, *"That's the second time this has happened!"* And the old parachutist's song, passed from class to class, *"Gory, Gory, what a helluva way to die!"* which went to the tune of the *Battle Hymn of the Republic* and contained the graphic

---

*A "stick" is composed of an arbitrary number of men who go out of the plane in one group.

observation, *"They poured him from his boots."* The jokes were not funny any more.

The plane had straightened out.

"CHECK YOUR EQUIPMENT!"

It was a perfunctory check, the last of a series. Each man slapped his neighbor's rear. The pace of their heartbeats mounted.

"SOUND OFF FOR EQUIPMENT CHECK!"

The last man in the line shouted first. "SEVEN O.K.!"

"SIX O.K.!"

"FIVE O.K.!"

Rice shouted as loud as he could, "FOUR O.K.!" The effort made him feel better.

There was a pause. The sun had disappeared under a small cloud. They could smell the rubbery odor of aluminum and paint in the cabin of the C-47. The crew chief, squatting like an Indian by the door to the pilot's compartment, gazed at them with an inscrutable face. Lucky devil, he didn't have to jump.

The engines throttled down. A red light glowed over the open door.

"STAND IN THE DOOR," shouted Jansen.

Thoughts ceased. They closed up, pressing against each other. Hearts pounded uncontrollably.

"ARE YOU READY?"

Their answer was a strangled roar.

A pause. The plane rocked again. Nobody said anything. Get it over with!

"LET'S GO!" And Jansen was gone.

Number Two man was gone.

Number Three man was gone.

Rice grabbed the edge of the door and swung around. Something inside him recoiled backwards. But the determination that had brought him to this point was too strong. Out he went.

4

Afterwards he was not certain what happened. Not until he had made his fourth jump was he a little more clear about it.

A blast of wind at ninety miles an hour struck his body with the impact of an exploding shell. The door of the plane was gone. For a fleeting second he was conscious of complete helplessness; his legs from his hips down were useless. He could not tell what position he was in. Partly by training, partly by instinct, he kept his head down, his arms clasped across his chest. He forgot to count. Out of the corner of his eye he saw a portion of the plane going away and realized that he was upside down. He did not see the ground. He did not think of anything. The world was a blinding confusion of noise, wind, buffetings, patches of meaningless sunlight.

When his parachute opened, the shock was so violent that his eyes blacked out for an instant. In less than a second he had been slowed from seventy or eighty miles an hour to zero. The blinding impact smashed the wind out of him; his helmet jerked across his forehead, cutting him on the nose.

But then there was peace . . .

The strangest thing he had ever known. There was no sound, no perceptible movement—only a gentle swaying back and forth. He looked down between his dangling feet and saw the ground far below: the small figures of men and the different-colored patches of grass at the center of the field. He did not seem to be falling; he was floating. The roaring had ceased; all noise had ceased; the only sound was a little swaying creak and rustle of the harness. He remembered to check his canopy. Sun flooded through the clean white silk. He could hear the shouts of other men in the still air around him. He was feeling wonderful. He had done it. And he was still alive.

As he approached the earth, the ground seemed to come up faster. Tension mounted. He began to oscillate violently. He see-sawed the canopy by pulling alternate risers. When he had steadied himself a little, he twisted his arms behind his head and pulled himself around to face the direction of the drift. He saw the red cross of the ambulance and someone standing by a still figure holding a red flag. A broken leg, probably. Little groups of instructors stood at points in the field, checking the landings, dodging a few steel helmets that split off, as 'chutes opened, and came down like small round bombs.

Rice was a hundred feet off the ground. The wind had turned him again and he was coming in backwards; he made a second body-turn. Close to the ground the breeze was stiff; he was travelling fifteen miles an hour forward and ten feet a second downward. A gust of wind caught him. He swung up. When he swung back, like a pendulum, he saw the patch of scrub and yellow grass where he was going to land. Then the wind bowled him forward again and in the very middle of the swing he was smashed into the ground like a pile driver.

Lying flat a moment later, he moved his feet gingerly to see if they were broken. When both of them obeyed him, he collapsed his parachute canopy and lay still on the sun-warmed earth. He had a grin on his face. Every inch of his body, from head to foot, felt happy. He watched, with profound and mysterious satisfaction, a small red ant climb up a blade of grass.

5

The men carried their parachutes to the waiting trucks. They were unable to contain their joy. There were shouts of "What an opening shock!" and "How'd you come in? I came in hard." "Not me! Soft as a feather!" Colonel Johnson chafed them happily; it was his sixth jump that morning.* Above their heads the C-47s continued to spill parachutes into the soft blue air, chain after chain of them—as they would spill them into the darkness fifteen months later on the enemy-held Normandy coast.

---

* Before he went overseas, Johnson made several hundred parachute jumps—no one ever knew the exact number. He kept the riggers busy. Asked once for the reason, he remarked that he was afraid of parachuting.

3
P.O.E

When parachute school was over, Colonel Johnson knew that
the crisis for his regiment—at least as far as its spirit went—
had come. His men had entered the army wanting to be
paratroopers. For the first three months of their training the
lure of a parachute jump had carried them irresistibly forward. Working towards it, knowing that eventually they would
get it, their spirit had been high.

Now that they had graduated, it was a different problem.
They had done what they had set out to do. Healthy, sun-
tanned, aggressive and confident, they believed that they
were ready for anything. And they were impatient.

To cool them off a little, Johnson gave them all a furlough.
He knew what most army commanders know: that men who
go home on furlough in the middle of their training are
not—generally to their own puzzlement—entirely comfortable
at home. They are set apart from their old environment.
Because they are not yet veterans, they have the vague suspi-
cion that they are wasting time. Part of their existence, no
matter how much they believed to the contrary, was left
behind with the regiment.

When they returned, Johnson told them they were going
overseas. From now on, he said, everything they did would
be aimed at that goal—the port of embarkation. They had
finished their basic training; they had qualified as paratroopers; now they would learn to fight together as a unit. The
specialists—the communications men, the demolitionists, the
truck drivers, the radio operators and the motor mechanics—
each would learn his own particular job. In the companies,
the mortar men, the machine gunners and the rifle men would
learn theirs. When it was over, they would go on maneuvers.
And then to the P.O.E.

"WHO'S THE BEST?" he screamed at them.

"WE ARE!" they roared.

"LET'S GO!"

But Colonel Johnson had no assurance that what he was promising them would actually come to pass. He thought it would; that was all. What sometimes happened to units like his was that long before the second stage of their training was completed they were broken up into small groups and shipped overseas as replacements. Even more common was the tragic case of regiments like the 366th Glider Infantry that completed their basic training, completed their unit training, passed the ground force tests for overseas, and then were shipped back to a new division to mark time for months and months, training the same men in the same elementary things and ultimately making them soldiers who—having started out with the same enthusiasm as every other movie-indoctrinated young American—became a cynical group whose only escape from their own uselessness lay in raising hell.

Johnson, of course, knew nothing of the plans for the invasion of Normandy. And no one knows what was in his mind when he shouted:

"WHO'S THE BEST?"

The next few months of training would tell.

2

In American newsreels, soldiers train by dashing madly through forests, climbing board fences, swinging on ropes across small streams (into which at least one, obviously a future reject, always falls) and jabbing straw sacks with bayonets. Jeeps are invariably driven at such a rate of speed that they are hurled bodily into the air from time to time in a cloud of highly pictorial dirt. Machine guns never fire anything but tracer bullets, and they always fire at night. Soldiers march with immaculate uniforms, exquisite precision and an expression on their faces that Mr. George M. Cohan immortalized for everybody in a song. All of these things take place, as everybody knows, to a background of music.

The films that afford the greatest amusement to soldiers, however, are not the newsreels. Soldiers sometimes relish the sight of a jeep being driven the way they have never been allowed to drive one. And if the public wants to believe that all a soldier does to train for battle is to hurdle brooks and vault over fences, they have no special objection. It certainly impresses the kid brother.

No—the films they hoot at are more pretentious. They are those dramas of Hollywood which purport to show, in seven or eight reels, exactly what happens to "the American Boy" when he goes away to war. Those are not sugar-coated pills; those are pills of pure sugar. In them, barracks are invariably spotless. Soldiers in freshly pressed uniforms study the *Handbook of the Soldier* and tell each other, like people explaining Why Dora Is Lonely These Days, the importance of knowing more than the next fellow if you expect to get a stripe or two. Kindly sergeants with an air of sticky good-fellowship explain the importance of brushing your teeth up and down, not sideways.

At inspections, an officer in full-dress uniform strolls sternly from cot to cot, convoyed by a small flotilla of lesser dignitaries (also in full dress) who carry note-pads like swagger sticks. Soldiers approaching such officers on the street snap to rigid attention, bracing for the inevitable, and those who make the fatal mistake of acting like an honest recruit are subsequently shown on K.P.—represented by cleaning garbage cans.

Everybody is very enthusiastic to get over and fight the Japs or the Germans and, when the lights go out at night, they hold philosophical discussions with themselves from cot to cot, in which it becomes evident that all soldiers are (1) just kids homesick for Mom's apple pies; (2) older men who are Grim But Ready, and (3) men with a Secret Past—the latter generally very surly and ready to pick a fight. The climax shows them in some desperate situation overseas, where, with dirt-streaked greasy faces (but no growth of beard), they continue to do almost as much talking as they did in the barracks. The film generally ends with a few strains of The Star Spangled Banner, leaving the women to wipe their eyes, the 4Fs to blow their noses, and the seeds of military glory in everybody's heart.

Films like that are a parcel of nonsense. Along with the military band, which Mr. Shaw called the greatest enemy of civilization, they are probably the outstanding single contribution, at least in America, to the secret craving of each new generation to be a soldier.

3

Johnson's men quickly found out what the motion pictures never told the public. Military training was exceedingly technical. Behind that moment when the bullets streamed out of a machine gun to lay crossfire on a defended area lay hours and days of study on assembly and disassembly of the weapon, care and cleaning, mechanical functioning, characteristics of fire, final protective lines, range cards and range estimation, practice in manipulation, practice in dry firing—all before the first bullet left the first gun. The mere recital of those subjects is dull, and the average reader will have skipped hastily over them. Soldiers could not skip.

Modern warfare is highly complicated. This typical instruction to the mortar gunner—Tom Rice, for instance—*"He checks the vertical line of the collimeter and simultaneously turns the adjusting nut and traversing handwheel in the same relative direction until the vertical line is laid on the left edge of the aiming stake"*—will never be repeated by a newsreel commentator. But the mastery of thousands of such details in weeks and months of training lay in the background of all the piffle turned out by Hollywood.

Rice had become a mortar sergeant. He was a typical line soldier, rapidly becoming a specialist. They all were. The jeep drivers were taught not only how to drive their vehicles but also how to repair them, to take apart the engine and put it together again and, most important of all, first echelon maintenance, which was driver's maintenance, and of which a great part emphasized the importance of never driving jeeps the way they were driven in the newsreels.

The demolitionists were similarly trained. It was spectacular to blow up a bridge; it was not so spectacular to know the formula, $N = 3/4R$, that was one small part of learning how to do it.

That was how it went for all of them—for Technician Fifth Grade Thomas R. Alcott of Donora, Pennsylvania, who was simultaneously studying Morse code, radio operation, wire-laying and map reading—and for Private Leo Greene of Burbank, California, who was learning the complicated differences between accountability and responsibility in company supply—and for Private Leo Runge, who was mastering the tactics of the squad and platoon and the advanced principles of field firing. The army had no more glamor. It was a place where barracks were sometimes dirty and seldom immaculate, where sergeants were too harried to be kind, and where junior officers were sometimes saluted and sometimes not.

But somehow Colonel Johnson, in spite of so much detail, kept a high spirit among his men. They were never allowed to forget that they were paratroopers and the best soldiers in the army. His almost demoniac frenzies at times roused them to a pitch of excitement where they wanted to chuck their studies and go after the Germans—evidently lurking in the Georgia hills—with knives and bare fists. They were raring for a fight. When they went on maneuvers in Tennessee they outmarched and out-fought almost all the other units, and when the maneuvers had ended they were fifteen miles inside the enemy lines, sitting on a road communications net—as they were later to sit on the road communications net of Bastogne— waiting for all comers.

Johnson's luck held. The promises he made came true. On January 1, 1944, a little more than a year from the time the first group of draftees had arrived at Toccoa with their hands in their pockets, he took to the port of embarkation near Camp Miles Standish in Massachusetts a group of paratroopers so wild for battle and so impatient to get there that the harmless little town of Charlotte, where they had started a small civil war of their own, would never forget them.

PART I

". . . .five hours before the seaborne landings. . . ."

4

"This Blessed Isle . . ."

It is difficult to remember what we thought about and how we felt in the days in England before the invasion of Normandy. That bleak winter before the last and greatest task of the war seemed afterwards to be dimmed out behind the great blaze of combat. Later we understood the fear of death, which was an animal fear of detached and recoiling flesh; but in England, before the invasion, when the gray winter days succeeded each other without change, and the rain came down forever, sometimes in dreary moderation, sometimes in vertical glittering lines, we lived always with the fear of the unknown. The future was an emptiness, a space, which no thoughts could bridge. We were ignorant. We worked blindly. There were the good hours and the bad hours, but we had always a tightness within us. Something was coming that we were powerless to prevent.

I do not think the soldiers of World War I knew anything quite like this. It had its root in the immensity of what we were about to do. And perhaps our airborne soldiers felt it most of all, for they knew from the beginning what they would have to do. Whether the invasion came in Italy or Southern France or the Channel shore or the Low Countries, they knew they would have to lead. It was not a question of getting up out of a muddy trench at a certain hour and going forward into fire already experienced and known; it was not even a question of struggling up through water to a shell-swept beach. It was a question of going out into the unexperienced, the unimaginable, at night and from a roaring plane.

On the surface, our lives were matter-of-fact. But disquiet lay deep within us all.

2

The area of England in which Colonel Johnson set up headquarters was on an old estate at Hempstead Marshall, two miles from Newbury, in Berkshire.

The tents were laid out in neat rows beside the elms. They occupied fields which were not quite gardens, not quite wilderness, but that casual mixture of the two which seemed to be the greatest charm of the English landscape. Behind the Nissen huts containing regimental headquarters and the messes, behind the rows of officers' tents and the drill fields, a small valley deep in grass gave pasturage to cattle living out their lives on its slopes. And beyond that valley the manorial estate continued in the same tranquillity: an indefinite repetition of greenhouses, gardens, cottages; greenhouses, gardens, cottages . . .

It had been raining for weeks when we arrived. The pools of water that had refused to soak into the ground had trickled underneath the sides of the tents and gathered in new pools around the stoves. Morning had succeeded morning with somber skies. Sometimes in the late afternoon the sun came out for a brief space of time, like a benediction, and made the great patrician trees sparkle. But then the sun set and inevitably the stars were hidden. Night followed night without stars.

A small group of officers and men had preceded the regiment overseas to lay out the base camps—both the one at Hempstead Marshall and another, for the 1st and 3rd Battalions, at a town called Lanbourne, eight or nine miles away. Lieutenant Strasser had been one of the leaders. So, as soon as the regiment had arrived, he was sought out and questioned.

"What the hell do you do around here in the evenings?" was the first demand.

"There, my friend," said Strasser, who enjoyed the role of humorist, "you have a long, sad story."

"It's simple, Lieutenant," volunteered an enlisted man. "You go to the movies in Newbury. A week later there's a new movie, so you go again. That's all there is to it."

"What's at Newbury besides movies?"

Strasser ticked off on his fingers. "A hotel. Ale and bitters every night. Scotch once a month. A bicycle store—"

"Good idea to buy a bicycle," the enlisted man interrupted.

"That's right. Put your name on the waiting list." Strasser went on: "Three or four antique shops. One English version of a 'Five and Dime.' One hardware shop, one junk shop, two flower shops and a church. After that you have the wide open countryside."

"How far is London?" someone wanted to know.

"About an hour. Trains every day."

"That's for me."

"One London pass once a month," continued Strasser. "Then you have Reading. Reading is a jolly little version of Waukegan. At Maidenhead you can rent a boat and go for a jolly row on the river. North of here on the Oxford road are the Downs, where you can go for a jolly constitutional. You can get a jolly cup of tea anywhere. And if you don't like any of those things you can stay in camp and go jolly well mad."

Everybody laughed. One of the officers asked: "Is there an officers' club?"

"Now you ask," said the enlisted man.

"Six miles from here," put in Lieutenant Strasser. "The Mill House. Two floors, a bar and a dance hall. A dance once a week, Bogart says."

"And that," said the enlisted man, "touches on the heart of the problem. The women. Who keep you from going jolly well mad."

Everybody laughed again. "What about 'em?" asked somebody.

"In Newbury," said Strasser, "you have an English military hospital—various assorted nurses of different resistances. Most of them blow a fuse under high voltage. If you want American girls, the 98th General Hospital will oblige. Or you can walk the streets and take your pick."

"How's the liquor supply?"

"Three pounds ten for Scotch. That's fifteen dollars a bottle in real money. Twelve dollars a bottle for gin."

"When do we start getting mail?"

Strasser grinned. "They have a very interesting system over here. All arriving letters are put into five categories for rerouting—by South Africa, South America, South Australia, South India and 'No delay.' Those marked for Africa, America, Australia, and India eventually reach you. Those marked 'No Delay' go to Ireland for the duration."

3

On an ordinary morning there at Hempstead Marshall we were awakened by an explosion of dynamite—a hair-raising sound that brought everybody out of a sound sleep. The band played reveille, and then the musicians marched around the area for a while, usually followed by numbers of mongrel dogs.

Breakfast was comprised of powdered eggs, a strip of flabby bacon, some cereal and coffee. For variety the cooks sometimes omitted the bacon. On Sundays there were pancakes, and on rare mornings, perhaps twice a month, there were cold-storage eggs. Those were a treat.

Everyone was at work by half-past seven. By eight o'clock the meadows and open ground in the area were in use by the platoons for calisthenics; at nine o'clock the company officers took their men for forty-five-minute runs along the roads to Newbury or Denford. Rest periods of ten minutes divided the hours. If the eternal clouds broke, everyone crowded into one of the dark Nissen huts for a lecture on map reading or the tactics of the squad, while the rain beat a steady tattoo on the corrugated tin roof. The neighboring villages were attacked with blank cartridges and considerable enthusiasm, while the villagers watched with dubious patriotism from the windows.

The latrines at the camp were all outdoors. The showers were called ablutions. There was never enough hot water, and often the rooms were freezing. For toilet supplies and other necessities, the P.X.—first set up in a tin hut and later in a glider crate—opened for business twice a week, selling liquor to officers as a sideline. Coca-Colas and beer were unavailable.

At night almost everybody went to town. The English girls were friendly, and no one worried much about conventions. From time to time a prostitute from London, called a Picadilly Commando, was caught in one of the tents, or out on the meadow behind the camp, but those incidents failed to ruffle the monotonous existence; and British "bobbies" appeared with pompous regularity to take them away.

England in 1944 was in its fifth year of war. Life there could no longer be compared to the bright and essentially still untouched life of the United States. With the end of the siege of London, the nation had entered a phase that resembled the long, bitter, gray pull of a windjammer rounding Cape Horn. It was not war in the picture-book sense, but it was war in the sense of a word that was almost as ugly: deprivation.

The people seemed alive and cheery. The children were ruddy-faced and in good health. Everybody had enough to wear. And the destruction of homes had not been so widespread as the news pictures, those incorrigible concentrators of tragedy, had led everyone to believe. England appeared to be quite all right.

But there were little things. Only the newcomers with discerning eyes noticed them. The girl at the railway station in Glasgow who served the hot tea had laughed when we asked whether she had any sugar. Civilian travelers who looked as though they might have been wealthy once upon a time wore square black patches on the knees of their trousers, or had sewed the edges of their coats with reinforced lining. Nobody showed any embarrassment at his shoddiness. On the sidewalks in front of the meat shops (which had bare windows), long lines of women waited in the rain for a few ounces of food. The grass was long in the city parks. Everybody's spectacles were horn-rimmed. And in the fields and gardens of the countryside where the houses with thatched roofs made the settings tranquil, the men who hoed and ploughed were old enough to have been our grandfathers.

"Got any goom, choom?" "Got any sweets?" Behind those innocent and familiar queries of the English children lay a starvation for sugar. Behind the soiled clothes that made them ragged-looking, and the griminess of the adults, lay not only an utter lack of soap but also not enough coal to heat water. The bus systems were inadequate, because there was not enough gasoline. The stores were empty-looking (except for useless luxuries like Chippendale furniture), because nothing was being manufactured to sell. And there were no restaurants with anything to offer the soldiers, because there was not enough food for the people of England.

English dignity was too deeply ingrained for them to allow the visitor—even the men who would fight by their side—full understanding of how the war had transformed England. The English believed, for the sake of their own pride, in keeping up appearances; they lacked the American trait, behind which lay another kind of pride, of honestly admitting they were hard up.

So we never understood the real story. Our criticisms of England were based on what the English allowed us to see— what they could not prevent us from seeing. And the curious distortion of this picture made our opinions tragic in their inconsistency and tragic in their finality. For England at war was the only England that most of us ever proposed to see.

5

Behind the Scenes

About four miles from Hempstead Marshall and on the other side of Newbury was an airdrome called Greenham Common. In a great English manor house at the edge of the airdrome was the headquarters of the 101st Airborne Division. Colonel Johnson's regiment had become a part of this division. The other regiments of the Division, like the 506th Parachute Infantry under Colonel Sink, the 502nd Parachute Infantry under Lieutenant Colonel Michaelis and the 327th Glider Infantry were stationed in the same neighborhood, where the small roads were fragrant with the scent of lilac and where the only people laboring in the fields were the Land Army girls, who liked to work in sweaters and shorts.

Whatever the future held would come to us through the 101st Airborne Division. On the second floor of its headquarters was a place called the war room, where the field orders and maps of the coming invasion would—when they arrived— be kept. As long as there was no guard on the door of that room, we knew that our quiet life would continue. So the officers or the enlisted men who had business up that way always glanced along the second-floor hall before they left.

Months passed. The cold dreary English winter drew to an end. And then one day the guard was there.

2

Just prior to the arrival of the regiment in England, Field Marshal Rommel had, at Hitler's direction inspected the coast defenses of the Atlantic Wall. Part of what he saw was evidently displeasing, for increased activity became evident all along the critical part of the French coast. Intelligence officers at SHAEF were kept busy identifying units moving in, units moving out. Much of this information came from officers and soldiers of the OSS, both British and French— and sometimes young women—who were parachuted secretly into France at night. Information radioed from those teams underlined the certainty at SHAEF that, early in May, only two infantry divisions were on the Cotentin Peninsula of France.

The work that was secretly taking place to establish these facts was not known to our paratroopers, or even, at least in the winter, by the division commander, Major General Maxwell D. Taylor. But our men could see the obvious. They were being trained in night assembly. They were practicing the support of seaborne infantry. As early as February 28th, volunteer soldiers and officers went to a secret school called "the pathfinders," where they were taught to operate radar sets and directional light systems to guide incoming troop-carrier planes. For the regimental fire problems the men used live ammunition. And when General Eisenhower and Prime Minister Churchill reviewed the American airborne troops at Welford Airdrome on March 29th, a year almost to the day from the time we had made our first parachute jump, everyone understood what it meant. The "old boys" were saying good-bye.

Tension began to mount.

In April, England was so weighted with invasion material that, according to one barrage-balloon girl worker, the island would have sunk beneath the sea if the balloons had been cut loose. More ammunition was stacked along the English country lanes than had been expended in the whole of World War I. Huge parks of tanks, trucks, bulldozers, ducks, jeeps, self-propelled guns were spread behind the hedges. Airfields were jammed with planes parked wing-tip to wing-tip beside the runways. The embarkation ports, according to Nazi radio reports based on reconnaissance flights, were "bristling—positively crammed to the breaking point—with all manner of invasion equipment." More than four thousand ships, not counting small craft—by far the largest armada ever assembled—would ferry the men and equipment across. Protecting the convoys and covering the landing would be a dozen battleships, scores of cruisers and destroyers, literally hundreds of gunboats, corvettes, destroyer escorts and other fire support craft.*

The date set for D Day, June 5th, was not chosen until a month before the landings. At that time, and only then, were the plans for the airborne operation completed. Only in part were the airborne troops to serve as a diversionary threat to the rear of the two enemy divisions. Our principal mission was dictated by the peculiar terrain of the Cotentin Peninsula— terrain which, properly employed by the Germans, was a threat to the success of the entire invasion.

3

The two slow, dirty rivers that ran down the Cotentin Peninsula—the Douve and the Merderet—flowed through areas of grazing farm land that were on the same level as the river water. Partly by seepage into the surrounding meadows, partly by overflow in times of flood, the two rivers had made wide areas of swampland. To control the water and drain some of the swamps, the French had built locks on the Douve, principally at La Barquette. When these locks were opened, a shallow lake formed in the lowlands below; closed, a similar lake formed above. This lake was not a barrier to the seaborne landings, but it was a barrier to any German regiment trying to move into the peninsula from outside. Seized and held, the La Barquette locks were an instrument of preliminary Allied defense.**

---

*From *Soldier of Democracy*, copyright 1945 by Kenneth S. Davis, published by Doubleday Doran & Company, Incorporated.

**In May 1944 it was believed that opening the locks would prevent the German command from moving reinforcements into the critical area, while keeping them closed would allow the Allied troops a ready means of extending their gains out of

Because of the inundated nature of the ground, the La Barquette area was one of only two points at which passage in or out of the peninsula was readily possible. The second of these was the firm ground between St. Lô d'Ourville and St. Sauveur de Pierre-Pont. The third critical locality in the area had nothing to do with the movement of German troops, and everything to do with the movement of our own. This was the flooded area between Quineville and Pouppeville. There swamplands lay directly in the advance of the seaborne troops and closed down their route to narrow causeways easily defended by the Germans.

The seizure of these causeways was assigned to the 101st Airborne Division. Apportioned to Colonel Johnson's regiment was the destruction of two bridges over the Douve River on the highway northwest of Carentan and the seizure of the La Barquette locks.

It looked good on paper. It worked out well in effect. But between plan and effect lay a time of tension, of unexpected moves by the Germans, of bad luck and of ordinary mistakes.

We learned of our assignments in France only when we moved to those temporary camp sites called the marshalling areas. These areas were within the barbed-wire confines of airdromes in Southern England—Merryfield and Welford for the 501st Parachute Infantry. There, guards were posted around the confines of the camp and, once we were admitted to the long green tents called war rooms, where the ultimate secrets of more than four years of work were given to the sergeants and the corporals and the privates, we were no longer allowed to leave the area. The time for casual "details" had also come to an end; meals were cooked and served by Negro service troops. The men had no further drilling, no further training, no further chance to make love to the English girls. This was a time for fitting parachutes and packing ammunition, for sharpening trench knives and going to church.

The regiment was to parachute into Normandy five hours before the seaborne landings. It would land north and east of

the peninsula. According to subsequent data discovered months after the invasion, the opposite was true: it was to the advantage of the Germans that the locks be kept closed. The facts on this point are not yet clear; so I have left the narrative as it was written at the ETOUSA historical section in Paris in May 1945. As the account stands, it represents the information on which the assault troops acted.

the town of Carentan. Two battalions were assigned the mission of seizing the locks at La Barquette and blowing the bridges over the Douve. The 3rd Battalion was to be in division reserve—an assignment that more experienced troops would have received with gratification.

But, unknown to everybody at the marshalling areas, something had happened to the plans. While the infantry troops were moving to the coastal areas of England, intelligence reports at Supreme Headquarters revealed that enemy dispositions on the Cotentin Peninsula had unaccountably changed. An entire new division had arrived. This was information of the gravest importance. With a total of three divisions opposing the Allied landings, the original plan of closing off the entire peninsula had to be modified to a smaller scale. Nothing could be done, however, about changing the plan for the airborne troops. Except for slight modifications, their strength could not be increased nor their mission changed. They would have to go—and success would be up to them.

4

June 4th was rainy and overcast. After a conference, the assault was advanced to the following day. Several convoys, already at sea, had to be recalled. The weather reports for June 6th showed a continuance of the same bad weather.

Kenneth S. Davis's account tells what happened behind the scenes at SHAEF.

Eisenhower spent the day anxiously scanning the weather reports which arrived almost hourly, gazing often at the fateful skies. That evening, Churchill, Smuts and De Gaulle all visited Eisenhower and sat with him for an hour, discussing the great decision which Eisenhower alone must make. At nine o'clock, after the three experts had left, Eisenhower held another staff meeting. This time three weather experts, who had arrived at their forecasts independently, were called in singly. Their forecasts confirmed one another, and they added up to a predicted improvement in the weather during the next forty-eight hours. Beyond that, the long-range forecast (always a "guess," the experts insisted) was decidedly unfavorable. In other words, a postponement now might mean an indefinite postponement.

It was tentatively decided to move on June 6th. The final decision was reserved for a conference to be held at four-thirty Monday morning, June 5th.

At four o'clock on the following morning, after a few hours of fitful sleep, Eisenhower was back at Southwick Park. There, around the conference table, he, Tedder and "Beedle" Smith met Montgomery, Ramsay, and Leigh-Mallory with their chiefs of staff. The weather men were called in. Again their forecasts tallied. Tuesday would be windy, but not stormy, with a reasonably high ceiling. Skies would probably clear at noon, and the wind would die down in the afternoon. The "guesswork" long-range forecasts remained unchanged; a "December depression" was moving in. Eisenhower then reviewed aloud the factors which must be considered and called for opinions. Ramsey and Leigh-Mallory were the ones whose opinions were most dependent upon the weather. If they could move, Montgomery and Bradley could. Leigh-Mallory indicated that he was willing to take what they all recognized as a gamble. Ramsey said, "If the 'air' thinks he can do it, the navy certainly can." There was silence. All looked toward Eisenhower, who was plunged now into one of those moments of terrible solitude which, again and again in recent years, had measured his inner resources. His subordinate commanders were good men, strong men, but the supreme responsibility was not theirs. It was his. He alone must make the decision.

There was nothing dramatic in the way he made it. He didn't think in terms of "history" or "destiny," nor did there arise in him any of that grandiose self-consciousness which characterizes the decisive moments of a Napoleon or a Hitler. He simply weighed rapidly in that remarkably logical mind of his the factors of the situation. The troops were all set; they'd never get that fine edge twice. A promise made to Stalin (we'd promised him a second front by the end of May) was already in default by several days. Public opinion in America and Britain clamored for action. Failure to move now might mean an indefinite postponement and consequent danger of a "leak," which would destroy the possibility of surprise. With luck, beachheads could be established firmly enough in one day to hold and the weather experts admitted that the weather might be better beyond the forty-eight-hour period than fore-casts indicated. Success now might mean a quick decision in Europe.

Adding them up that way, the risks of delay outweighed the risks of immediate action—even though, as it turned out, we had the worst weather in forty years in Normandy.

"All right," Eisenhower said, "we move."

5

At Merryfield Airport, Colonel Johnson faced his assembled paratroopers. It was thirty minutes before plane time. His high-pitched voice was even louder than usual.

"I'm proud of you!" he yelled. "You've shown me what you can do! You've shown yourselves what you can do! I have confidence in you! Tomorrow night you'll be fighting Germans! Are you ready?"

A roar was his answer.

"We've worked together—sweated together—played together! Now it's the end of playing! What we do tonight and tomorrow will be written in history!" He stopped and reached for his jump-knife. Raising the blade in the air, he poised it dramatically. His voice became a scream. "I swear to you that before tomorrow night this knife will be buried in the back of the blackest German in Normandy!"

Overwrought by tension and wild to go, the men were on their feet cheering.

During the afternoon, General Eisenhower had visited the airfields where units of the 82nd and 101st Airborne divisions were lined up beside their planes. Kenneth S. Davis writes further:

He was gambling with the lives of these superbly trained troops. He knew it. They knew it. Many on his staff had strongly opposed the move, and at least one of them had asserted that to land these men behind the Atlantic Wall, in view of the doubtful weather, would be "murder." He had calculated the risks carefully. If the beachheads did not hold, these troops, certainly, could not be evacuated. On the other hand, Eisenhower had pointed out that the beachheads would be much less likely to hold if the airborne landings were not made. "Never risk men in operations that cannot achieve a decisive result" was one of his battle mottoes, and its reverse implications were clear enough: to achieve great decisions, great risks, if necessary, are justified—and this, above all others, was to be a decisive operation. Yes, he was sure his decision was the right one. Nevertheless, no anxiety of D minus one weighed more heavily upon him than the doubtful fate of these splendid men.

Murder! The word rang in his ears as his Cadillac drove up to airfield after airfield and he dismounted to move among the men. Only with extreme reluctance had he permitted the four correspondents who were assigned to his personal headquarters to accompany him on this, the most dramatic and heartfelt of his inspections. He ordered them to keep at a distance. He wanted nothing to interfere with his direct, personal relationships with these young Americans on whom so: much depended, and who were now, very many of them, so soon to die. They stood at ease. Many of them had already colored their faces with cocoa and linseed oil, and one of them, as the general passed, was licking the mixture from his lips.

"Does it taste good?" Eisenhower asked.

"Damn good," said the boy, laughing.

Where are you from? What did you do in civilian life? How many bushels of wheat do you raise on your Dakota farm? Is there anyone here from Kansas? He was delighted when at last he found a paratrooper from Kansas. . . . It was evening when he drove up to the last airfield. There, as he watched the men climb into their planes, a spasm of emotion broke through his iron self-control. He swallowed heavily and his eyes blinked rapidly. He raised his hand and shouted, "Good luck!" He climbed to the roof of a headquarters building to watch the planes roar down the sky, southward toward the coast of France, and he raised his hand again and waved and said softly, "Good luck and Godspeed."

NORMANDY

When the airborne troops landed in Normandy, they were scattered over a wide area of enemy-held territory. They had to fight as individuals or in small groups. Sometimes they died within hours; sometimes they managed only to stay alive. But for each regimental objective there was at least one small group who struggled doggedly to seize it: and because of them the airborne assault of the continent was successful.

6
From Flak to Foxholes

The night of June 6th was sullen and rainy. Fitful gusts of wind rocked the planes. Twilight was late in England at that time of year and, though the planes did not take off until 10:21—in military time 2221—a desolate blue light still showed behind the storm clouds. The C-47s climbed to their formations and straightened out, at two thousand feet, to head for France. Within the cabins we sat with darkened faces and stared out at the lampless countryside far below. Those of us who had taken the round, pink seasick pills felt drowsy. The wild excitement characterizing the scenes at the field prior to the takeoff had subsided, and no one talked very much. In the planes ridden by the Catholic and Protestant chaplains, the men said short prayers, bowing their blackened heads where they sat. Forward, by the pilot's compartment, were equipment bundles waiting to be kicked out the open door; on racks under the planes, like bombs, were more.

Over the English Channel a familiar and tranquil moon came out. Looking down to the indigo water, we could realize for the first time the stupendous effort of which we were a part. As far as the eye could see on the rough surface of the Channel, extending from beneath the plane to either wing-tip and dissolving into the far-off murk, were the ships of the Allied invasion. The thought crossed many of our minds that, down in each one of those tiny fragments, were men like ourselves, sitting in darkness and waiting dry-mouthed for the unknown. And suddenly it seemed as though we could see the whole great, sprawling, disconnected plan, which had begun at the induction centers ("Did they ask you about the paratroops?''), coming together into a single arrow of assault. And we were the tip.

The man who is going into combat does not feel much

different from the man who is going to make his first parachute jump. What lies ahead of him is too unfamiliar to be
frightening. He may realize that his heart is beating a little
faster than normal, that the skin of his face is hot and his
hands are cold. Otherwise he feels all right. But all his
faculties are keyed up to abnormal alertness. And if the inner
nervousness has not made him drowsy—which is one effect
of tension on the system—he is acutely aware not only of
himself, his physical presence in the plane or ship, but also of
everything around him. From the moment he leaves the security of the rear to go forward he lives completely in the
present.

The weather was clear across the Channel. By the time the
planes began to encounter scattered clouds near the French
coast, most of us were asleep. We were awakened by an
unfamiliar sound, like the close-by popping of an outboard
motor. Looking out the celluloid windows, we could see what
it was: we were being fired at. The tracer bullets were speck-
ling up into the sky in streams, thousands of them. Curiously
enough, they were all colors—red, green, yellow, blue. It
seemed unreal; it gave the darkness a nightmarish quality,
like a multicolored blast furnace.

For all of us, pilots and soldiers alike, this was our first
instant under fire. Nobody stopped to analyze his feelings.
But if we felt anything at all it was surprise—surprise that
anybody actually hated us enough to want to kill us. It was a
feeling that tightened us in around ourselves painfully. And if
the reader is interested in knowing what causes the gulf
between a civilian and a veteran soldier, it is simply the
difference between a man who has lived all his life in a
reasonably friendly world, compared to the one who has
existed where other people are literally trying to spill his
brains on the earth.

The machine-gun bullets turned on Tom Rice's plane. They
appeared out of the darkness below as little colored specks
and whizzed past at the same instant. The popping noise
sounded, oddly, as though it were close underneath the plane.
It was not a loud noise, but it was distinct above the roar of
the motors.

At the shouted order we shuffled to our feet. Hooking up,
we checked our equipment. The familiar rote of parachute
school was reassuring. But then we had to wait, pressed close

against each other in silence. And we were having a hard time keeping on our feet. Almost at the first shots from below, the inexperienced pilots—men who later were to take us through enemy anti-aircraft fire as nervelessly as on a bomb run—had begun evasive action. This was contrary to orders. Their formations loosened up. A cloud bank near the Merderet scattered them still further. Sergeant Rice's plane dipped and turned, sometimes rising a hundred feet in a second or two, buckling the men's legs under the pressure.

All this had taken only a few moments. Now there was a new sound in the sky—the noise of explosions. The distant ones made an odd, enveloping *wop,* like a sound curling in on itself; close by, they had the concussion of dynamite. A noise like the rattling of chains beat against the walls of the plane; it was expended shrapnel. Nothing had prepared us for the surprising discovery that flak made noise. A glare lit up the sky. Rice saw a plane on fire as it dipped down below him, curling off on one wing. One—two—three dark figures hurtled out of it; then flames enveloped the cabin. In his mind's eye he saw the men shriveling up inside—maybe Suarez, maybe Colonel Johnson . . .

He wanted to get out of the plane . . .

A red light glowed over the door. There were more explosions. All semblance of formation had been lost. In the steady popping of the machine-gun bullets, the *wham wham wham* of the 20mm. tracer shells and the explosions of the 88mm. flak, the sharp arrow of the invasion seemed hopelessly blunted. One or two pilots slammed the doors of their compartments and circled back for England; they had had enough. But for the most part the planes blundered on. Men got sick and vomited on the floor; shrapnel tore up through the greasy pools or through the seats they had quitted. In the planes carrying loads of high explosives known as Composition C-2, the men held their breaths, waiting to find out what it would feel like to be blown to pieces.

"Take it easy, boys!" yelled Lieutenant Jansen at the door of Rice's plane. "It'll all be over in a minute!"

Fifty-caliber machine-gun bullets tore through the wings like the chattering of gravel. Rice's plane was much too high. Everything was going wrong.

Over the door, like a signal of relief, the green light went on. *How the hell did the pilot know where they were?*

2

A K ration bundle lay in front of Lieutenant Jansen. He kicked it out the door. That was the last they ever saw of it. The second bundle weighed three hundred pounds. Before he and the crew chief could get rid of it, sixty seconds had passed. In that time the plane, going too fast anyway, had traveled almost two miles. What none of the men realized was that those chance sixty seconds were taking them—as in Colonel Johnson's plane, where a similar delay occurred—to La Barquette.

The anxious men dove out. Rice was wearing too much equipment; his left arm caught in the door. For three seconds he hung outside in the hundred-mile-an-hour wind. When he was torn free, the metal edge of the door scraped his skin almost to the flesh, taking with it his hundred-and-fifty-dollar wrist watch. He scarcely felt it. But his body position was so bad that the opening of the parachute almost knocked him unconscious. Dazed, he floated down. The only sounds were the sharp cracking of bullets that struck the edge of his nylon canopy. One arm was almost useless; with the other he slipped to earth as fast as he could. It was dark. He lay still on the ground for a moment. Machine-gun bullets firing to his right were thirty and forty feet in the air. He could hear the explosions of mortars and the sounds of planes going away, going back to England . . .

The pilots were hopelessly confused. The area had looked right; that was all. How could anybody be sure of anything in all this confusion? But it would work out. It had to work out . . .

All over the Cotentin Peninsula the parachutists were coming down that way. Out in the English Channel the great armada of ships moved steadily towards set destinations— beaches later called Utah and Red Leg and Omaha, where hundreds of infantrymen died in the bleak daybreak. But that was four hours away. Meanwhile, we had no encouragement, no assurance, even, that the seaborne invasion would actually take place. And we were scattered. Where we had expected to land in selected drop zones, to assemble as complete battalions, each man found himself virtually alone.

A prize military secret—the dim locator lights on the equipment bundles—was quickly rendered useless; the German machine gunners fired on the lights. Later they booby-trapped the abandoned bundles. The biggest secret of them all—the pathfinder radar devices, the operators of which were dropped in Normandy half an hour before the first wave of planes— also turned out poorly: the operators were unable, as a rule, to reach their sets. All over Normandy, that night, the long prepared plans and the careful strategy were going awry.

Small groups of men worked their way across country, collecting more men as they went. Privates or sergeants or colonels led them—whoever kept his wits. Staff Sergeant Clarence J. Tyrrel of Georgia, who had been dropped twenty miles beyond his objective, gathered enough men to act as a tactical unit and on his way back through the darkness destroyed two light tanks. Lieutenant Colonel George Griswold and Captain Eldia Hare collected another group of men and brought them to the division command post at Hiesville, knocking off a horse-drawn German ammunition train enroute. But some of the groups were so small and so thoroughly lost that they fought for days before they learned that the invasion had really taken place.

This scattered fighting in the darkness seemed useless at the time. In effect, however, it worked out all right. The German soldiers had been accustomed to a pattern of formal war, with front lines, outposts and command posts. They found themselves fighting all around the clock. They themselves had developed vertical envelopment at Crete and Holland, but counter-offensive had evidently not occurred to them. There was nothing in their books to prepare them for situations where fire came from one direction one moment and from another the next. War waged by small independent groups of soldiers without leaders or without strategy was inconceivable. It was not war; it was chaos. How were such men controlled?

The Americans were not controlled. They just killed Germans.

Colonel Johnson was near Sergeant Rice when he landed. A dark building suggested one way of finding out where he was. But he left it alone—it was a German command post— and worked his way along the ditches in the general direction of the south, killing his first German when an enemy soldier opened up at him with a machine pistol. He was looking for La Barquette. He crawled for half an hour before he met anyone. Then he encountered a small group from one of the other battalions. None of the men knew where he was. Johnson was convinced that the locks lay to the south of them, so he and the group continued that way.

Tom Rice, meanwhile, had done all right. He and a small number of men moved into the apparently deserted village of Addeville. Finding no Germans there, the platoon leader, Lieutenant Rafferty, set up a temporary command post. Addeville had not been an objective. Everybody knew it. But just then they were not thinking about the plans that had been laid out for them in the sanity of England. They considered themselves lucky to hold what they had.

General Eisenhower, listening to the first word of the seaborne landings early next morning, had no idea of what had really happened to his airborne troops. But neither, as a matter of fact, had his airborne troops.

7

The Pattern Begins to Shape

"What the hell town is this?"
  "Addeville."
  "Any 506 men here?"
  "You 506?"
  "Yeah. He's 327th."
  "Well, make yourselves at home. We got everybody."
  "Any other 327th men here?"
  "Some."
  "What's going to happen next?"
  "I dunno. We got patrols out."
  "Think there's time to eat?"
  "Yeah. You can eat."
  "What a mess! There ain't even a battalion in one piece!"
It was true. Of the 1st Battalion, which was supposed to

blow the bridges over the Douve and seize the locks, only a hundred-odd men were assembled in the town of Addeville. A similar group at the town of Les Droueries represented the 2nd Battalion and another at the town of Hiesville represented the 3rd. And so far, not much—tactically—had been accomplished.

The quiet-voiced lieutenant colonel named Robert Ballard had landed close enough to his planned drop zone to recognize terrain features—particularly a junction of five roads. His part in the La Barquette-Douve River assignment, as commander of the 2nd Battalion, was the seizure of the neighboring town of St. Come du Mont. With that town captured and held, the Germans would be doubly prevented from crossing into the peninsula with fresh troops.

When Colonel Ballard had landed, unhurt, the tracers from a machine gun on the hills behind him were thirty or forty feet above his head, firing down. He could hear voices on the road, but the men who were talking disappeared before he could find out if they were Germans or Americans. He moved cautiously along the road. Presently he encountered a man from D Company, and shortly afterwards ran into Major Bottomly, furious because he had hurt his ankle so badly that he had to crawl to move. Eventually, they encountered more of their men, some from the 506th Parachute Infantry, and one group of parachute engineers who were too scared to move from the ditch. Theirs was not the only case of funk that night: Colonel Griswold had encountered a similar group of glider men who refused to be led anywhere.

The difference between a good combat leader and a good combat soldier is that the good soldier is intent upon doing his job, while the good leader is intent upon reaching his objective. Colonel Ballard was concentrating on the seizure of St. Come du Mont. He had no long-range radio and consequently no idea of how other units were faring. But, he figured, they would be doing all right and would depend on him to do the same. So when he and Major Bottomly, with the help of some non-coms, had gathered a workable force, he started them towards the town. He had expected to be leading a battalion of 700 men. He actually had a hundred.

Just before they left, he heard the sounds of firing from the direction of Addeville, half a mile away. Not knowing that a strong force of Germans lay on the high ground between himself and the other village, he dispatched First Lieutenant George Sefton of Anderson, Indiana, and a few enlisted men to make contact and return. That simple round trip of a mile took the determined (and successful) Sefton twenty-eight hours.

Long before Sefton could shoot his way through to Addeville, however, the situation there had crystallized.

2

The dawn was both windy and overcast. With the day-break, we saw that Addeville was scarcely even a village. The four streets, fifteen or twenty feet wide, were deep in the same mud as the countryside. Islanded in it were thirty or forty houses of brick and rotting plaster, with red-tiled roofs. There were no stores, and the large barns attached to the houses gave the community a rural air. It not only looked desolate, it also looked far from home. And the weird part of it was the indifference of many of its inhabitants to the fighting that was going on.

They were Normans. They had lived in a part of France little troubled by the German occupation. At the first unex-pected explosions late at night they had gone down into their cellars. But when daybreak came and nothing happened to them, many came out. Most memorable of all to us was a plump Frenchwoman who, during one of the fire fights on the outskirts, sat between the two lines calmly milking a cow.

Major Allen was in charge of the men in Addeville. They were heavily engaged with the Germans by the time Colonel Johnson arrived there.

"We're going on down to the locks," said Johnson. "You'll have to withdraw and come with us."

"I can't," said Allen. "We'd be overrun. And how long will you last at the locks if we don't hold off here?"

"ALLEN," he yelled, "DON'T TALK TO ME LIKE THAT! DO AS I SAY!"

"Think it over," said the other.

Knowing Allen, Colonel Johnson thought it over. He needed men at La Barquette—especially if he expected to blow the Douve River bridges. Evidently there was nothing left of the 1st Battalion. Where the hell was Ballard? Ballard could help. He finally contacted Colonel Ballard with a 300 radio. But

Ballard, heavily engaged at Les Droueries, could send no reinforcements. Johnson walked away angrily.

While he was deliberating, one of the communications men picked up a broadcast from the BBC in London. Johnson listened, transfixed.

"At latest reports," said the sober British voice, "all seaborne landings are going satisfactorily. Allied troops are a mile inland in the vicinity of Le Bain. Casualties so far have not been excessive, and Field Marshal Montgomery and General Eisenhower have expressed their satisfaction with the progress. The operations of the airborne divisions are meeting with success."

Johnson went back to order Allen's men out of Addeville to their objective. The hell with the Germans at their rear!

Among the soldiers who had found their way to Addeville was one of the most respected and best-loved officers in the regiment. He was Francis Sampson, the Catholic chaplain. A tall, heavy-set man, broad-beamed and heavy-boned, he bore a slight resemblance to Irvin S. Cobb. His habit of rubbing his hand over his face in moments of amusement heightened this Falstaffian air. He was a hearty and jolly man, deeply loved. He himself loved all human beings, but especially the Catholic boys, "his boys" as he called them. His faith was so deep that, when he was saying Mass under sporadic shellfire in the later assembly area at Vierville, he would have died at the altar before he ducked.

During the first stage of a parachute invasion a chaplain usually works at an aid station—often, in the absence of medical personnel, establishing one himself. Father Sampson had done this once during the night and then, leaving that station under the care of another chaplain, made his way overland eight miles through enemy territory to join the meager forces of his own regiment at Addeville.

There were fourteen wounded men in the little town. When Colonel Johnson gave the order to withdraw from contact with the Germans on the outskirts and march to the regimental objective at La Barquette, one thing in the midst of so much uncertainty was certain: the wounded men would have to be left behind.

Major Carrel, the regimental surgeon, a mild and capable man who hated war, detailed an aid man to remain behind with them. This was the best he could do. His own duty lay with the regiment.

"I'll stay behind with those men," Father Sampson told him.

Carrel told him the Germans would come into the town as soon as the 501st men were gone. Father Sampson glanced at the makeshift aid-station where the fourteen men would be abandoned. "I'll stay with them," he repeated.

"The Germans are shooting prisoners."

"Shooting these prisoners," said the huge priest, "is what I can try to prevent."

Carrel, a warmhearted man, shrugged.

Later, when Johnson and the lead party had gone, and Allen was ready to withdraw with the remainder, Allen also tried to persuade Father Sampson not to stay behind. Knowing Colonel Johnson, Allen even made it clear that, by remaining behind, the chaplain was disobeying orders. There is no record of Father Sampson's rejoinder, but it seems evident that he considered himself under orders of somewhat higher Authority. So when the last paratroopers had gone and the little village was silent—silent, that is, except for the noise of roosters and the occasional random shots from the unopposed but wary Germans just outside—Father Sampson stood in the door of the aid station with a large white flag and waited to be taken prisoner.

3

The countryside on the road to La Barquette was comparatively open. Moreover, there was high ground to the north in the direction of Carentan and St. Lô; the enemy could watch from there. To move about openly in the combat zone was an uneasy sensation, we found. But we walked steadily down the road, one line of men on each side and each man a score of yards from his neighbor. Bringing up the rear was Lieutenant Farrell, who had parachuted into Normandy as a naval fire adjuster for the airborne troops.

The quiet was ominous. There were no houses, and the only signs of previous habitation were the dead cows here and there, already beginning to look a little bloated. The fields were heavily turfed with sod, interlaced with small canals. Under the low clouds the small patches of poplar trees looked funereal. Around them here and there were flooded fields with bullrushes, evidence that the water had been there a long time. The whole land had that aspect which marks an area close to the fighting—it was empty of human life. The only signs of war were the multicolored parachutes flapping in the wind and the discarded canvas of equipment bundles.

We found it hard to believe that on the coast the infantrymen of the invasion were fighting towards us. The land was too still.

As we reached a turn in the road north and west of the village of Peneme and close to the locks, the unexpected happened. We heard the whistle of an 88mm. shell. An instant later, mortar shells, artillery and small-arms fire tore up the Norman road in clouds of exploding soil. The men who were still alive a second later dove into the ditches. We could smell the ammoniac stink of cordite. The shells that were coming down made a high thin shriek, like a tearing sheet; it was a sound that lasted no longer than the tire screech before a motor crash. The slight *swish* of the descending mortars was inaudible unless you were close, and those who had been close in the first moment lay helplessly on the road, their faces or legs a pulp of blood. Panic-stricken horses thumped about the sodden fields.

Unable to fight back, Colonel Johnson ordered the group forward. Inching their way along the ditches, the men moved towards La Barquette. They felt what most men feel under heavy shellfire—that movement was more sensible than lying still. Thoughts were driven out of their heads.

The only one who seemed to go on thinking was Colonel Johnson. He was worried. If the Germans could see his men along the road, they would certainly be able to see them at the locks. And in two or three days of a barrage like this, how many of them would be left alive?

Angrily he pushed the group towards the river.*

*In the official War Department history of the La Barquette action, Colonel Johnson is shown to have seized the locks at dawn and left a token force to guard them while he went up to Addeville to collect Allen's forces, which he brought down in the afternoon. However, the men of Allen's force who were questioned on this point testified unanimously that when they arrived at La Barquette the locks and the surrounding area were deserted; moreover, Colonel Johnson seemed to take this desertion for granted. Since Colonel Johnson was dead at the time the interviews were conducted, it was impossible to resolve the disparities in the two accounts, so the official version, being unconfirmed, was not used.

The locks at La Barquette seemed peaceful enough when they got there. Across the muddy water was a small granite bridge. On the far side of that bridge, beyond the locks, was a house where the lockkeeper lived. It was later found to be deserted. A few poplars stood up funereally at the approach to the stream, and by them was a granite house and barn. The locks were closed; the rural countryside was empty. The only evidence of civilization was a paratrooper of the 506th, who lay on the far bank of the stream with one leg blown off. He was still alive.

Mortar shells began to fall sporadically. The first man to cross the bridge, Private Campos, lost his eye and broke his arm when a mortar shell exploded close to him. But the men followed in short dashes and within a few minutes the locks were secure.

"Dig in," went the order. Johnson sent patrols towards the Douve River bridges. The words of the radio announcer kept running through his mind—" . . . the airborne operations are meeting with success . . ."

4

At 6:30 that morning twenty assault groups of the seaborne 4th Division had landed at Utah Beach. Opposition at the point was not so heavy as had been expected; even the Luftwaffe was absent. In a very short time the infantry and tanks were moving across the sand dunes towards the parachutists; one of their objectives was the narrow causeways through the marshes that led to Pouppeville and Carentan.

Tanks reached the outskirts of Pouppeville at noon. But they were held up outside the town while a group of infantrymen, who had approached Pouppeville from the opposite direction, cleared it of enemy snipers.

This group consisted mainly of Colonel Julian J. Ewell's 3rd Battalion. Ewell had assembled about a hundred men. His tiny battalion had been in division reserve earlier in the day, while the 506th Parachute Infantry seized—or was supposed to seize—Pouppeville. But reports from the 506th had been fragmentary, and General Taylor, worried about the approaching 4th Division, at last committed Ewell's group.*

Ewell and his men fought their way into Pouppeville against stubborn but disorganized resistance. The first two German machine guns at the outskirts of the town were knocked out singlehanded by enlisted men; Sergeant Meryl W. Tinklenberg of Edgerton, Minnesota, reduced one, and Corporal Virgil Danforth (though creased in the skull by a bullet) reduced the other.

A lieutenant from New York put his head around a building and was promptly shot through the eye, the bullet coming out the other side of his head. Private James F. Hubbard of Gaston, N.C., started through an open gate by the road and was also shot. But this resistance came from snipers on the outskirts, and after the first hundred yards the going was easier.

The only villagers seen by the troops, as they worked their way through town, were a group of Frenchmen laughing and talking among themselves in a yard. Private Jesse C. Garcia of Chicago, Illinois, and one other man went into the yard to investigate. A German soldier stepped from behind a fence and fired eight bullets into Garcia. Then the German disappeared. The second soldier discharged a clip of submachinegun bullets above the heads of the Frenchmen, and nobody ever saw them again.

First Lieutenant Luther Knowlton of Florence, South Carolina, and a sergeant from his platoon worked their way to the far side of Pouppeville, where the resistance was light.** In the distance beyond the curve of the highway they saw the protruding hull of a tank.

"German?" asked the sergeant.

"Damned if I know."

"The hell with it," said the sergeant. He opened fire.

But in a moment an orange identification panel appeared on the side of the tank.

"Cease firing!" Knowlton yelled excitedly. He tossed an orange smoke grenade in front of him.

---

* Colonel Ewell, who read these pages in manuscript form, scribbled a notation at this point that in the division group at Hiesville were three generals—Taylor, McAuliffe and Higgins—supervising his hundred men. "Never," said his note, "had so few been commanded by so many."

** This passage is from Knowlton's testimony to the writer.

The sergeant was the first down the road to the tanks. An American captain, approaching from the other direction, flung his arms around the enlisted man and pounded him on the back.

"Never in my life been so glad to see a total stranger!" he shouted ecstatically.

5

That was how the seaborne troops met the airborne.

Ballard at Les Droueries, Johnson at La Barquette and Father Sampson at Addeville could only guess at these things, happening half a dozen miles away. They were having troubles of their own.

As Johnson had expected, the Germans on the high ground towards Carentan and St. Come du Mont had opened fire again. Visibility was excellent from both sides, and the paratroopers at the locks could see German troops coming and going on the road between Carentan and St. Come du Mont. They could even see the faint smoke rings made by the German mortars. But they were helpless. Their own weapons were too light.

Casualties began to mount.

Colonel Johnson raved at the hopelessness of the situation. Little by little, hour by hour, his force was dwindling. He had no air support; he had no artillery support; he could expect no reinforcements; he had nothing. He ground his teeth in rage.

But then he stopped. Damn it!—THE NAVY!

Disregarding the shell fire, he went in search of Lieutenant Farrell, the artillery officer.

"Can you contact a ship? Bring fire on those positions?"

"I think so," said Farrell.

"Then for God's sake, man, do it!"

"Give me the coordinates."

While Farrell and the radio man made contact, Johnson fixed the coordinates of the enemy positions. Farrell reached the U.S.S. *Quincy,* a modern cruiser riding offshore on the English Channel nine miles away.

When the fire order was passed to the warship, our group on the French road waited tensely. Five . . . ten minutes . . . then all at once we saw the billowing clouds of gray smoke from the heavy artillery, splintering out on the rocks of the enemy positions.

It must have been a considerable shock to the Germans.

Our men cheered.

"Over!" Johnson yelled excitedly. "Over, fella'."

He radioed Allen in Addeville to watch. The second salvo of six-inch shells then fell directly on the enemy positions. Farrell radioed to fire for effect. In a few moments the gray smoke had mushroomed out like fungus on the slopes of the high ground beyond them. The enemy fire slackened off.

"How do you like that, Allen?" Johnson yelled over the radio.

"Try it for Ballard," Allen radioed back.

Johnson agreed. Ballard was not in radio contact with Johnson, but he could reach Allen. So he had to relay his co-ordinates from the vicinity of Les Droueries to Addeville, from Addeville to La Barquette and from La Barquette to the *Quincy*. Back and forth like that for some time the strange sequence of fire commands was forwarded.

"Tell Ballard to get his ass up here!" Johnson finally radioed. "Tell him we're being wiped out. Tell him anything. Just get him here."

His patrols towards the Douve River bridges had been stopped dead. And steadily the opposing German troops moved down towards the locks.

6

The order to go to La Barquette angered Colonel Ballard's group. After hours of heavy fighting one force of men had seized a critical road junction; another, under Lieutenant Walter Wood, had seized a second. Resistance was just beginning to melt away. Withdraw!

If Colonel Ballard had known that the second of his two crossroads had been seized, he would have continued towards St. Come du Mont. But his contact with Wood was by runner—two hours to go and come. He ordered the withdrawal. His troops would assemble at Angoville au Plain and move down to join Colonel Johnson.

This was more easily said than done, however. The naval gunfire from the *Quincy* had been of no permanent help.

Allen told him the disturbing news that, unless he could get to La Barquette, Johnson's force would be wiped out. Yet, between his group and where he was supposed to go lay a wide-open stretch of marshy, semi-inundated land, crossed by a single road. The patrol which he dispatched out there as a test drew so much fire from the enemy on the high ground that the men were lucky to get back alive.

The marsh was impassable by daylight. Darkness was four or five hours away. If Ballard waited that long, Johnson's group . . .

Tired, discouraged, hungry, he and his men turned back to fight for their former positions. If they could get around the marsh that way, they could reach La Barquette through Addeville.

On their faces was a stubble of beard. They were coming to their second night without sleep; dirt fouled their bodies; lines of weariness compressed their mouths. The skin around their eyes was screwed up in the squint of killing, of being killed. They looked like nondescripts, stragglers. They no longer had any idea of what they were doing. They went on killing men whom they didn't hate, because that was their job. But for the first time in their lives they began to understand what it meant to hate war.

Night fell and they went on dying.

A few miles away, at the aid station in Addeville, Father Sampson was making dinner for his wounded men. The Germans outside the town evidently considered the sudden quiet from the American side a trick, for they made no move to enter. Enemy records, later captured, indicate that no estimate of the situation was made by the German General Staff until hours after the invading forces had landed, and in the absence of unmistakable authority, which was the keystone of the German military machine, aggressiveness was missing. Father Sampson left the white flag in the door of the aid station while he prepared dinner.

One of the soldiers in the aid station, suffering from shock, was out of his mind. To prevent him from demoralizing the others, Father Sampson put him in the connecting barn and assigned the aid man to watch him. Among the other wounded, the one who was closest to death was a soldier whose leg had been partially torn off by the accidental explosion of a hand grenade in the pocket of his combat suit. Though Sampson gave him blood plasma several times, the man died in a few hours. There was no time to bury him. The priest wrapped his body in the silk shrouds of a parachute and put it in another barn close by.

"You think the Krauts will shoot us, Father?" asked one of the men.

"Not while I'm here," said the big priest, cheerfully.

To himself, he wondered how long he could keep up their spirits. The dinner he had cooked for them, a scraped-up formula of cocoa and hash, had been of some help. From a Frenchwoman down the street he secured a couple of bottles of *vin ordinaire*, and he was able to give a little wine to those whose injuries were not too great. Nonetheless, some of the men were so badly hurt that they moaned continually. Two of them had to be put in a small adjoining room, where the horror of what had happened to them was spared the other wounded. The priest continued to administer blood plasma. When midnight came and the little farm house was silent, and after he had said a prayer for the men, he went back to the doorway and waited, flag in hand, for the Germans.

They were certain to come by daybreak.

7

Unknown to Colonel Ballard his small force was islanded a few miles away in the midst of German forces shifting east and west to meet the rapidly consolidating threat of the beachheads. He was bypassed several times by enemy forces strong enough to wipe him out. These forces, later engaged by other elements of the 101st Airborne Division (the 506th under Colonel Sink in particular), missed him only by chance. But at dawn, when Ballard had begun to despair either of reaching Johnson or of being of any real usefulness in the invasion, a curious incident took place.

A German officer and two German soldiers put their heads over the bushes to the rear of the command post. The Americans took them prisoner.

A few minutes later, Ballard's tiny force observed a battalion of Germans approaching from the rear. The command post personnel—only a handful of men—opened fire.

To their amazement the enemy battalion refused combat.

Veering off, the long lines of men moved across the swamp
road and vanished in the direction of La Barquette.

Ballard, watching them go, wondered helplessly if this
would be the end of Johnson.

8
They Didn't Know How They Did It

Vivid actions are easily overestimated. In fairness to the
thousands of airborne troops who fought and died in the first
three days of the invasion of France—and especially in fairness to those men who were assaulting the beachheads—it
should be understood that the fight at La Barquette was not a
major key to the success of the invasion. The Germans had
evidently overlooked the strategic value of the locks and, in
the time they were held by Colonel Johnson and our men, the
attempt by the Germans to seize them never became a serious
threat.

But after the Germans around Carentan and St. Come du
Mont recovered from their initial surprise, they discovered
that a very determined group of men were deployed around
the La Barquette locks. Defense of an area they could understand; it was organized and recognizable warfare. Whether
they understood the military value of the locks will never be
known. But after the confused insanity of the first scraps with
the airborne troops, they seemed glad to fight the way they
had been taught.

The area was called "Hell's Corner," because the road to
St. Come du Mont made a bend like a hook where it passed
by Johnson's provisional command post. Approaching along
that road on foot on June 7th, after a long walk alone from
where he had landed, Sergeant Val Suarez saw a few houses
and the ruin of an old stone building shadowed by a scraggly
orchard. Near the ruined house was the artillery officer,
Lieutenant Farrell, who was sitting in the shelter of an equally

ramshackle wall, trying to establish contact with another vessel offshore. The crackle of his set was the only sound.

Suarez didn't know much about the situation, but he was too hungry to care. He had lost his canteen and his K rations during the jump, and the only equipment he retained, besides his gun, was a torn part of his parachute (which he wanted to take back as a souvenir) and a photograph of his wife in Mishawaka. When he had reported to Major Allen, he went in search of food. Everyone, he learned, was just as hungry as he was. The only thing he could do was draw some of the foul water from the pump, decontaminate it and mix it with cocoa, of which there was a little to spare.

Earlier that morning, the men had slaughtered a calf that had been running wild through an adjacent field. In the lockkeeper's garden they found cabbages, potatoes, onions and a few strawberries. They cooked it all together and, when it was ready to eat, carried it back three hundred yards to the wounded in the aid station.

The area was quiet. A few men were strolling about, collecting water canteens from the dead. Some of the men were riding horseback along the road, recklessly trying to draw fire from the snipers on the high ground. One horse, on which they had tied a bright yellow parachute, wandered about the road looking like a stray from Barnum and Bailey. A general atmosphere of confidence prevailed; since the naval bombardment, everyone believed the worst was over.

Down on the line by the locks were a number of dead Germans. Some of them had approached to within a few feet of the American lines during the darkness. One of those Germans had had a wild time before he died. Creeping along the canal during the night, he had reached the defended knoll before he was challenged. When he failed to reply, he was fired on. The sentry missed. The German jumped into the canal and swam to the far bank. As he reached it, one of the men on that side shot him three times in the shoulder. The German screamed. His weapon fell into the water. Still alive, he stripped off his webbing and ran around the barn, screaming for mercy. Tripping, he fell into an empty foxhole.

One of our soldiers had pulled the pin on a hand grenade. As he was about to throw the grenade, the German came struggling out of the hole, staggered forward a few feet and fell into a slit trench, moaning. The American tossed the grenade into a nearby pond, where it exploded harmlessly, and, going over to the prone German, stabbed him to death.

At about four o'clock the following afternoon Suarez was at the command post with Colonel Johnson. Someone had just arrived with the information that a large body of troops was approaching their position across the marshy flatland to the rear.

Johnson grabbed binoculars. Suarez scurried about and found another pair.

"What is it," somebody whispered at his elbow, "the Fourth Division?"

"Can't tell."

"Hot dog! The seaborne!"

"Better wait."

The operations sergeant, Charles O. Hill, alerted some of the line; Bud Dorman of Philadelphia alerted the rest. Suarez, peering through the glass, saw only a long column of tiny figures in blue green—the same color, at least from a distance, as the American uniform. The countryside at that point was flat and marshy; it offered virtually no cover at all. Our men were disposed in dug-in positions roughly forming the shape of a U, the deep end of the U being nearest the locks.

Everybody waited. Whispers ran up and down the line.

"Americans?"

"Hell, no! What do you think Americans are doing out here?"

"Let's open up on them."

"They're too far away."

That was how the battalion that Colonel Ballard had contacted a few miles away at Les Droueries walked into La Barquette.

When the Germans came within rifle-shot and were recognized, they were caught on the open ground. The fighting that developed was the kind of fighting familiar to every soldier who has ever been under fire, in which neither side sees very much of the other, but each, from what cover it can find, bangs away at hazard.

In this case two things favored our own badly outnumbered force—better cover and (oddly enough) a higher morale. The Germans' almost timid reaction to their first brush with Ballard's group had not been evidence of a determined move towards Colonel Johnson, but simply a desire to keep out of trouble.

They were rattled. Like a great many Germans on the Cotentin Peninsula in those days, they believed that the airborne invasion was bigger than it really was.

Winning, a German soldier fights more efficiently and methodically than the American soldier. Losing, he is defeated quickly.

After an hour of fighting, Colonel Johnson saw evidence of disorder on the German side. Faint cries of "Kamerad!" came to him over the crackling of rifle fire. His own ammunition was running low. Casualties had been numerous on his side. He badly needed a German surrender.

Private Nicholai, a stolid soldier, volunteered to act as interpreter. Private Norman D. Blanchette of Acushnet, Massachusetts, a quiet man with a round face like a moon, volunteered to carry an orange flag.

A sparse crackling of fire still came from the German lines. Johnson waved the orange flag. But the firing continued sporadically, and even his own men were reluctant to stop shooting while they were being shot at.

At length, in spite of the firing, Colonel Johnson, Nicholai and Blanchette started forward.

"Don't be a damn fool, Colonel!" shouted one of the staff officers. "You'll be shot."

"This is what they pay me for," Johnson called back.

But he felt uneasy walking across towards the enemy. He was encouraged by the bearing of Nicholai and Blanchette.

They had reached a point about a hundred yards in advance of their own line when an intermediary from the German lines approached to meet them. Back in the American lines, a captain drew a bead on the German intermediary. His shot dropped the man instantly. Fire sprang out on both sides again. Johnson and his two men had to go down. By squirming and crawling they regained their own lines. Johnson, blazing mad, searched for the offending captain.

"What the hell's the idea?" he screamed.

"Colonel," the captain pleaded, his voice breaking, "those Krauts have been killing our men all day. And now you won't let us shoot them." He broke down and cried.

Colonel Johnson kicked him. "Get in the C.P.!" he shouted. "Get in there and stay there!"

The slow business of quieting the line had to begin all over again.

On the second attempt, the parley in the center of the field was successful. Johnson's instructions to the Germans were to throw down their weapons and come out one by one, with their hands behind their heads. If they behaved themselves they would not be shot. They had half an hour.

Greatly pleased, Johnson returned to his own lines. The firing still was sporadic. But about twenty minutes later, the men saw the first Germans come out and file across the field with their hands behind their heads. First there were fifty, then a hundred, then a hundred and fifty. They did not all come at once; some waited to find out if their comrades would be shot. But in the end they all surrendered, and the only men lying behind the German lines were the wounded and the dead.

It was the first real battle victory for the 501st.

2

The first American surrender of any size had taken place, meanwhile, at Father Sampson's aid station in Addeville.

With the dawn, the tardy Germans came. The priest saw them when they were a little distance down the wide main street of the village.

"Here they come, fellows," he told his men. "Just take it easy now." And carrying the white flag he went out to meet them.

The Americans inside the aid station felt queer when they heard the Germans outside. One of the men, less gravely wounded than the others, stood near the door to watch.

"They've taken him," he announced for the benefit of the others.

"What? Who?"

"Two Krauts. They're taking him up the road somewhere."

"What're they going to do with him?"

"How the hell do I know? Looks like they're going to shoot him."

There was a little silence in the aid station. The men felt sick at heart. Next moment a German soldier jumped into the doorway and shoved a machine pistol into the stomach of the paratrooper who had been standing there. The German said something unintelligible and pulled the trigger.

The gun failed to go off.

The German pushed the American into the room and entered. He was followed by several others, all enlisted men. The aid man attempted to point out that everyone except himself was wounded and helpless, but the Germans waved him back and made an inspection of their own.

Audible in the room that instant was the sound of a distant shot—one and then another.

Bending their heads or closing their eyes, whichever they could do, the wounded men said prayers for the man who had stayed behind to save them. Then they waited for their own death.

3

Johnson, a few miles away, was wildly pleased with his bag. Prisoners were concrete evidence of success. Suarez, who watched him supervise the collection of dispirited German soldiers, remarked to Bud Dorman that his antics reminded him of Hitler's dance when France surrendered.

Meanwhile, however, a more resolute group of the enemy on the far hills by Carentan and St. Come du Mont had observed this spectacle. Whether they realized that it was a surrender will never be known. But through their field glasses they could see, down behind the little stone house in the orchard, a great crowd of men—an unmilitary horde—the target of an artillery man's lifetime.

With 88mm. guns and mortars they opened fire.

The first shells killed or wounded thirteen of the defenseless Germans. The remainder, though guarded by armed soldiers, showed signs of panic. When the second barrage of shells whistled down, the armed guards were forced into the shelter of inadequate ditches. Captain MacReynolds, the regimental adjutant, stood his ground and almost single-handedly controlled the crowd of frightened and uncertain men. They stayed where they were—and that was how Captain MacReynolds died.

Suarez was in the orchard when the first shell whistled in. He dove behind a tree. The shell exploded so close that he was banged sidewards into the air. Shaken but unhurt, he saw Charlie Hill dive into a foxhole, Bud Dorman after him. The next shell exploded close to that foxhole and Bud Dorman was killed.

Then a shell got Suarez.

He was making for the command post. When he heard the heartstopping, thin shriek of the incoming steel, he dove behind the shelter of the wall, his legs and hips exposed. The explosion on them felt like the kick of a mule. But there was no special pain. Suarez didn't know that he had been hit. He got up and ran as fast as he could for the shelter of the already overcrowded ditch.

Slowly, the shelling moved over the entire area. Only when it lifted did Suarez realize that something was wrong. He could hardly move. There was blood in the water of the ditch. Feeling along his back with his hands, he could find nothing wrong. But he told the man next to him that he thought he'd been hit.

"You sure have," said the man, helpfully.

Suarez could hardly walk. Hobbling brought great pain. But others were in greater need of attention than he, so after a little while he made his way, foot by foot, back to the crowded aid station a quarter of a mile down the road. Because the doctors were busy, he sat at the side and waited his turn. He was dazed and aching. When Major Carrel had examined and tagged him, he hobbled into the barn behind the aid station and lay down to sleep. For Suarez, the invasion of Normandy was over.

4

Only a few miles away, the drama was continuing for Father Sampson.

The two German soldiers who had taken him prisoner on the street made him drop the surrender flag and then walked him up a road to a bend where they were out of sight of the others. The Germans carried their weapons at the "ready" position; when they made Father Sampson put his back to a crumbling stone wall that flanked the road, there could be no mistaking their intentions.

It was a still, pale day. In the bushes and trees, birds chirruped like blithe spirits, indifferent to good or evil. Father Sampson, convinced that this would be his last morning on

earth, said a hasty act of contrition. The two soldiers stepped
back to the far ditch at the edge of the road.

Then there was a shot. It came from higher up the road. It
was followed by another shot. The German soldiers were as
startled as Father Sampson. Looking up, they saw the distant
figure of a German officer running towards them, his pistol in
the air.

In the angry disciplining that took place on the road in the
next few minutes Father Sampson (not quite the disinterested
bystander) managed to make the German officer understand—by
pointing to the silver crosses on his shirt, the Red Cross
brassard on his sleeve—that he was a chaplain. When this
fact was established, the German officer's manner changed to
cordiality, even obsequiousness. He and the two chastened
soldiers, who followed like coon dogs deprived of their coon,
accompanied Father Sampson back to the aid station in the
village. While the American soldiers concealed their amazement and delight, the German officer satisfied himself that all
of the men were disarmed, ordered his own soldiers out of the
house and, saluting Chaplain Sampson, gave back to him the
aid station intact—an island of inviolate American territory in
the middle of the German lines.

Higher Authority, it seemed, had returned the priest's applica-
tion with an indorsement of approval.

5

Colonel Ballard, still at Les Droueries, and still worried
about Johnson, finally managed to make contact by radio with
division headquarters at Hiesville. Outlining his situation to
Colonel Kinnard, he repeated Colonel Johnson's order to
withdraw.

"Stay where you are," advised Kinnard. "Something's
brewing."

Ballard stayed where he was. He couldn't go anywhere,
anyway.

The radio contact had come on the heels of a decision by
the division commander, Major General Taylor, for the next
move.

Of the division objectives, the 502nd Parachute Infantry,
under Lieutenant Colonel Michaelis, had captured the cause-

way leading out of the peninsula and held the Germans to the north of the beaches.

The 506th Parachute Infantry, under Colonel Sink, had pushed the German forces back towards St. Come du Mont.

Colonel Johnson had seized and was holding the critical locks at La Barquette.

Colonel Ewell and his men had taken the causeways at Pouppeville and had made contact with the seaborne 4th Division.

But St. Come du Mont and the bridges over the Douve River still were in enemy hands. The seizure of the former and the destruction of the latter would accomplish the last of the division missions. This made it clear that Colonel Ballard's then impotent force at Les Droueries, though unable to achieve anything by itself, offered a wedge into enemy territory which could be used as a jumping-off point for St. Come du Mont. The decision to launch a coordinated attack from that direction lay behind Kinnard's allusion to "something brewing."

So the 506th Parachute Infantry—not a regiment, just then, but the gathering skeleton of one—and Colonel Ewell's equally shorthanded 3rd Battalion, whose men had already been encouraged by their success at Pouppeville, pushed overland to join the exhausted forces under Ballard. With medium tanks in support, they were to attempt what Ballard had been trying to do, against outnumbering forces, for two days.

Coincidentally, the advancing seaborne artillery, other armed forces, and some naval ships made plans for a night barrage of sufficient intensity to paralyze the entire organization behind the German lines. The barrage, with interdictory fire, was to cover all of the known enemy territory, including the town of Addeville—where reports clearly indicated that only Germans now remained.

9
Night Barrage

Evening fell. At Les Droueries, Colonel Sink, establishing a joint command post with Colonels Ballard and Ewell in the shell hole, gave the attack order for the morning. At La Barquette, what was left of Colonel Johnson's men settled down for a second night at the locks, with ammunition and food so scarce that their presence was largely a bluff.

Father Sampson, in the aid station at Addeville, was ignorant of the entire situation in Normandy. He knew nothing of the seaborne invasion, nor even of the success of the parachutists, and his only word from down the road where Johnson and Allen had disappeared was the steady *"wop-wop"* of incoming shells exploding at La Barquette. Nonetheless, he was in good spirits, and the German soldiers who occupied the town ignored him as they went about their own business.

None of the wounded men had died. Father Sampson had tended them without relief, administering blood plasma intermittently throughout the day and evening. With nightfall and the inevitable lowered spirits which accompanied the darkness, he heated more coffee and made a new meal of provisions foraged from the French. Then he led the men in prayers and settled them for the night. He himself had not slept since the night before the take-off from England, but, when the men were dozing in the dark room, he stayed awake to watch them. And he was awake several hours later, when it became a certainty that the distant roll of a heavy, incoming artillery barrage was getting closer and closer to Addeville.

A heavy artillery barrage, like saturation bombing, is one of the really terrifying forms of destruction in modern warfare. While it lasts, there is nothing a man can do to help himself. He must listen in silence, generally without moving, while the heavy shells explode with a shattering thunder, so all-encompassing in its violence that no doubt is left in the mind of one's chance of surviving a near miss. With each roar the earth shakes, the walls bulge, the windows rattle or burst inward as though underwater. What is worse, each explosion is anticipated by a high, thin and unearthly shriek—unearthly because it comes from something moving faster than instinct comprehends.

As the barrage from the American guns moved closer and closer to Addeville, the wounded men woke up. They said nothing to each other. Father Sampson lifted those who were lying on beds and put them on the floor, placing two of the more seriously wounded underneath the mattresses, where they would be sheltered from falling plaster. He checked on the demented man in the barn and on the two men—already near death—who were in a separate room at the side of the aid station. When he had done everything he could, he led the group in prayers again. By this time, the incoming shells were on the outskirts of the village.

Within a few moments the whole town was under fire. The explosions were so heavy and the firing so intense that, between the bursts, the screams of the wounded Germans were audible. The house rocked. Window-glass shattered; plaster crashed down from the ceiling on the men; Father Sampson threw himself across their bodies; dirt fell; boards fell; the house next door erupted in a thunderous flash; the courtyard exploded; the Germans opened fire with small arms; bullets splintered the wainscoting of the windows, smashed into the plaster walls above the Americans; in the barn the demented man began to yell; fires started down the street. . . .

With a blinding flash, a shell struck the adjoining room. Tons of plaster, tile, and wooden beams crashed down on the two men who were in there. Groping his way through the dust, Father Sampson tore at the beams and rubble. He unearthed the head and shoulders of one man, who gasped "Father" and died. The other was already dead.

Shells were exploding in the courtyard. Jagged fragments of shrapnel spun through the walls with a "*pang,*" like a bent saw released. Out of the open gap torn in the walls at the side, Father Sampson could see a lighted flashlight. It had evidently been blown into the courtyard and lighted by the impact. He went outside to extinguish it before it drew more fire. Close by, a German boy had been blown into the creek, where he lay moaning in the water. The priest lifted him out and put him on the bank, where he died.

Inside the house, a ricochet bullet struck Father Sampson's trousers and set them afire. He beat out the flames with his hands, but the skin of his thigh shortly began to blister. Meanwhile, the falling plaster had opened some of the men's wounds. Kneeling in the fiery darkness, Father Sampson administered more plasma. Then he joined the group in prayers. Little by little—though it seemed to take hours—the rolling barrage moved away from the demolished houses of the town and beyond to St. Come du Mont.

It was almost morning.

In the first light, Father Sampson walked down through the little village to see the damage that had been done. When he returned, he knelt down at the side of the room and bowed his head.

Of all the houses in the little town, only his aid room was intact.

2

The barrage had been carefully guided around the Sink-Ewell-Ballard combination waiting to push off at dawn from Les Droueries. They had planned a barrage of their own from the tank guns, just prior to the advance. Afterwards, the tanks and the men would go forward together.

The tanks would go forward, that is, if they could get through the hedgerows.

Hedgerows were the chief difficulty of the fighting in Normandy. Centuries of cultivated growth had formed them into heavy tangled walls, deep-rooted and almost impenetrable. They were generally paralleled by a ditch. Fighting took place between one hedgerow and another, where the light blue haze of smokeless powder was the only visible evidence of the enemy.

For a man to crawl directly through the hedgerows was almost impossible. The twisted roots were close together and immovable. He could climb over the hedgerow, but, if he did, it was unlikely that he would be alive to reach the ground on the other side. So if he was ordered to advance and seize the next line of hedgerows, he had to crawl along the ditch until he found a break, generally by a tree or at the junction of two hedgerows. And the enemy, anticipating an advance through these points, had them zeroed-in with mortars and artillery, or else mined.

All over Normandy our troops were finding out the meaning of those hedgerows. They partitioned the local battles into squares or rectangles like a rural checkerboard. Men died crossing them, or they died in the fields between. Like desert warfare, hedgerow fighting became associated with the land itself, so that long afterwards the sight of them in other countries recalled the mosquitoes at evening, the taste of soil, and the ammoniac smoke in the meadows where the crickets piped.

Dawn had not yet come. The spring darkness was cold. Colonel Ballard and some of his men went down to the lines to wait for the preliminary barrage. Behind them, out of sight of the enemy, the tank gunners loaded their weapons. Three minutes to go . . .

Somewhere there was the bassoon piping of frogs.

Two minutes . . .

A light scattering of rifle fire rippled along the lines.

One minute . . .

The men who were going to attack waited, their hearts pounding, their lips dry. Here and there was the click of a canteen.

FIRE!

Colonel Ballard and his group dove for the ditch behind. The fire was close—too close for comfort. The night seemed to heave up in quick, sharp, yellow flashes, billowing upheavals, torn hedges, trees, and torn men. Shells came, shell after shell, as rapidly as the tank men could load and reload; so fast that the Germans could only hug the ground.

Then the tank motors coughed into life. The tanks and the men started forward together, the machine guns on the Shermans spraying the fields. The tanks were not stopped by the hedgerows. And in fifteen minutes the line had advanced farther towards the retreating Germans than Colonel Ballard had been able to advance in two days.

10
Attack on St. Come du Mont

The combined attack towards St. Come du Mont represented the first attempt by the 101st Airborne Division staff to act with forces in excess of the scattered "Indian bands" which had done most of the hard work up to that time. The two illustrations in this chapter make clear, better than words can do, the unbelievable hodge-podge of the offensive. But it is interesting to observe that, through the maze of conflicting routes and dead ends illustrated on the map of battle, one line of advance leads directly from the point of departure to the objective.

That line was made by the men of the 3rd Battalion of Colonel Johnson's regiment, under Lieutenant Colonel Julian J. Ewell.

In addition to Ewell's 3rd Battalion, elements of six companies of the 506th Parachute Infantry Regiment, one battalion of the 401st Parachute Infantry (a glider unit), and Ballard's weary mixture of soldiers participated in the attack. Many men of Sink's 506th group were just as tired as Ballard's men, and this may have been one reason why the general plan of attack went to pieces during the action. The soldiers were too tired to listen to the attack orders. Ewell's men were comparatively fresh, however, and the success of their operation at Pouppeville had fused them into a unit.

They were supposed to attack straight through, aiming at the main highway just below St. Come du Mont. For quite a while after they had started they were able to make good progress, although Ewell could see that he was being cramped on the right by D Company of Sink's forces, which seemed to be drifting to the left. On Ewell's own left was the 401st group, so he was unable to give ground.

Just at the edge of Les Droueries the assault platoons encountered the enemy. As the artillery barrage lifted to make

71

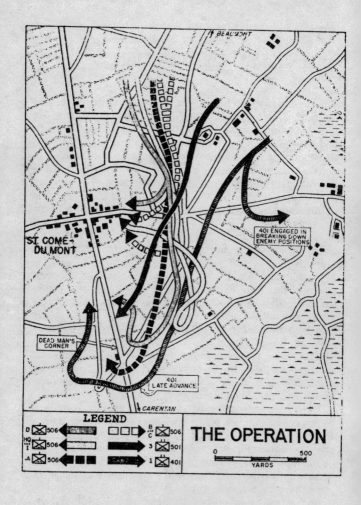

BEAUMONT

ST. COMÉ
DU MONT

401 ENGAGED IN
BREAKING DOWN
ENEMY POSITIONS

DEAD MAN'S
CORNER

401
LATE ADVANCE

CARENTAN

LEGEND

D ⊠ 506
HQ and I ⊠ 506
A ⊠ 506

B C ⊠ 506
3 ⊠ 501
1 ⊠ 401

THE OPERATION

0   500
YARDS

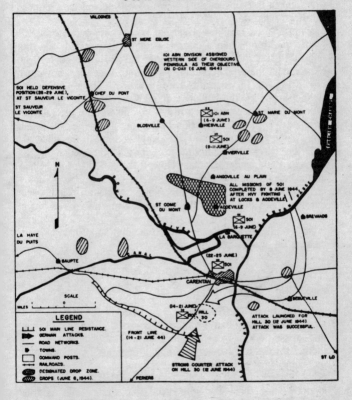

CARENTAN, FRANCE
6 JUNE – 29 JUNE 1944

way for the American advance, the Germans were pulling out of their foxholes. Ewell's men went forward at a run. Hedgerows intervened and, although the Germans continued to retreat, the paratroopers could only put a screen of fire ahead of them, and never succeeded in coming to grips with the scared enemy soldiers. But the charge broke the enemy line, and in the subsequent process of withdrawal the German positions were destroyed in detail.

Ewell's men had not advanced much farther towards St. Come du Mont when a curious situation developed. On the left the 401st men, having become heavily engaged by the Germans in the prepared defenses around Addeville, began to crowd towards the road that Ewell was using for his advance. At the same time the D Company men, who had no clear idea of what they were supposed to do, continued their drift to the left. And at the road junction below Les Droueries all three units came together—with Ewell squeezed out in the middle.

Drily, Ewell halted his men. After a conference with the adjacent commander, Captain Howell, he called Colonel Sink and asked for orders. Sink talked to Howell.

"Move your battalion to the right," he said. "Take up a defensive position—keep the Germans from moving in from the west."

As events proved, this was not the solution. But at least it cleared the way for Ewell.

2

In the fields to the east of Les Droueries, platoons and whole companies had become hopelessly entangled. Units had crossed and recrossed each other's lines of advance, and the hedgerows had further scrambled the mixup. So badly had the companies become wrapped around each other that nobody was moving. The 401st men on the left flank had also stopped—nobody knew why. And into the middle of this lugubrious hodge-podge—from which, for this account, the unprintable comments of the soldiers have been excised—the Germans around St. Come du Mont began to throw artillery.

Annoyed, Ewell moved his men on. It was then eight o'clock in the morning and the air was fresh. The men still were confident of their abilities, and the decisiveness of their own commander, coupled with their swift movement forward, reminded them of an old song:

> *The Third Battalion will win the war, Parlez-vous.*
> *The Third Battalion will win the war, Parlez-vous*
> *The Third Battalion will win the war,*
> *So what's the rest of the army for?*
>   *Hinky-dinky parlez vous!*

This optimism was not to be long-lasting. As Ewell's force moved down the road, they came abreast of the German main artery of communications. Ewell could see some signs of movement among the enemy forces in St. Come du Mont—a few wagons getting out, small groups of men moving along the hedges—which made it clear that the Germans were withdrawing towards the west. For a while he thought of circling in that direction and getting behind them, to block their retreat. But his own force was too small for this. So he continued straight down the highway, intending to seize the causeway and the Douve bridges.

From the houses around the Pont de Douve, however, heavy fire broke out. It came from at least two machine guns, one anti-tank piece and a considerable force of German infantrymen. The men and their commander hesitated. Ewell tried to call for artillery support, but found that his wires had been cut. Next moment German 88mm. artillery shells from Carentan were falling among the men. That resolved Ewell's indecision and he withdrew.

In the action that followed, Ewell's position after his withdrawal was the factor that decided the battle.

Germans in great numbers were coming down the main St. Come du Mont road. It was a counter-attack. As Ewell's men deployed and moved out of the area of resistance around the Pont de Douve, they heard the crackle of rifles and the fast *"brrrrrrrup!"* of German *Schmeissers*. The bullets were going overhead. As the Germans worked their way forward along the hedgerows and ditches, the noise became steadily louder and the aim better. It was soon obvious that the entire weight of the German offensive would fall squarely on Ewell's skeleton battalion.

It did: from the first skirmish at 9:30 in the morning until four o'clock in the afternoon. Ewell and his men sustained six enemy attempts to drive them back from the road. Each attack was a little better organized than the one which preceded it. Each time, the volume of fire built up more threateningly. Each time, the Germans closed to within one hedgerow of the battalion's forward line. And each time, met by unyielding fire, the survivors faded back. Ewell's judgment of ground had given his men the advantage of a sound defense line; early in the day twenty-five of his men had, at his order, taken by storm a ridge of high ground that straddled and dominated the line.

At 4:30 the Germans made their heaviest attack. And this time the fire became too hot.

Ewell's right flank almost dissolved. The men fell back one hedgerow. To Ewell, who was then at the base of the hill, it seemed as though the whole position was about to collapse. As fast as he could, he sprinted to the top of the hill.

"Follow me!" he shouted to the men positioned there.

When he turned back at a run, the paratroopers were at his heels.

At the base of the hill a hedgerow extended out to the right. The greatest pressure from the attacking Germans had become concentrated beyond the field on the opposite side of that hedgerow. Some of Ewell's men had begun to withdraw when he and his scratch force of wildly excited men charged down along the line. The commander of a battalion is generally a little to the rear of his assaulting or defending companies. When the soldiers saw their commander not only on their own dissolving front line, but also leading his group in the one thing they could best appreciate—a direct charge—they were confirmed in an opinion of Colonel Ewell that they were never afterwards to lose.

Two American tanks had arrived at this moment. As Ewell and his group sprinted around the edge of the hedgerow and took the Germans with machine gun and rifle fire from their flank, the tanks went forward in a frontal attack, and the men behind the hedgerow line fell in behind the tanks. This unexpected counter-attack at the very moment when the Germans thought resistance was beginning to melt away broke the spine of the enemy push; under its pressure the Germans fled, leaving their dead and wounded behind them.

3

By this time it was quite late in the afternoon. Ewell thought that he and his men had fought without support long enough. His lines to the rear had been cut, however, so the only way he could find out what had delayed the remainder of Sink's forces was to go back on foot. Doing this, he found the 401st glider men still disposed in their all-day positions outside Addeville. Ewell used their telephone lines for a talk with Colonel Sink and persuaded the latter to order the 401st to Ewell's support.

They were too late. By the time the glider men had moved into support positions the Germans had made their last attack of the day. Taking place in Ewell's absence, it had cost his battalion more casualties than any of the enemy attacks during the day, killing the tank commander, three battalion officers and about twenty men. Ewell's troops, fired by the example of their commander, had yielded no ground. But when the 401st men closed in to support the 3rd Battalion of the 501st, the enemy had already begun its withdrawal—not only from the road, but also from St. Come du Mont. At 4:30, when two battalions started moving west, Ewell could see files of Germans in the distance, retreating down the railroad embankment. Even the forces around the Pont de Douve, where Ewell's men had been stopped earlier in the day, drew back and out of the fight. And when a patrol from the 1st Battalion of the 506th Parachute Infantry entered St. Come du Mont they found the town deserted.

Ewell, who had started with 160 men, had only 120 left.

Just about the time that he and his remaining men entered their objective, tired but satisfied with themselves, Field Marshal Rommel conferred with three of his principal subordinates in the Normandy area. The forces they had used to oppose the Sink-Ewell combination at St. Come du Mont had been the remainder of the German 6th Parachute Regiment—one battalion of which seemed to have disappeared during an engagement at La Barquette. Evidently Rommel had a poor opinion of the 6th Regiment, for he agreed with his subordinates that what was left of the group had fought better than he had expected.

In Rommel's opinion the main factor in the Cotentin Peninsula operation was now the defense of Carentan. Loss of that town to the Americans would only strengthen and consolidate the American front.

Accordingly, the 6th Parachute Regiment was ordered to regroup at Carentan and defend that town "to the last man."*

11

The Walking Casualty

Fighting his way down to relieve La Barquette with two jeeploads of ammunition and rations, Lieutenant Sumpter Blackmon of the 1st Battalion passed through a wrecked town that appeared on his maps as Addeville. No house in the town seemed to have escaped destruction. But for the sake of reasonable precaution he fired rifle grenades and machine gun bullets through the ruins as he went. The few Germans who returned sporadic fire on the outskirts were retreating as rapidly as they could, and Blackmon let them go.

It was not until he reached the besieged force at La Barquette and talked with Major Allen that he heard about Father Sampson's aid station. On his way back he stopped at Addeville to see if the priest's group were still alive.

Eleven of them were—eleven and Father Sampson.

With Lieutenant Blackmon to help, Father Sampson evacuated all of his wounded men to the division hospital at Hiesville. Evening was at hand before the job was done—his third night without sleep. Only one other priest was at work in the hospital, however, so, when his own men had been cared for, Sampson sent that man to bed and continued in his place all night. And when, in the early hours of the next morning, a liter of Type "O" blood was needed for a dying soldier, Sampson furnished the blood.

Most heroism in battle is a heroism of destruction. It

---

* From the war diary of the German 7th Army High Command.

normally takes place when a man has reached that pitch of nervous excitement where he is only half-conscious of what he is doing. Father Sampson's heroism was of a rarer sort: deliberate, premeditated, selfless. It was characteristic of the priest that when the War Department confirmation of his Distinguished Service Cross for those days in Addeville reached the regiment months later, he had become a prisoner of the Germans at Bastogne, Belgium.

2

Suarez was evacuated from La Barquette the next day at noon. Firing was still moderately heavy, and one of the evacuation vehicles, loaded with wounded men, was struck squarely by a mortar shell as the vehicle made its way out of the area. Legs, arms, bones, and viscera were scattered along the roadside. Suarez held his breath when his own turn came to be driven out. He was taken to the division hospital at Hiesville, where Father Sampson had been working, and sent on from there to Utah Beach by ambulance—a short time after Father Sampson left and half an hour before the hospital was blown to pieces by a German bomb.

Accounts of battle seldom deal with that other factor in the equation of success—the wounded man. It is interesting to follow Suarez back from La Barquette and Hiesville to the hospital in England.

What struck him forcibly as he rode in the ambulance along the dark roads to the beach was his own hunger. Except for the cocoa and a few pieces of the meat of a calf, which he had boiled over a makeshift stove until they were soft enough to chew, he had had nothing to eat for three days and three nights. The stiffening aches of his wounds (shrapnel had penetrated his back) intensified his emptiness. He was too miserable to care very much when the convoy of medical vehicles became lost on the black roads, and he managed to rouse himself only when, for a long stretch, the vehicles ran through water so deep that the edges of the road were invisible. He was quite sure that, military efficiency being what it was, he would die long before anyone troubled himself about him. Old wounds uncared-for make it difficult for any man—

especially a man with an empty stomach—to think of much besides himself.

He wasn't comforted when a tired surgeon at the beach hospital said, "Let's take a look at you, fella." After a quick examination, the man said, "You'll be operated on in England," and tagged him a walking casualty. Suarez was convinced he was not a "walking" casualty; he could scarcely hobble. His depression increased when he was left to his own devices for the remainder of the night. Hunger weakened him more than his wounds did. Scrounging among the tents, he stole a couple of blankets and, wrapping himself in these, lay down on the cold sand to die—thinking of all the newspaper accounts being written that moment, back home, about the tender care and expert treatment given the wounded men of the invasion. This comparison between the ideal and the real kept him reasonably happy until it began to rain. He was too sick to move. He pulled the blankets over his head.

Suarez didn't die, however. He survived the entire next day along the beach, idle and still unfed. The only incident of any note gave him the grim satisfaction of a man who considers his own worst suspicions justified. A German plane dove out of the low-lying gray banks of clouds to strafe the beach. Anti-aircrafters promptly shot it down. When it was followed by two more planes, the busy anti-aircrafters shot those machines down, too—and discovered, only after one pilot had managed to parachute to safety, that they had destroyed two American fighters.

The war was in its clumsiest stage just then.

At three o'clock the following morning Suarez and his group were moved aboard a steel LST which had been converted into a temporary hospital ship. He was beginning his fifth day without food. When the LST lay in the harbor hour after hour Suarez became so hungry that he took his camouflaged parachute, which he had carried all the way from the drop zone in France, and traded it in the galley for something hot to eat.

Not until six o'clock that evening did the LST sail. It reached Portsmouth, England, at noon the following day. Suarez had no idea of what hospital he finally reached, but when organization and efficiency at last took up again, he felt as Dante must have felt at the last circle of Purgatory. His

wounds were washed and dressed. He was put to bed in a
fresh cot with clean sheets. And an American nurse came in
and said with a smile, "Here you are, paratrooper," and
handed him a full chicken dinner.

12
Assault of Hill 30

The 101st Airborne Division had accomplished all of its
missions. The one exception was the demolition of the Douve
River bridges; this the enemy himself had accomplished. The
over-all airborne missions had been accomplished on schedule, too—though at a cost of 1,500 airborne troops killed or
captured and sixty per cent of all equipment lost.

The 501st Parachute Infantry assembled and reorganized at
a dreary little French town called Vierville. Even at that late
date, almost a week from D Day morning, parachutists who
had been lost, and fighting alone until then, came straggling
into the town. Except for the lack of gaiety—a quality of
spirit wholly absent from combat zones—the streets sometimes looked like an American Legion convention.

"Joe, you old son of a bitch! They said you were dead!"

"I am."

"Heh! There's Sciaccotti!"

"They can't kill him."

"You seen Bud Dorman?"

"He's dead. La Barquette."

In England before the take-off, General Taylor, the division commander, had said that the men would be out of the
fighting three or four days after their assault landing. It was
rapidly becoming evident to the paratroopers, however, that
nothing of the sort would happen.

2

The seizure of Carentan by the regular infantry had proved more difficult than anticipated. The Germans, recovering from their initial shock, had reorganized and strengthened their own lines of resistance. The gains made by the Allied forces in the first week of the assault showed promise of being the only gains they would make for a while to come. But Carentan had to be seized; it was a communications center vital to the consolidation of the lines. So the 101st Airborne Division was chosen for the assault.

Carentan was a city of about 65,000 persons. It lay at a bend of the Douve River, where it was approached by a highway and a railroad. Eastward beyond the town the land rose gently until it reached a crest about two hundred feet above the level of the surrounding terrain. Save for sparse shrubbery, hardly thick enough to afford concealment, and for a criss-cross checkerboard of hedgerows, the slopes of this high ground were almost bare.

The rise was dubbed "Hill 30" by the paratroopers. The Germans had fortified its slopes and crest with machine guns and 20mm. cannon. Even from the first hedgerow these emplacements commanded the approaching ground; from the summit their weapons overlooked the entire town of Carentan— its church spires, its wide, geometrical, but unmistakably old-fashioned streets, its river and railroad. Any troops attempting to attack up the slopes of the hill had to cross not only the Douve River, but also a wide stretch of marshy land under direct observation from the fortified German positions on the commanding slopes.

It was clear that if Carentan were to be held after it had been seized, Hill 30 outside the town would also have to be secured. This became the mission of our men—specifically the 3rd Battalion under Lieutenant Colonel Ewell, and particularly H Company under Captain Felix Stanley.

Stanley was a heavy-set and rather phlegmatic man who came from Waco, Texas. His features were mild, and even in repose they appeared good humored. A faint squint to his eyes gave him the suggestion of quizzicalness. He was not severe with his men, but he was imperturbable in battle and

he had that trait which Tolstoy considered indispensable to a
battlefield leader: the capacity to accept an unexpected rever-
sal as though it were part of his own plan.

In the direction of the Douve River the 327th Glider Infantry occupied front lines facing the river, the marshland, and
the rising ground. While Stanley's men spent the night in a
field behind the lines, he and the other company commanders
made what is called a preliminary reconnaissance along the
forward positions. Except for occasional gold-colored flares
from the German side, the night was quiet. Few shots were
being fired anywhere. As quietly as possible, engineers brought
rubber boats forward to the near shore of the Douve. Preparations had been made for a thirty-minute artillery barrage just
prior to the scheduled time—five o'clock on the morning of
June 12, 1944—when the troops would cross the line of
departure. In addition, mortar smoke shells would screen the
Douve River until the troops had gained the enemy side.

It is hard to convey the state of mind of soldiers who know
they are facing a difficult attack. No one talks very much.
Fear is more common than is readily admitted, but it is a
physical fear: a dry mouth, cold hands, hot skin around the
cheeks and temples, and a weight on the heart that makes it
hard to breathe. Only soldiers who can see no further into the
future than their own noses are wholly untroubled. The immi-
nence of death creates a state of mind impossible to remember
when the event is over; a soldier may remember what he did
during a battle—and sometimes the queer, irrelevant detail of
mud in ditches and hopping crickets—but he cannot afterwards remember how he felt. Combat is foreign to all other
experience; nothing in ordinary life reminds one of it.

3

When the first blush of light had appeared in the east, the
men moved silently to the line of departure. They knew as
well as did Stanley, as well as did Colonel Ewell, that
crossing the river to the flatlands and the base of the hill
would be as difficult as the assault of the high ground itself.
When they drew up along the line of departure to wait for the
preliminary artillery barrage, they were only two-dimensional

figures in the cold dawn, as insubstantial as the mists that drifted down from the quiet-running Douve.

They waited.

They waited fifteen minutes. The morning was silent. A half-hour passed. Still there was no barrage.

Colonel Johnson radioed Stanley. "You've got your orders. What are you waiting for?"

It occurred to Stanley that he was waiting for Johnson's artillery barrage. But he made no comment. In silence he and his serious-faced men moved out.

The scouts that Stanley had dispatched ahead of him to the Douve River returned with the information that, although the railroad bridge had been demolished, men on foot could still get across it.

The sky was growing lighter. Stanley had not yet called for smoke, and he waited until his men were ready to cross before he radioed back for it. As he had expected, a spattering of fire broke out from the enemy as soon as the smoke was laid down. But his men filed across the bridge steadily, one by one, carrying their weapons at the ready position, and the entire company gained the opposite shore without a casualty.

So far, so good. While his company grouped again for the push across the marshes, Stanley sent patrols ahead. Moments later, he ordered the company in their path.

Men are fatalistic when they are walking towards an unseen enemy. Everyone knows that sooner or later someone will be shot. On this morning there was an inexplicable silence everywhere. The first explosions came when Stanley's lead scouts discharged some German land mines. To avoid the mined area, Stanley led his men directly through the swamp, where they had to struggle forward, waist-deep in water, holding their rifles and mortars above their heads. Still the enemy was silent.

When at length they reached the foot of the hill, they discovered the reason for the silence. The two German 20mm. guns, neatly emplaced to command the ground over which they had just advanced, were abandoned. German packs and rifles around the area indicated the gunners were not far distant. Whatever it was that had called them from their posts at the one time when the dull vigil of guard duty would have been rewarded, Stanley could only conjecture. He reorganized his company once again for the assault up the hill.

The action that followed was to rank with the sand-dunes fight at Eerde and the Bois Jacques offensive near Bastogne as one of the bitterest actions of them all.

The German gunners, returning, opened fire on the left flank of Stanley's company. Almost immediately afterwards, the enemy on the hill above opened fire point-blank on the first line of advancing paratroopers.

4

If Stanley or his troops had hesitated at that point, the capture of Hill 30 would have cost more lives and taken more time than it did. Instead, he and his men charged forward directly into the enemy fire, going so fast that the first mad rush took them halfway up the slope without cover. Yet, only two men were wounded—one hit through both legs, and the other struck through the shoulder as he dove into a ditch. The man in the ditch didn't even know that he was hurt—telling someone near him that he'd jerked a crick in his neck.

But by the half-way point, enemy fire had become intense. Stanley halted his company in a ditch behind a hedgerow, where the men regrouped. As the day broke, the mists were beginning to clear. The 20mm. cannon were giving more trouble than the machine guns, so Stanley sent a few small groups of men to work their way along the connecting hedgerows and, with hand grenades, put the guns out of commission.

By that time he was pinned down. The fire made it impossible to move. The enemy mortar gunners, who were so close that he could hear their shouted fire orders, began dropping a systematic barrage of mortar shells along the ditches and hedgerows where the men lay. Simultaneously, the Germans launched a counter-attack on the left flank of Stanley's company. Within a few minutes there were thirteen casualties.

Stanley radioed for white phosphorous and more smoke. Much to his satisfaction the counter-attack stopped as quickly as it had begun. But the enemy worked around to his right flank. . . .

During this time the support platoon had come up to Stanley's position. Stanley sent that platoon to the right flank and then took a few moments to direct the evacuation of the wounded. In the midst of that work some American white-phosphorous shells exploded over the exposed wounded men. In streaming sheets of smoke the burning particles fell and lodged on the already torn skin and bare flesh of the men. The wounded screamed helplessly. Stanley himself was burned. But there was nothing he could do except get the wounded out of there as fast as he could.

Meanwhile, his men had begun to spot some of the enemy positions. When Stanley returned, he found Sergeant Robert J. Houston of Theresa, New York, walking up the slope under intense enemy fire carrying a mortar, a bipod and ammunition. A one-man mortar squad, Houston set the mortar in position, fired a round, ran to the hedgerow to observe, returned to adjust his fire, then corrected the fire again, and continued until he had put one of the enemy gun emplacements out of action. He kept that position, though clearly visible to the enemy on the hilltop, and continued to fire while the rest pushed up.

Sergeant Amos G. Casada of New York, Private Lloyd J. Lein of Minnesota and Captain Stanley worked their way along a hedgerow towards another 20mm. gun position. They had approached to within a score of yards, when a round from Sergeant Houston's mortar landed close to the enemy gun, the explosion spreading out around the enemy field piece in a cloud of gray smoke. The crew, though unhurt, ran for their foxholes. Taking advantage of this momentary confusion, Stanley, Casada and Lein dashed forward. Their pell-mell rush overran the gun position, where they killed two of the gunners and wounded the remainder.

By this time the action had become savage. The 2nd platoon, advancing wildly on the left, forced the enemy machine gunners to withdraw, then shot them down as they retreated. A German tank pulled up to one of the commanding hedgerows and fired three rounds into the American positions; someone opened fire with a bazooka and the tank withdrew.

Stanley led the company up the hill in a wild running assault. The German mortar crews, terrified out of their positions, were killed as they moved. Paratroopers dashed about the hillside throwing grenades into the enemy foxholes. Yelling like madmen, the Americans—those same Americans who once had stood uncertainly in line at the reception centers— swept up and overran the last of the positions on the hill, shooting, stabbing, blowing up, until the enemy had surrendered and Hill 30 was in American hands.

Men do strange things in time of great stress. Killing becomes butchery and necessity the father of violence. Conversely, the habits of civilized and courteous people are sometimes so deeply ingrained that not even bloodshed and sudden death will altogether erase them. A young cook of Stanley's company, jumping into a foxhole during the heat of the battle, found the foxhole already occupied by a scared German soldier. He shouted, "Oh, excuse me!" and jumped out again.

13
The First Job Done

"Where's Sheer, Ed?"

"Dead. Les Droueries."

"They got Bud Dorman, too."

"I know."

"And Captain MacReynolds and Colonel Carroll and Johnnie Clapper and . . ."

"Talk about something else, will you?"

"When are we going back to England?"

For the airborne troops the campaign of Normandy was almost at an end. Since the assault, there had been ten or twelve days of heavy, continual fighting and the same length of time in defense.

But what has been written here tells only a small part of the story: the story of those men who—by luck or by initiative— found their way to the regimental objectives. What cannot be told here is the stories of those hundreds of men who were dropped miles from anywhere and had to fight the enemy, sometimes alone, sometimes in small groups for many days without food, without water, and sometimes without hope. In one particular group, lost for five days, a French-speaking American soldier donned French working clothes and walked openly through German-held villages, getting food and information from the villagers. Another group of men, surrounded in a castle, fought off superior forces of the Germans for several days and then made its escape by creeping through a marsh under cover of darkness.

Afterwards, the SHAEF studies of the airborne invasion retold the military significance of so much scattered fighting. At no time could the Germans get an accurate estimate of the strength opposing them. Though in retrospect it seemed suicidal to scatter little forces of men all over the coastal area of the peninsula, where they had to fight without support, the total effect—unplanned as it was—made chaos of the stiffly formal German defenses. Everywhere the Germans found the stiff thorn of one more small group of fighting men.

It is interesting to observe, parenthetically, that the soldiers of the 101st Airborne Division were green troops. When they parachuted onto the Cotentin Peninsula in the early morning of D Day, five hours before the seaborne landings, they had never heard a shot fired in anger. Much has been said about green troops in extenuation of reverses suffered by units which had had no previous battle experience. But there would seem to be some truth in the observation that green troops are not the main factor of defeat in battle. Spirit can sometimes overcome that greenness—can even overcome the equally hazardous factor of green commanders.

We were not bitter about the pilot error that had scattered us over a wide area of enemy territory and taken the lives of so many of our comrades. Having succeeded in our own missions despite the error, we were scornful, but it was not until late in the following winter, under slightly unexpected circumstances, that the Troop Carrier Command entirely redeemed itself in our eyes.

2

For two weeks after the struggle for Hill 30, the 501st Parachute Infantry remained in a static holding position on the high ground behind Carentan, rotating battalions into a rest area called Basin à Flot. Basin à Flot was a peaceful place. High on each bank of the canal were double rows of poplar trees with small roads running between them. On the canal, boats or barges passed from time to time, occasionally using green parachutes as sails. A quartermaster shower had been set up for us, and we could rest, get clean and eat the new ration called "Ten-in-One."

On the line positions around Carentan, life was not much more lively. The routine was varied a little by frequent excursions into that rosy world created by hard cider, Calvados or wine. Casualties continued, however. In the little town of St. Quentin, visible from the high ground, was an old gray-colored granite church. From its tower the enemy could adjust artillery fire on the American positions. Eventually our own artillery knocked off the church roof and part of the steeple, but the original builders had constructed too well and modern shelling never entirely destroyed the place.

The Germans had a few machine guns around that church and one day, when a small artillery observation plane flew too close to the tower, the Germans shot it down. Nobody ever found out what happened to the pilot.

The *Wehrmacht* usually admired the military, even when it was the enemy. Within the defensive area on the high ground, which had once been a prisoner of war enclosure for captured Americans, were the graves of three Americans and seven Germans. The two nationalities were separated by about four feet of clear space. Except for that, the American graves were as carefully constructed as the German. The plots were about three feet wide and seven feet long. In each the enemy had piled a smooth mound of earth; and on it they had laid the camouflaged American parachutes. The men's helmets had been placed at the foot of the graves, and at the head of each was a small black cross with the soldier's name neatly lettered in German script. The dog tags, those final identifications, were carefully attached.

But the Germans had no respect for civilians. A dead Frenchman lay about thirty feet distant. The earth had been dumped on top of him, leaving half of his body still uncovered.

The living men on the line slept in handmade graves of their own. Most of them lived in two-man foxholes, covered with heavy wood or sheet iron. American ingenuity was at its best with foxholes, and some of them became quite elaborate. The visiting chaplains—Father Sampson or Chaplain Engels—were always shown those foxholes first; they were a point of local pride.

Life seemed quiet enough for a division ceremony at Carentan, where a group of officers and soldiers were awarded Silver Stars. But somehow—perhaps from a treasonable Norman—the Germans found out about the gathering and put a few shells into the square of the city. When the first shell exploded, the line of troops wavered like grain in a wind. One of the generals on the platform shouted, "Hold your ground!" But in a moment or two the soldiers, evidently preferring a little longer life to a needlessly heroic re-enactment of the boy on the burning deck, melted away to the cover of the buildings, leaving the generals to demonstrate, if they wanted to, the proper method of stopping shrapnel.

The French people were the ones who were injured. A little French girl, eight or nine years of age, an interested spectator of five minutes before, was carried away a bloody mass; several other people were wounded. After that, these ceremonies were held in England.

3

At the end of June the regiment moved to St. Sauveur le Vicomte and then to coastal guard in the area of the recently seized (and heavily stocked with brandy) German garrison at Cherbourg. The 501st men had a few days of that *de luxe* war known only to rear echelons. Finally, on July 19, 1944, thirty-four days after their parachute drop, they were taken by landing ship tanks from Utah Beach to Southampton.

The first job was done.

PART II

Inscription on glider:

"IS THIS TRIP REALLY NECESSARY?"

14
No Rest for the Weary

Habit is one of the few things a soldier really values. If he has been a soldier for any length of time, he has learned to dread a change of station as most civilians dread losing their jobs. Perhaps the reason is just that he must change stations so often, and each time he does the circumstances are the same—he packs his few belongings and his heavy weight of equipment into a barracks bag, slings the bag over his shoulder and leaves behind, not just an empty cot, but a way of life. He may resume that way of life at his new station, after he has been there for a while, but during the period in between he feels somehow as though he could remember nothing else in his experience except the weight of a duffle bag on his shoulder, the cold station platform and the dirty train.

So to return to Hempstead Marshall was an overwhelming joy. We were returning partly to familiar surroundings, partly to English friends, but above all to old habits. We could take them up again as though no break had intervened. Nothing had changed. The evening bus schedules to Newbury were just as they had been before the invasion. The crows were still noisy in the great trees at sundown, and the English girls on bicycles still gathered at the camp entrances to talk, very much against the rules, with the guards. It was not long before the English children were trotting from tent to tent to collect the men's laundry, as they had done in the cold winter months after our first arrival, and, when the small English truck arrived in the morning to empty the "honey buckets," as the latrine receptacles were called, all of us knew that we were home again.

In the first days after the return of the regiment, Hempstead Marshall was transformed astonishingly. Anyone would have known where we had been. Along the walls by the tents little yellow German flags with skulls and crossbones warned of mines—*Achtung Minen*. Bullet-torn parachutes hung on the guy-ropes to dry. Men compared notes on captured Lugers and P-38s, on twenty-year-old Martel brandy, on Iron Crosses, and on friends who were in France under another kind of cross.

Although almost everyone had brandy, no one would say where it had come from. The only known fact in the mystery was that Colonel Johnson had loaded a great number of cases into a truck while he was in the Cherbourg area and, by the time the truck reached Utah Beach, its load had disappeared. Everybody had a different solution to offer; but everybody also had brandy.

French bicycles, German field switchboards, ordnance repair kits, parachute delivery containers—every imaginable kind of valuable and valueless loot, including a few pairs of the wooden sabots worn by the Norman peasants—were strewn between the tents. It was the souvenir stage of the war. Several days passed before the area looked military again, but the change was managed good-naturedly and no one guessed what repercussions were later to come from looting of a more serious nature in Holland.

Affection for the town of Lambourne had become so strong in the 2nd and 3rd Battalions, the personnel of which were billeted there, that during combat Chaplain Engels had remarked that the sound of incoming shells said plainly, *"Youoooooooooooooooo aren't going back to LAMbourne!"* So the men of the two battalions were disappointed when Colonel Johnson moved them to a new extension of the tent camp at Hempstead Marshall, where they were within walking distance of regimental headquarters. Johnson probably remembered his vain orders to get Ballard away from Les Droueries to La Barquette, a personal disagreement that only the European Theater historian was able to straighten out. Or perhaps he only wanted to get his regiment under unified control. Whatever the reason, by mid-July the regiment was together in one camp.

England to us meant civilization and reasonable comforts. Even powdered eggs and dehydrated potatoes were a luxury. The people of Newbury and Lambourne looked at us with friendly eyes. Places like the Regal and the Forum theaters, the Chequers Hotel, Greenham Common, Reading, Piccadilly, had become as familiar as the Barringer Hotel in Charlotte or the Henry Grady in Atlanta. We were beginning to realize there was something rather nice about England.

It was full summer then and, though the eternal rains continued, the air had grown milder. Because of war hours, known as "British double summer time," the twilight lasted very late, and on clear nights the sun was shining at ten o'clock. But time had become precious, and the longer the day the longer the life that remained. Only the new men made any inquiries about the next mission. The old men knew that sooner or later it would come, and when it came there would be time to talk.

The Troop Carrier Command, perhaps a little anxious to be friendly, flew everyone up to Scotland for a week of leave. Colonel Johnson went away for a while, too. But life overseas had no meaning for him when he was away from his regiment, and he returned after two days to begin the task of writing letters of condolence to the hundreds of parents of men who had died—a task that began in July 1944 and was to continue uninterruptedly, under different regimental commanders, until Admiral Doenitz arrived in Reims in May of the following year.

2

Several hundred new soldiers had come to Hempstead Marshall to replace those who had died in Normandy. They had sailed from New York City on the *Queen Mary* on June 7th. While Tom Rice was in Addeville and Colonel Johnson was at La Barquette, those replacements, officers and men alike, had watched the submarine net close behind them at the entrance to the narrows and seen the shore of Coney Island disappear at the end of the wake. Now, after a tedious journey from the Firth of Clyde to a replacement depot near Chester, and finally to the 101st Airborne Division at Greenham Common, they had come to the regiment. And they were feeling a little forlorn.

The combat replacement finds himself in a difficult position. If he is an officer, he must take command of battle-experienced troops, all of whom remember their old commander and measure the newcomer against that man's achievements—not the least of which was his death under fire. The replacement officer, who must follow the training schedule like everyone else, finds himself instructing veteran soldiers on subjects of which they have had a great deal more practical experience than he. It quickly becomes obvious to him that only a baptism of fire will unite him with his men, and in occasional moments of bitterness he is apt to feel that only his own death in combat will raise him to the stature of the man he has replaced.

The soldier replacement also has a difficult time. He is as valuable as a fresh supply of ammunition, but until he has been under fire he is used by the older men chiefly as a sounding board for exaggerated anecdotes of former battles. He receives no mail for at least a month or two after his arrival. Often, he has not been paid for several months. He gets the impression after a while that he has nothing to offer his new organization except his physical presence: a numerical addition of rather dubious fire power.

Reticence about battle, among veterans, usually begins when the soldier is back home among surroundings that make the experience seem unreal. Overseas, where there are new battles soon to be fought, most men are talkative about their experiences in combat. And since the American soldier almost always exaggerates, replacements get a distorted conception of what they will be up against on the next mission. It was not long that summer before the new men understood that Hell's Corner had been the Gallipoli of World War II, and St. Come du Mont had been seized with a valor approaching that of the charge at Balaclava.

Veteran—veteran—veteran. The new troops, some of them with several years of service in the army, felt like rookies.

The replacement is the most underrated man in a war. Our regiment was to receive many replacements before its job in Europe was done—men who came to the organization in Holland, in the dreary little camp of Mourmelon, in Bastogne after the siege, and along the snow-bound winter lines of Alsace-Lorraine. By the time the regiment was stationed at Berchtesgaden in the Bavarian Alps, the old men were only a few scattered handfuls among hundreds of new soldiers. But the replacements were all American, and they were all paratroopers; what the regiment accomplished in the long, difficult winter of 1944-45 was due largely to the fresh spirit added by the new men to the spirit that had been there before them.

3

Duties at Hempstead Marshall were comparatively light just then. We had to train the replacements to work together with us as a team. But for the most part it was tacitly acknowledged that the regiment had won its spurs in Normandy, so the men yawned their way through the lectures and waited impatiently for that hour when they could go to Newbury.

The most onerous chore for the junior officers was censoring mail. No one was glad to get back to this task. Each night, just at that hour when everyone was impatient to dress and go to town, six or seven bored junior officers had to sit down in each orderly room of each company and painfully struggle through two or three hundred handwritten letters. Very seldom was this task enlivened by any literary merit. Once in a while a letter would contain an entertaining bawdy joke, or a shrewd comment obviously intended for the censor's eye. But for the most part the letters were homespun, painfully illegible, and a little touching.

There were letters like this—

England, July 16, 1944

Dear Mom,

I can't tell you how we're living or what we're doing. They cut that out if I do. I'm doing allright. We have some rotten officers but we have some good ones too. It rains all the time here. I can't wash any clothes because they won't dry. Tell Nancy I love her. Ask her to write. Give Sis a big hug for me. I'll send Eddie a German helmet as soon as I can get one. Nobody has any German helmets left. We haven't been paid in a month and a half so I'm broke. I don't need any money though. Send me a pen so I can write you. I don't have nothing but this pencil and you can see it won't last long. Don't forget to give Sis a big hug for me.

Your son,
Joey

Ps: Please Mom ask somebody to write me. All the fellows are beginning to get letters but me. I don't care if Nancy don't want to write, but ask Eddie and Sis and some of the gang to write. I got your letter. It's the only one I got so far.

Censorship regulations prohibited, among other things, any reference to the weather. So the censor who read a letter like this had to pause over the sentence, "It rains all the time here," and decide whether to make it, "It———all the time here," which would only pique the curiosity of the people back home, or cut out the sentence in its entirety. No matter which decision he made, the family who received the letter would inevitably feel that Joey's best and happiest thought had been lost. Censors never won.

Love letters were a profound bore. We could always tell when one of the other officers came to a love letter, because a peculiar expression crept over his face, quite impossible to describe. This was too bad, because such letters were always written with deep feeling:

> . . . I'll never forget you. Every night I have you close to me the way I had you that week and nothing matters except that. I keep thinking of the way you looked at me and the things you talked about and I love every bit of you. It's hard to wait. . . .

Fortunately, the love letters could be scanned; they never contained any information.

A great many of the men had trouble at home. One man's wife was going to jail for a third conviction of shoplifting; he had to find a place for his children. Another man's mother had cancer and not enough money for treatment; he was trying to persuade his wife to turn over some of the allotment to the sick woman. And there was the usual miscellany of letters to bored young fiancées on the point of striking out for themselves, to parents who complained of getting no mail, to parents who were getting a divorce. After a while we came to associate the signers of these letters with the men of our companies and then it was difficult to discipline them harshly when the men exploded, as they sometimes did, on Saturday nights.

Neither soldiers nor officers were supposed to criticize the English people. Once in a while, from the small percentage of enlisted men who were unable to adjust themselves to anything, we got a letter that had to be returned to its writer. The men were not allowed to write "S.W.A.K." on the envelope, nor to put X's for kisses: such hieroglyphics were easily made into code. Without a doubt some of the soldiers were able, by private codes of their own, to tell their families where they were living in England, or where they had been in Normandy, but those were risks that had to be taken. In each case, almost without exception, the soldier was just trying to outwit the "brass."

Because censorship theoretically had to end somewhere, officers censored their own mail. In order not to expose them to any undue temptation, however, every third or fourth officer-letter was checked by the base censors. Perhaps somewhere, somehow, someone checked the base censors.

15
Thunder in the East

Following its initial successes on the Cherbourg peninsula, the Allied invasion ground to a halt, with a screech of headlines, at Carentan and Caen. Days passed with reported moves of a few hundred yards one way or the other. To the 501st men, busy pretending to train, it seemed as though the next combat mission would be in the same hedgerow country they had left behind.

England just then was a place of tension. The war had not yet taken form; and nobody knew what was going to happen. Some believed that the present lines in France would remain fixed for months to come and that fighting in Northern Europe would reach the same deadlock reached in Italy. Others believed a new invasion was in the making—probably in the Scandinavian countries. But the plans of Supreme Headquarters were unknown to ordinary privates and ordinary colonels in those days; and all any of us could tell, reading *The Stars and Stripes* each morning, was that for a long time in the future nobody could think of going home.

By the end of July, Caen and St. Lô had been captured. After bloody fighting, Hill 192, commanding the road from St. Lô to Bayeux, was in Allied hands. Since the fall of Cherbourg, 7,944 Americans had been killed and 39,549 wounded—yet the enemy was only halfway out of Normandy.

Suddenly, on July 26th, six Panzer divisions of the German Seventh Army were pinned down on the right flank of the Allied line by a concerted British drive on a four-mile front along the Caen-Falaise road. On the left flank, where only two German divisions were disposed, 1,575 heavy bombers of the Eighth Air Force, followed by 1,000 medium and light bombers of the Ninth Air Force, dropped 4,400 tons of bombs on a six-mile enemy front—and incidentally almost made an early end to Ernie Pyle.

Under a rolling artillery barrage, the 1st, 4th, 9th, and 30th Infantry Divisions of the 1st Army gathered force and drove out against the German flank. Following them, General Patton's 3rd Army turned south towards Coutances. In a few days the entire picture of the front lines had changed. As fast as the English papers could appear on the streets they were out of date. So liquid was the mobile line that one German commander, later captured, confessed that his only accurate information about the situation had come from BBC news broadcasts out of London.

Within eight days the Americans had advanced thirty-five miles, captured 18,587 prisoners, routed five enemy divisions, and turned the entire German left flank.

The battle of Normandy was becoming the battle of France. But the Germans were not retreating in haste just then; they were pouring more troops into the Falaise-Argentan pocket. Either they were misinformed as to the gravity of the situation or—as some paratroopers ingenuously believed—they were committing military suicide to force a peace within their own country. Whatever the reason, the Falaise-Argentan gap closed tight on six full enemy divisions and the fragmented elements of two more, giving the Allies—when those divisions surrendered—25,000 more prisoners. After that, the Germans went into full retreat towards the Seine.

And General Eisenhower flew back from Europe to address his assault troops.

2

It was a still, mild day. The entire division was assembled on an open field near Hungerford, including even the Troop Carrier Command—the pilots being jeered at a little, softly, as they passed the paratroopers. We waited half an hour. Then a car bearing a four-star plaque drove up to the speaker's stand, and we saw again that honest friendly soldier from Abilene whom we had last glimpsed on the flying fields of Merryfield and Welbourne the night of the invasion of France.

General Eisenhower spent an hour and a half reviewing the battalions. After a short award ceremony he stepped to the microphone.

"Will the soldier at the extreme rear of this group"—he paused with a grin, noticing the startled faces—"raise his hand if he can hear me?"

Half a dozen hands went up eagerly.

"Any man in the world," said the General warmly, "would feel honored to meet you. I want to express my gratitude for what you have done in the past. But for your services, the great operation proceeding in France perhaps could not have taken place.

"But the accomplishments of the past are only a part of what the future holds.

"I want to announce the First Allied Airborne Army, under an American air force general, Lieutenant General Brereton, of the Ninth Air Force. I brought him along with me today to see you men.

"It is through this command that we hope all the airborne troops and the Air Transport Command* will become brothers, as conscious of each other's successes as they are of their own. We want it so that when pilots return, the first thing they will do is report to their commanding officer that their troops were dropped where they were supposed to be.

"In the airborne operations lies one of the great futures of our success. My pride in what you have done in the past is not nearly equal to my confidence in what you are going to do in the future, for we have an opportunity to end this war far,

---

* General Eisenhower meant the Troop Carrier Command.

far quicker than we could do without you. The United States of the future is going to be deeply indebted to you. All the democracies will remember all your future and past exploits. I am proud of you and of what the Air Transport Command has done.

"I was talking to a soldier and noticed he did not wear his campaign ribbons. As old soldiers, I do not care whether you wear your ribbons from former wars, but as a personal favor to me, I ask you please to wear your ribbons of these campaigns. They will be something worth while remembering."

Next day the English papers in Newbury carried banner headlines: EISENHOWER HINTS NEW AIRBORNE INVASION.

3

On August 10th electrifying news came from southern France. On the coast between Toulon and Cannes, General Patch's Seventh Army, preceded by British, French and American airborne units fused into the 1st Airborne Task Force, landed against comparatively light resistance and drove inland 140 miles in eight days. Spearheads reached up to the north to join the rumbling forces of Patton. This was the beginning of the end of the battle of France, and the French Underground, climbing into the daylight, put on uniforms, shot people, shaved heads and took prisoners.

As onlookers in England, we were sure the end of the war was in sight. Obviously—and despite General Eisenhower—nothing more would happen to us.

16
Confusion at the Top

At midnight on August 12, 1944, the regiment was alerted.

It was a chilly, clear night. The only lights in the encampment were the glimmers from the blacked-out tents. Far up overhead in the black sky bombers were going past on their way across the Channel.

The excitement within the sealed tents was electric.

"How's this webbing look?"

"Don't bother me, will ya?"

"Help me shift this box. . . ."

"Want these slippers, Butterball?"

"What the hell do I want slippers for now? Why didn't you give 'em to me a month ago?"

"Stick 'em in the duffle bag. If you live through this you'll be glad to have 'em."

Someone in the darkness outside the tent was singing at the top of his lungs: *"Standing in the lamplight, waiting in the rain . . ."*

"Nobody ever knows the right words to that song," said somebody inside the tent.

Sergeant Fontana read from a magazine on his cot: " 'Our troops are singing this song from the deserts of Tunisia to the apple orchards of Normandy. . . .' "

"Where the hell are we going this time?"

"What difference does it make? Lead poisoning, any way you look at it."

"Nice way to make a living. I think I'll apply for assistant base camp commander."

Outside in the blackness of the camp, trucks roared. There were shouts of men. In the spells of silence the noise of baggage being loaded onto trucks was audible. Voices spoke in the darkness.

"Who's that? Harmon?"

"Yep."

"Where's Major Butler?"

"At Supply."

"Roger. See you at the field."

In the morning the marshalling area was a bustle of concealed tension. By the edge of the airdrome long lines of enlisted men in green combat suits filed past the supply tents to receive their ammunition and grenades. Here and there men sat in the open sunlight, sharpening knives. A few had prematurely pinned onto their sleeves the small American flag arm-bands which were the badge of assault troops. Over at the hangars, by the row on row of silent troop carrier planes, other soldiers were fitting parachutes.

"Where's that rigger, Joe?"

"Help me take this thing up."

"Let's see what's wrong with you."

"I'm leaving mine loose. I was twenty minutes getting out of the damn harness in Normandy."

"You've got your leg straps reversed."

At the edge of the field bareheaded men knelt for Mass. The gold and white robe of the Catholic chaplain seemed odd against the background of olive-colored C-47s and gliders. The sun came and went through a sky watery with ragged white light. The priest intoned softly . . . *"Dominus vobis-cum. . . . Et cum spiritu tuo. . . ."* Planes droned high in the windy clouds, like a murmur of what was coming.

The objective was France again—this time in the rolling grain fields around Chartres and Rambouillet, at the rear of the Falaise debacle. Platoons of men were led into the long, green war tents where the maps, the aerial photographs and the sand tables were spread out for display.

". . . Orange is the assembly color. This small patch of woods by the main road junction is the assembly point for the 1st Battalion. Fix that in mind. Enemy opposition is expected to be very light. . . ."

Someone laughed.

"The nearest enemy force is two hours distant. There may be a machine-gun emplacement at this road junction here" —pointing with a stick that trembled slightly. "Following the assembly . . ."

For some reason hard to explain, none of us felt quite right about this new operation. Someone even booed General

Taylor when he remarked, in his farewell address, that
everyone was eager to get back into the fight. And on the day
of the take-off, when a rumor spread like lightning that
Rambouillet and Chartres had been overrun by American
armor, there was rejoicing for everybody.

The regiment returned to Hempstead Marshall.

Within a week, however, we were once again alerted and
sent back to the marshalling areas—this time for an airborne
assault along the Belgian border in the vicinity of Lille and
Tournai.

2

We approached the second operation with a jovial cyni-
cism. We listened all over again to the farewell speeches,
pocketed our newly issued Belgian money, and sprawled on
our bunks to wait and see. We didn't like the idea of a limited
assault and we couldn't understand why the British would
have trouble with Belgium.

As a matter of fact, the British did not. And the mystery
deepened still more when, on September 5th, the second
operation was cancelled. Our disgusted paratroopers returned
wearily to Hempstead Marshall.

It should be remembered that few experiences are more
emotionally intense than preparations for a combat jump. The
paratrooper goes to battle swiftly: in the morning he break-
fasts on a peaceful air strip and by noon he may be dead.
There is no gradual toughening, no march through villages
that successively condition the mind. For the paratrooper,
going to battle is a sudden and terrible leap from morning in a
sunny field to midnight in a flaming town.

It was then September 5th. By the 11th all was evidently in
complete confusion at SHAEF. Ten separate and distinct
airborne operations were ready to be used almost overnight.

The operations were:

Operation Comet, desired by the Northern group of armies,
to drop on the Rhine bridges from Arnhem to Wesel and
facilitate an advance on the Ruhr from the north;

Operation Infatuate, a landing on Walcheren Island to aid
in opening the port of Antwerp by cutting off or harassing the
German retreat across the Scheldt Estuary;

Operation Naples I, an operation behind the Siegfried Line to the east of Aachen;

Operation Naples II, to secure a bridgehead over the Rhine in the vicinity of Cologne;

Operation Milan I, to breach the Siegfried Line at Trier;

Operation Milan II, to assist in crossing the Rhine between Neuwied and Coblenz;

Operation Choker I, to assist in breaching the Siegfried Line at Saarbrucken;

Operation Choker II, to assist in crossing the Rhine between Mainz and Mannheim;

Operation Market, to seize the vital bridges across the Maas, Waal,* and lower Rhine and establish a corridor through Holland and into Germany for the British Second Army;

Operation Talisman, in the event of a German surrender to seize airfields in the Berlin area (to facilitate the establishment of a SHAEF force there) and to seize the German naval base at Kiel.

Viewed from the chilly heights of strategy, any one of these operations would have helped to advance the Allied lines. But from the low vantage point of the ordinary troops, who had to go on cheerfully writing home, the two fiascos at the marshalling areas had convinced them that someone, somewhere, was an "Eager Beaver."

17
No Fooling This Time

In the very northerly regions of the European battlefront, beyond the north tributary of the Rhine in Holland, was a sector of the German border which aerial reconnaissance had showed to be more lightly fortified than any place along the Siegfried Line. This sector lay beyond the three great water barriers of the Maas, the Waal and the Neder Rijn, which

* Rhymes with "wall."

were not streams, but great rivers like the Danube. Secure behind these natural barriers the Germans were—if aerial photographs and reports of the underground could be trusted—off guard.

It was in this direction that General Montgomery's 2nd Army had been advancing. Amid the wild hurrahs of the Belgians, the Tommies had rolled northward as far as the Albert and Escaut canals, their ultimate objective to seal off Holland, liberate Antwerp and open the Scheldt River estuary to Allied shipping. But there was an even remoter objective. It was to reach the good tank country of the Westphalian plain in northern Germany. Once across the water barriers guarding this area, a strong armored force could, with good luck, outflank the Siegfried Line and shorten the war by months.

Unknown to any of the soldiers in the 101st Airborne Division, this plan had been under consideration for some time. General Montgomery wanted an airborne salient all the way to Arnhem. Various important officers disapproved of the plan. If it took place, supplies would have to be diverted almost entirely to the British advance. Moreover, as General Eisenhower was later reported to have pointed out, the position of the airborne troops at the extreme tip of the salient, beyond the three rivers, was extremely hazardous.

Nonetheless—to quote General Brereton's diary—

"All considerations favored Operation Market as likely to produce the greatest results. The enemy's forces were badly depleted and broken up in the Falaise gap, in the retreat across the Seine, and in Eastern France and Belgium. Operation Market, if successful, would outflank the Siegfried Line, trap thousands of Germans to the west and put us across the Rhine and in a position to encircle the Ruhr and catch the bulk of the enemy's forces west of the Rhine. . . ."

So, on August 14, 1944, we returned wearily, and for the third time, to the marshalling areas.

The forces for Operation Market comprised the greatest airborne assault in history. They were as follows:

Headquarters, British Airborne Corps, commanded by Lieutenant General Browning;

1st British Airborne Division, commanded by Major General R. E. Urquhart, C.B., D.S.O.;

82nd Airborne Division, commanded by Brigadier General James M. Gavin;

101st Airborne Division, commanded by Major General Maxwell D. Taylor;

1st Polish Paratroop Brigade, commanded by Major General S. Sosabowski.

General Brereton's diary adds:

"The mission was to capture and hold the crossings over the canals and rivers that lay on the British Second Army's axis of advance from inclusive Eindhoven to inclusive Arnhem. The British and Poles were to capture the bridges at Arnhem and establish a bridgehead around them so that the Second Army, led by the Guards Armored Division, could pass through without delay on their advance northwards. The 82nd was to capture the crossings at Nijmegen and Grave and to hold the high ground between Nijmegen and Groesbeek. The 101st was to seize the bridges and defiles between Eindhoven and Grave.

"Operation Garden was the code name for the British Second Army's advance from the general line of the Albert and Escaut canals in Belgium to the Zuider Zee in Holland, a distance of about 99 miles. The advance was to be on a very narrow front, with only one road most of the way. The British Second Army, which had advanced about 280 miles between late August and 11 September, did not have a surplus of transport and supplies.

"We were all glad to be getting into action. In the 40 days since the formation of the 1st Allied Airborne Army, we had planned 18 different operations. . . ."

2

The town of Veghel* lay midway in the sector assigned to the 101st Airborne Division: it was north of Eindhoven and south of Uden. Strategically, it was an important town, for

*Rhymes with heckle.

one of the main waterways in that part of the country—the Willemsvaardt Canal—lay just at the outskirts, where it was bridged by a single span for the highway and by railroad bridges to the northwest. So the primary mission of our men, to whom this area was assigned, was to prevent the Germans from blowing those bridges.

By the night of the 16th the attitude of the men in the marshalling area had undergone a subtle change. Our resentment had disappeared. Everyone knew somehow that Operation Market would not be cancelled. Most of the men were curious about Holland. And, in the week preceding the jump, there had been a general feeling that the war would last a long while yet. How this impression changed would be hard to say: perhaps it was because the newspaper correspondents and the BBC announcers had begun to talk about the Siegfried Line. Whatever the reason, we went to sleep in the clear autumnal night of September 16th feeling only that we were about to resume what we had begun in Normandy.

For the English people the night of the 16th was one of the memorable nights of the war—a turning point in the five years of dreary struggle.

On that night a regimental courier for the 501st Parachute Infantry rode by jeep from Hempstead Marshall to Newbury. It was after dark. The clouds had thinned over the sky and a few stars were visible.

As the messenger and his driver passed through the quiet streets of Newbury, both were aware of a strange difference. The town was not the same. Under the street lamps little children stood and stared and talked among themselves. Here and there, people leaned out of open lamplit windows, gazing around them. Through cautiously half-opened doors, groups of old men pointed and waved and clapped each other on the back.

The driver and the messenger stared. It was a moment or two before either of them realized what had happened.

The lights were on in England.

HOLLAND

The airborne invasion of Holland failed because Arnhem could not be held; otherwise, the salient might have been as important as the later crossing of the 1st Army at Remagen. During this campaign, however, the struggles of individual soldiers were replaced by the struggles of companies or of single battalions. In all its phases could be seen the growing maturity of a combat organization.

"I think that the prominence the press and radio gave the failure at Arnhem overshadowed the absolutely heroic work of the 82nd and 101st Divisions, who accomplished every one of their objectives . . . In the years to come everyone will remember Arnhem, but no one will remember that two American divisions fought their hearts out in the Dutch canal country and whipped hell out of the Germans."

LIEUTENANT GENERAL LEWIS BRERETON

18
Getting in Dutch

The Invasion of Holland was taking place at that stage in the war when *Festung Europa* had been supplanted, in the minds of the Germans, by the concept of *Festung Deutschland*. The *Wehrmacht* was falling back on its second phase of defense, which was the Siegfried Line. Except near Trier, the resistance had not yet steadied, however. While a few American troops experienced that bitter fighting of the border lines which was soon to discourage hope for an early end to the war, the majority of our units in Europe had been somewhat disorganized by their long push forward from the beachheads. France and Belgium had been liberated too speedily. And if the airborne invasion of Holland took the Germans completely by surprise, as it certainly did, there is some evidence to indicate that it surprised the Americans, too. We were in Holland before we knew it.

2

Among the replacements who had joined the regiment after Normandy was a soldier named Davis Hart, from Grand Island, Nebraska. He was about twenty years old and had lived all his life on the farm. He did not have much schooling, but he had a good deal of native intelligence and a natural sense of humor. He had never been away from home before, much less in a war, but he was pretty sure that combat was not as bad as it was supposed to be.

He had fractured his arm in England before the invasion and had been ordered by the regimental surgeon to remain at the base camp. Because he didn't want to miss the fun, and because he was miserable left to himself in the base camp, he

got up early on the day of the take-off and dressed in combat
clothes. His fractured arm was in a sling. Carrying a carbine
in the other hand, he persuaded Captain Bogart's jeep driver
to take him to a marshalling area where the gliders were
waiting. He thought he could stow away.

The driver had some difficulty finding the right field and,
by the time Hart arrived, the C-47 tow-ships were warming
up. He jumped from the jeep, shouted a thanks to the driver
and ran down the apron, looking for someone he knew.

The gliders and their tow-ships were parked almost nose to
tail. Nevertheless, Hart had to run for quite a while before he
came to the headquarters group of his own regiment. A
soldier named Tony Wysocki shouted at him.

"Hey!" shouted Hart in return, "Got any room?"

Tony, a regimental driver, was sitting in his own jeep. The
rear of the vehicle was piled high with equipment of all kinds,
but the seat next to Tony was vacant. With the help of the
pilot, who probably thought that his new passenger had been
authorized by somebody else, Hart struggled aboard. He did
not have a "Mae West." His name was not on any manifest.
If he were shot down, his parents would never know what had
happened to him.

But he was feeling fine.

It was a beautiful day. As the glider lifted into the air at the
end of a short run, he looked down at the pleasant countryside
of England with the emotions of a man who had accomplished the impossible. He was not afraid of the immediate
future and he was delighted to realize that he felt quite
normal. Perhaps a little excited, that was all. He watched
with great interest as the glider passed out over the English
Channel. The V-shaped door at his elbow was open, and by
leaning over the side of Tony's jeep he could look down
through 2,000 feet of space to the shimmering waters. For
some reason, this struck him as being very funny. He gave
Tony a resounding smack on the shoulder and began to sing.
Tony was working on the bolt on his carbine.

Over the bright, sunny land of Belgium, where the farming
country reminded him of home, Hart thought of his younger
brother and his two sisters. He supposed that soon they would
be sitting down to breakfast. Tomorrow morning, at this same
hour, they would read in the newspapers about the airborne
invasion of Holland and then they would know where he was.

This didn't strike him as being particularly sad. What struck him most keenly was the thought of being in Holland. It was a long way from Nebraska.

The roar of the wind was so loud that he was unable to share these thoughts with Tony, so he contented himself with looking out the open door or watching the pilot adjust the trim. It never occurred to him that within an hour the pilot would be dead and the officer next to him horribly wounded—nor, above all, that Tony would be captured by the Germans before nightfall. He felt as most of the American soldiers were supposed to have felt in the first World War: that he and everybody else were on the adventure of their lives.

He was startled that moment by what sounded like the popping of an outboard motor.

Looking down over the side, he could see that the atmosphere of the countryside had strangely altered. A haze—either imaginary or real—had crept over the sun and darkened the land. By a railroad embankment and a ruined bridge a vehicle of some kind was on fire, the luminous orange flames vivid in the steel-blue monotone below. Elsewhere there was utter desolation. But Tony punched his arm and pointed, and when Hart leaned over to look out Tony's door, he gazed straight down into a cone of tracer bullets coming up around the plane.

His first reaction was one of dumbfounded astonishment. Somebody was trying to kill them! It was inconceivable. But then his mind was lifted into the high key of combat and his only possession became his heartbeat.

The pilot and the parachute officer in the cockpit up ahead were sitting very still. The plane went on steadily, while bullets cracked around it in visible red streaks. Then Hart saw that the cone of fire had turned to the planes behind him and he relaxed a little, just enough to realize that he was unharmed. At the same instant, however, an angry dark upheaval of fire burst in the air a little to the right and above the wing, and in the thunderous explosion the glider rocked.

In a few minutes all the planes had passed beyond the immediate sector of the front lines into an area where the firing temporarily ceased. Hart sat back in the seat and grinned at Tony. But there was no meaning in the grin; humor seemed to have drained out of him. He could tell by the clamminess of his skin that he was pale. He could see that Tony was pale, too. Hell—Tony had been in Normandy! No wonder he had been so quiet on the flight across!

Hart closed his eyes for a few minutes, trying to re-establish his identity. When the firing and explosions were repeated for a brief space, he kept his eyes shut. He wished he had a parachute. Dying by gunfire was one thing, but, if a wing came off . . .

During this time the land had become quiet again. The wind roared with a little different sound. When Hart opened his eyes, he saw that they were flying much closer to the ground. He saw fields and trees and canals, and he could guess by the way the pilot was looking out the window at the ground that they were close to their destination. The plane was about 800 feet in the air. Tony, on the seat beside him, was arranging his equipment. Hart did the same, suddenly aware that he was scared stiff.

Almost at the same moment that he saw a field littered with gliders and edged with banks of linden trees, there was a sudden movement from the pilot in the seat ahead—a loud crash—and then, except for a little whistling of wind, silence. The glider had been cut free.

So steeply was the ship banked away from the previous line of flight that Hart had to grasp the edge of the open door to keep himself—as he imagined—from falling into Tony. The pilot maintained the same steep bank until he had made a three-quarter turn. Then, about 400 feet off the ground, he straightened out and headed in a gentle quiet glide for an open space of meadow ahead of them. Hart realized with relief that there was no firing.

The light plane had side-slipped gently at the very end of its turn and was just recovering, when a dark object appeared in the air to one side. Hart, glancing up, was startled to realize that it was another glider. Evidently the pilot of the second ship was unable to see below him, for instead of veering off, the plane collided with Hart's ship. There was a crash—so violent that Hart, who seemed to have become the detached spectator of his own destruction, thought it strange that such light ships could come together with such a violent collision. The next instant he felt a strong downward swoop and a stunning blow against his forehead; he caught a glimpse of a grass meadow and a fence; then he knew nothing at all.

Afterwards, he wondered what had really happened. The

planes had been about 300 feet above the ground when they collided. Either he had lost consciousness in the collision—which was unlikely, since he could remember the subsequent dip towards the ground—or he had lost consciousness in the crash on the ground below. If it had been the latter, then his memory had blacked out in between. Later he was able to piece together most of what had happened after the crash. The jeep in which he and Tony were sitting had been forced forward over the pilot and the officer on the front seat, killing the former and seriously injuring the latter. The vehicle had then become wedged in the framework, and nearby glidermen had to dig out the survivors.

Hart's helmet had a long dent in it. Later, with the butt of an M-1 rifle, he tried to make a similar dent. Not all the force he possessed was sufficient.

3

He came to his senses in a forest. He was leaning against the side of a ditch with a number of other American soldiers, none of whom seemed particularly surprised when he looked at them. Evidently he had been unconscious for some time.

It was rather dim in the woods. There were no sounds of firing, and nobody seemed to be doing anything. Hart didn't see anybody he knew and he was ashamed to ask why they were there, so after a few minutes he got up out of the ditch and walked in the direction of the thinning trees. No one stopped him.

Emerging from the forest, he found himself at the edge of the glider field. It was empty of human beings. On the road at the side, however, was a German car with three persons sitting in it, one of them a woman. The fire that had destroyed the machine was still licking up in little tongues of flame around the rubber tires, and when Hart approached, he saw that the three figures sitting in the car had been burned to death. They were naked. Their bodies were shriveled and black; and out of their skulls drifted faint wisps of blue smoke.

He gazed unemotionally at the dead people and moved on.

He had no idea where he was or where he was going. But in the distance, by what seemed to be a main road, he saw an

American hospital tent, so he headed in that direction. The
sky had become almost wholly overcast by then. No wind
blew; the leaves on the trees were still; and though he saw a
tower or building to the right of the road junction near the
hospital, there were no human beings anywhere. It never
occurred to him that he was in enemy territory.

Within the hospital tent an American major shone a flashlight on Hart's forehead. Taking a piece of gauze, he touched
the skin lightly and when he brought the gauze down Hart
saw his own blood. Not until the doctor had worked on him
for a while did he realize that blood had caked dry in his hair
and over one side of his face.

"Where are we?" he asked, when the doctor made him lie
down on a cot.

"Zon."

"Which medics are you?"

"Kangaroo."

Kangaroo was the code name for the 101st Airborne Division. The 501st Parachute Infantry was called Klondike.

"How far is Veghel?" asked Hart tonelessly.

"Hey, Joe," said the doctor to someone across the room.
"How far is Veghel?"

"Ten or fifteen miles."

"Which way?"

"You lie there," said the doctor. "You're not going any
place. You've had a concussion."

"I feel all right."

"Maybe," said the doctor. "But if you move around
you're likely to have a brain hemorrhage." He tied a casualty
tag on Hart's blouse, tossed his carbine onto a pile of discarded weapons at the side of the tent, and went away.

The sling had long since come off Hart's arm. When he
moved the arm gingerly, it obeyed him. His head was wrapped
in tight bandages, but he felt no pain. He felt a little queer,
that was all. His thoughts were disconnected. For the first
time since awakening in the woods and wondering why nobody was doing anything, he remembered that he was part of
an airborne invasion. His company was at Veghel. They
might need him.

Lying quite still on the cot, he waited perhaps half an hour.
When at last all the doctors moved to the other end of the

crowded hospital tent, he got to his feet uncertainly and made his way outside. He had to get to Veghel.

To his stupefaction, night had fallen.

For a little while after this discovery he stood uncertainly in the darkness. But when he heard the sounds of the doctors in the tent behind him, he walked quickly into the cover of night. The steel helmet over his bandages made his head ache a little, and his mind was oddly lacking in direction, so when he stumbled against a glider in the darkness he climbed inside and stretched out on the floor to sleep. Another man was sleeping there, too, and beside him was an abandoned but unused emergency parachute. Pulling the rip cord, Hart spilled the silk around him for warmth and closed his eyes.

He awakened hours later, aware of being crowded by the man who shared the glider with him. Freeing his good arm, he shook the man.

"Move over a little, will you, fella?"

There was no sound.

Hart shook the man again. The form spilled over in the darkness, one arm stuck queerly into the air. Reaching over, Hart touched the man's face.

The flesh was ice-cold.

For a moment Hart was motionless. Then, pulling the parachute closer about him, he lay back and went to sleep.

4

The morning was brisk and sunny. On the road at the edge of the landing zone a few German cars were going by, marked prominently with the fluorescent orange panels of the invasion troops. The traffic had a quick, businesslike air, as though the invasion had been going well. As Hart walked towards the highway, he realized for the first time that he was deep within the enemy lines, but he felt no apprehension. As a matter of fact, he had been feeling nothing at all since the day before, and even when he remembered that he had left his carbine in the hospital tent, he made no effort to recover it.

He was picked up at the side of the road by a sergeant named Peter Frank, who was one of the members of the prisoner of war interrogation team. Frank was returning in a jeep from division headquarters, which had been set up in the village of

Zon. Most of the 501st headquarters personnel who had come in by glider had been ambushed by German mortars on their way to Veghel. Tony Wysocki was one of the missing.

"What about the jump?" asked Hart, as a Dutchman wearing an orange armband waved them into a side-road detour, under trees loud with birds.

The paratroopers, Frank said, had landed against almost no opposition. The battalions had been able to assemble as tactical units and within three hours all of the objectives had been secured. The 506th had had a little trouble at Eindhoven, which was at the extreme southerly end of the salient, and there had been rumors of trouble in the north, where the 82nd Airborne Division had landed. But that was about all. Around Veghel, Peter Frank said, the land was nice and quiet. Ewell had outposted the village of Eerde.* Johnson had set up a command post in Veghel. Supply—S-4—under Major Butler, was in a lumber yard by the Willemsvaardt Canal. And the Dutch villagers were having a hell of a celebration.

"How long's it going to last?" asked Hart, as the car regained the main highway.

Frank only shrugged.

"Have the British got through to us yet?"

"Not a sign of them."

Hart was silent. He still felt a little queer. Between this moment and the morning of the day before, when he had set out from England in such high spirits, stretched a gulf of time that was like time in a dream, not longer than ordinary time, nor shorter, but somehow different. He had lost touch with his own past. He watched incuriously as the car crossed the tiny canal bridge at Veghel, where engineers were building a second span of timbers, and gazed expressionlessly at the crowds of rejoicing Hollanders in the streets of the town.

At the regimental command post the car turned up the driveway into a formal garden, where soldiers were digging foxholes in the grass. As Hart got out he met the sergeant major, whose name was Gordon.

"Thought you weren't coming," said Gordon.

"I got a little delayed."

Gordon grunted. "O.K.," he said. "How about giving us a hand?"

---

* Pronounced Aifdee.

19

The Short-Lived Carnival

As Peter Frank said, both the town and the canal bridges had been seized by the regiment within three hours of the parachute landings. On the first night one group of Germans attempted a sharp fire fight by the main bridge, but they were driven away by daylight on the 18th. On that day the 3rd Battalion, in the neighboring village of Eerde, was heavily engaged for several hours. But after that the local Germans evidently decided to await reinforcements, for the sector was quiet. And within the town the holiday went on.

Veghel, before anything happened to it, was a neat, cheerful, and homey little town. It was much nicer than most American small towns of a comparable size, because it had no outdoor advertising at all. This gave it an atmosphere of peace even in the midst of war. The homes of the Dutch people were of red brick, slate-roofed, and two stories in height. On the main street were a few stores, but for the most part Veghel seemed a residential community, with plane-trees, macadam streets, and a village square. There was a town hall at the square. There were also a canal bridge and a small hotel, where it was possible (if you didn't mind cold water) to take a bath.

Much to our disappointment, there were no tulips around Veghel, nor many windmills. As a matter of fact, the only windmill in the vicinity was outside of Eerde, just across the Willemsvaardt Canal from the town.

Colonel Johnson found himself in the sort of setting he liked best. It was bristling with comic-opera war. The underground men were so numerous that eventually one of them had to be hired to stand at the door of regimental headquarters and screen them according to reputation. It was possible to get information on almost anything, even the internal state of Germany. The underground men used the town hall as their headquarters, and all day long sober-faced young men with orange brassards on their arms and German rifles over their shoulders hurried in and out on obscure errands of state. A great many of them mingled with our soldiers across the street at the hotel bar, where the setting and the characters suggested a short story by Ernest Hemingway.

The collaborators were routed out of their homes for a long-delayed retribution. The girls were mostly rather young and sensual-featured, and they went undemonstrably to have their hair shorn; they seemed to accept it as an expected fate. There is always something to be said for both sides in these cases—as anyone who has seen German prisoners shivering in the snow can testify—and the Dutch crowds who watched the tonsorial administration of justice displayed none of the sickening and almost animal glee that French crowds showed on similar occasions. They were amused, that was all. The male collaborators were put in the hold of a barge on the canal front, where anyone could go and look at them without charge.

The gaiety in the streets was contagious. Young girls, who wore scarves of parachute silk, formed chains and danced from block to block, singing songs that, except for *Tipperary*, none of us had ever heard before. Tall clerics on bicycles saluted everyone who wore an American uniform. Nuns smiled out from within the cloisters of their hoods. Even the mongrel dogs seemed to have caught the mood of the occasion and trotted through town with a comical air of preoccupation— evidently on their way to the front.

Johnson's command post was the center of activity. It was in a house that belonged to a tall, Prussian-seeming, Dutch medical man. His wife was small, serious, and gentle. She and her husband valued principles more than property, for they cheerfully watched the private soldiers dig foxholes in the fine expanse of their garden lawn; they willingly and happily donated as much of the house as the regiment wanted; and they insisted upon utilizing their servants and provisions to serve the staff. As a consequence, the staff officers, who had expected to be eating K rations in a foxhole on the first nights of the invasion, sat down to supper at a mahogany table, where they were waited on by two rosy-cheeked Dutch maids.

It was not like Normandy at all.

2

The war that had been waged in Europe since the assault on the Cotentin Peninsula was mostly to the south of the new positions just then. The airborne salient had achieved complete surprise, and from the nearby town of Eindhoven to the junction with the 82nd Airborne Division north of Uden the entire division sector was quiet.

The news of the landings to the north still was fragmentary. But evidently the 82nd Airborne Division, which had seized the bridge over the Maas, was having a stiffer task at the other end of its own sector, where the Nijmegen Bridge crossed the Waal. The Waal was the first of the two most formidable river barriers between the northernmost American division and the British paratroopers in the region of Nijmegen.*

The situation of the British paratroopers was critical. They had been surrounded and cut off within an hour of their landing. Arnhem, a communications center vital to the German occupation of Holland, had been heavily garrisoned with troops, and, though the airborne landings had been unexpected, recovery was quick. Documents later captured from the Germans told of the speed and efficiency with which the *Wehrmacht* reacted. This was German organization at its best—and in the hours of delay at Nijmegen, while the 82nd fought for the Waal Bridge, and the delay above the Escaut Canal, where Dempsey's army was held up, the heavy span across the Neder Rijn was demolished by the Germans. On August 19th, when the British 2nd Army broke through to the salient, the only gain was the seizure of the Waal Bridge.

Nothing of this was known to our indulgent, faintly amused men of the 501st as we watched the column of British vehicles press north on the morning of the 19th, thirty-six hours late.

*We pronounced it Nigh-may'-gan.

3

Unknown to us, a German general, himself a refugee from the debacle in Central France, had organized a command post somewhere between the airborne salient and the English Channel. During the first two relatively quiet days after the parachute landings, he halted all of the demoralized German units drifting north towards Antwerp. As rapidly as he could, he organized them into new units, and when they were tactically operative, ordered them east against the walls of the salient. Of these forces, on the second day, the underground men began to bring information: and it was not long before Colonel Johnson could see that the holiday in Veghel would soon end.

It ended on the afternoon of the 19th. At about two o'clock the first German shells whistled in.

The change in the pleasant town was tragic. Almost in a twinkling the happy crowds vanished. At the town hall, which had been the center of underground activity, there was no one to be seen, nor was anyone at the hotel bar. At the regimental command post the doctor's wife, the two maids, and the children disappeared into the cellar and came out again only for a brief space to take mattresses from the beds. As each sickening whine of a shell passed overhead, the soldiers in the foxholes scuttled out of sight like prairie dogs. In the space of minutes the whole Dutch town had become gray, silent and deserted, like a town abandoned for a hurricane.

The soldiers and officers of our regiment witnessed a great many tragic sights during the war in Europe. But it would be hard for any of us to name a time when the bleak misery of war seemed more unjust, more pointless, more tragically wasteful than it did on that autumn afternoon in Holland. Veghel was like a town in America, an ordinary country town in Maine or Illinois, and as we watched the night fall on the sharp wreckage of so many good homes, we could feel, in a sense, what this would have meant to us back home.

20

The Mysterious Attack on Schijndel

Colonel Johnson was worried. Anyone who studied the operations maps at regimental headquarters could see that the Germans were steadily building up strength between the lines at Eerde and the fortified communications center of s'Hertogenbosch. Dutch underground men reported almost hour by hour (and sometimes with the same information twice) about new forces of enemy troops building up to the north and west. For the regiment to remain in a static position while this went on, Johnson was sure, would only give the Germans the opportunity they wanted. In a day or so, perhaps even sooner the *Wehrmacht* would strike.

Earlier, the commander of the 1st Battalion, Lieutenant Colonel Harry W. O. Kinnard, had persuaded Johnson (though not without a great deal of argument) to let him take his battalion on a limited offensive along the canal. There is no record of what Johnson thought would happen, but what actually did happen was that Kinnard, at the cost of two men wounded, returned with a bag of 480 prisoners and a clean sweep of the canal as far as Heeswijck and Dinther.

Johnson was impressed. Studying the map, he realized that he could use Kinnard's strategy on a regimental scale. If the main strength of the German forces was building up in the vicinity of Schijndel,* as the underground reported, then he could send two battalions on a pincer movement through that area, squeeze out the Germans in the middle, and stop their attack before it could be launched.

On the day after Kinnard's action along the canal, therefore, Johnson called a meeting of the battalion commanders. At the conference he detailed Kinnard's tired 1st Battalion to approach Schijndel from the north, crossing the canal outside

*Pronounced Shin-del.

Veghel. Ewell's 3rd Battalion, with a line of departure near
Eerde, would move up on Schijndel from the opposite direction. Johnson would keep Ballard to the southeast of Veghel
for defense of the town.

From division headquarters, Johnson got the support of
thirteen tanks from the 44th Royal Tank Regiment, a British
armored unit temporarily attached to the 101st Airborne Division. This armor was assigned to Kinnard because Johnson
thought Kinnard would have the tougher assignment.

The attack, Johnson said, would be at dawn the next
morning.

What happened after the meeting broke up has never become entirely clear. Even the historical records of the European Theater show, for this portion of the action, no
explanation. For Kinnard and Ewell had just returned to their
command posts and called a meeting of their company commanders, when each received a telephone call from regimental headquarters to attack at once.

To attack at once seemed out of the question. No preliminary reconnaissance had been made; the company commanders had not been briefed. Kinnard, positive that a mistake had
been made, tried to argue by telephone with Major Allen at
regimental headquarters. But Allen said that Johnson was not
there. To add to the confusion of the moment, a second order
from regiment transferred the thirteen tanks from Kinnard to
Ewell.

As Ewell, a West Pointer, later remarked, "When that
attack order came in, I was ready to turn in my soldier suit."

2

The night was thinly overcast, with no moon. It was very
dark and quiet on the lines. The men knew they were going to
attack within the hour, but they had only the vaguest notion
of what they were going to do and where they were expected
to go. At the appointed time they simply got out of their
foxholes and started forward. There was no cover, and they
walked in a crouched position, as though bracing themselves
against a high wind. They crossed a wood bridge and then an
open field, noticing without much thought that the clouds and

VECHEL, HOLLAND
17 SEPT — 3 OCT 1944

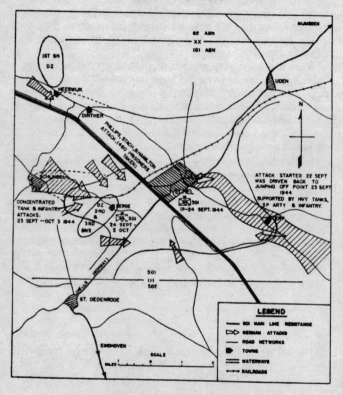

trees and rustling bushes made a setting like that of many ordinary nights at home.

Lieutenant Joseph Forney of Berkeley Springs, West Virginia, was in the lead of a G Company platoon. As he and the men approached a blackened house, in which the glass of the windows and the wood door had been knocked in, leaving only gaping holes, they heard a strange sound. It seemed to be a chant, and it came from underground. It was the strangest noise Forney had ever heard. He realized what it was, only as he came abreast of the dark ruin: the Dutch people in the cellar of the house were praying.

Forney's company was on the extreme left flank of the 3rd Battalion, paralleling the railroad track that led north to Nijmegen. About a mile away, Kinnard's 1st Battalion men were moving openly along the St. Oedenrode highway. They had gone about 500 yards when, from a house on the highway where a .50-caliber automatic weapon had been reported, a 20mm. cannon opened fire. Kinnard heard the fire go well overhead, but he saw the entire first half of his column melt away as the men took to the ditches.

"Keep moving!" he shouted, running forward. "That fire's going way high!"

"Maybe it is, Colonel," replied a private in the ditch. "But we already have eight men hit in the legs."

This was true. A machine gun, firing low, had opened up simultaneously with the 20mm. cannon. So Kinnard's men stayed in the ditches for a while, until enough of them had worked forward to bring a heavy volume of return fire on the enemy position. Presently they heard the motorized weapon start off down the road, retreating towards Schijndel. They followed it swiftly.

Over at the 3rd Battalion the advance was slower. At the first encounter with the enemy the low-spirited American troops had dropped down. It was hard for the non-coms and officers to make them go forward. For a few moments the Schijndel attack seemed to hang in the balance. Then one or two of the non-commissioned officers put their heads together, reminded themselves of the days at Toccoa, and, without further hesitation charged towards the first German positions with the old yells of Johnson's training. This spectacle galvanized the remainder of the men, who took up the charge behind them, and in a little while the Germans were retreating towards the crossroads of the Schijndel-St. Oedenrode highway.

Lieutenant Forney, following the railroad track, passed what seemed to be an old blockhouse of cement. Something on the stone caught his eye. It was a German canteen. Bending over, he peered through an aperture admitting into the blockhouse. There were no sounds inside, and nothing was visible. As he went on, however, one of his sergeants caught up with him.

"Lieutenant," said the man. "I think there's Germans inside that thing."

"All right," said Forney. "Go find out."

The sergeant took a couple of men with him. One of them poked a bayonet into the black hole. A jabbering of German voices broke out from the darkness inside, with frantic shouts of "Kamerad!" and as the Americans waited, eight Germans clambered out of the fortification to surrender.

3

The 1st Battalion encountered very little resistance after the retreat of the 20mm. gun. The outskirts of Schijndel were reached shortly after midnight, while the 3rd Battalion still was moving up to position on the St. Oedenrode highway. Company C, under Captain Phillips, undertook the seizure of the business district. Encouraged by their progress, the men were almost casual. Though they received several bursts of enemy small arms fire after they had advanced a couple of blocks, they scarcely paused. Breaking into every third house they routed astonished Germans out of bed. Other Germans, encountered in the streets, flung up their hands. Schijndel had been taken completely by surprise. The paratroopers moved through the town without difficulty, taking prisoners as they went, and when a heavy burst of fire broke out after Kinnard's command post had been set up, Lieutenant Harry Howard of Headquarters Company ran outside with four men and headed directly for the enemy gun a half block away. The men fired as they ran; the German gun crew quit; and three minutes after the fire had broken out, Howard was back in the C.P. with the gun and eight more prisoners. Except for snipers, the town was completely in hand by 1:15.

The 3rd Battalion on the other side of town, was held up at
the crossroads by fortified German positions in a couple of
abandoned houses where the battalion was to make its turn.
Ewell had no tank support, for the British commander had
refused to move his armor cross-country in the darkness. So
the entire battalion waited while a couple of lead soldiers
crawled forward towards the fortified houses and tossed phosphorous grenades through the windows. There was a *"ping"*
and a hiss. Next moment the interiors of the rooms lighted up
as though flash powder had exploded. The soldiers who had
been looking in that direction were temporarily blinded. Everyone heard howls and wild cries. The Germans dashed
outside, beating at their clothes and screaming and Ewell's
men made them lie down on the ground with their hands
behind their heads.

A 20mm. gun—the same one that had fired on Kinnard's
group—opened up along the Schijndel highway. By keeping
to the ditches Ewell's men managed to get forward. Almost at
the same time, Kinnard, relatively secure in Schijndel itself,
was listening to the report of a Dutch priest, a member of the
underground who said that a majority of his group were
hidden in a factory near the twin windmills and would do
whatever the Americans wanted.

This seemed rather like a Hitchcock melodrama. However,
the priest was in earnest. What chiefly concerned Kinnard,
who was not yet sure that he could hold Schijndel, was to
find some means of preventing the Dutch inhabitants from
coming out of their cellars in the morning, displaying orange
bunting and otherwise showing their pleasure at the arrival of
the Americans. So he directed the priest to bring back a man
who could speak good English, and when the priest returned
with a little bald-headed Dutchman, Kinnard told him:

"Keep your people off the streets. Tell them not to get out
their bunting, and to act as if we're unwelcome. Get that
word to them tonight."

The Dutchman agreed. He added that if the colonel was
interested, there was a considerable force of Germans at the
Schijndel station and on the *heidi* (moor).

"Can you send two small patrols of your men on bicycles
to both of those points and have them report to us what they
find?" asked Kinnard.

The Dutchman agreed and disappeared.

At the first light, Ewell's advance scouts made contact with Kinnard's force in the town. As Ewell later commented, "Those buildings looked pretty good to me." The Dutch underground man had dutifully carried out Kinnard's instructions to the inhabitants, and there was no sign of life anywhere. But when a few of the soldiers stopped to rest by a shuttered window, the shutters opened and anonymous Dutch hands thrust out steaming cups of coffee.

Schijndel was in American hands.

4

Captain Stanley, who had fallen behind on the highway in the rear of the attack, found himself the solitary guard of half a dozen empty German vehicles. Near him was a dark farmhouse. He left the house alone for a while, but the place seemed so deserted that finally he opened the door. To his astonishment, eleven Germans filed out, their hands behind their heads. Stanley didn't know what to do with them. Within a short time, however, an S-2 patrol of two paratroopers came by, and with their aid Stanley collected the remainder of the German soldiers inside the house. The total bag was approximately thirty prisoners. Stanley and the other two men then started for Schijndel with this group, casually tossing hand grenades into the houses along the way. By the time they reached Kinnard's command post they had fifty prisoners.

When Stanley reported in, Sergeant Henderson was sent with four men to bring the abandoned German vehicles into town. As he and the others got the trucks under way, one of the men leaned out of his cab window to shout to Henderson:

"Hey! See what I see?"

Moving across the adjacent field in plain sight was a full company of German infantry.

The Germans evidently had no idea that the convoy of German trucks was driven by American soldiers. They continued their march. Henderson slowed the column of vehicles, and as the first enemy machine gunner reached the ditch by the road, the American sergeant tossed a Gammon grenade at him. The grenade was a British type that exploded upon contact. It blew arms, legs and machine gun into pieces.

Instantly the company of Germans went flat. When a moment later they began running pell-mell for Schijndel, Sergeant Henderson's party killed or wounded most of them.

Among the other sidelights of the night attack was an incident that happened to Lieutenant Wilcombe. He had stopped in a ditch to relieve himself. While his pants were down, three or four Germans suddenly jumped into the ditch with him. Since there was nothing else Wilcombe could do, he put his hands behind his head in surrender. The Germans wanted to shoot him. But he demonstrated in sign language that he was an officer and persuaded them that he possessed a great deal of valuable information. So they took him back to a German aid station where one of the German medical officers spoke English.

Wilcombe, in answer to a question, told the medical group that he came from Hollywood. Was he, asked the medical man, a friend of Jean Harlow and Marlene Dietrich? Yes, said Wilcombe, he was on intimate terms with both women. The Germans clapped him on the back, gave him something to eat and let him go to sleep.

His whereabouts was discovered by his own battalion when three enlisted men—Fred Baker of Kentucky, Henry Boda of New York, and Maurice Pumphrey of Washington, D.C.— and an officer who was a friend of Wilcombe's set out into enemy territory to look for him. Near the aid station a small force of Germans opened fire. Both sides exchanged a spattering of shots, and then a German jumped onto the road in full sight, yelled "Kamerad!" and gestured for the Americans to approach—after which he jumped back again. This ludicrous pantomime was carried on at intervals for about a quarter of an hour, until the Americans grew weary of getting nowhere. When the next two Germans jumped onto the road, both were shot.

A white flag appeared on the German side. Presently a young German soldier came forward to persuade the Americans to surrender. The Americans took him prisoner, retreated from the position to avoid being outflanked by the angry Germans, and on later questioning found that there was an American officer at the aid station who knew Harlow and Dietrich. Later that day the line pushed out to seize the aid station, and Wilcombe was recovered—sound asleep.

21

Tight Spot for Everybody

There was intermittent sniper fire through the town all morning. A few men, more energetic than the others, undertook a house-to-house rat-hunting campaign to eliminate this nuisance. The remainder of the troops of both battalions went back to sleep in the ditches or maintained a drowsy guard behind hastily fortified positions at the outskirts. A few Dutchmen put their heads out, but the sniper fire kept most of them indoors.

Those whose concept of street fighting is derived from the newsreels may be surprised to know that, even while a battle is taking place, the people who live in the town still are there. A few of them may take to the roads, with their belongings in a handcart or wheelbarrow, but the majority—unless they are warned in advance of an aerial bombing—just go to their cellars, lie flat on mattresses they have taken down there, and pray that the house above them will be lucky enough to escape destruction. If there is an aperture from the cellar to the street above, there is the chance that a soldier may toss down a grenade. But most soldiers know that in street fighting it is the upper stories that bear watching. So the greater part of the civilian inhabitants are alive when the battle is over.

While Schijndel still was deserted, two things were happening. One of them was not to become known for several hours. It was a German drive in force across the highway north of Veghel to sweep down and seize the town from the unexpected direction of the east. Johnson had left Ballard's battalion to secure Veghel, and, in the interest of the second situation which developed that morning, he almost forgot his main responsibility. The second situation was a heavy enemy attack from the west on the lines of the 502nd Parachute Infantry, just south of the newly occupied Schijndel. Being in

Schijndel, Johnson found that he was to the rear of the German forces pressing on the 502nd.

His soldiers had fought all night. Kinnard's group had been fighting for two days. No one was in a mood to go on. Nevertheless, everyone was routed out of the ditches around noon and sent across the fields south of Schijndel to attack the western enemy at its rear.

The break-through of the German armor to the north of Veghel was a threat to the security of the entire salient. This was the break-through that Ballard had to contain alone. Traffic on the road was brought to a halt while General Taylor at division headquarters diverted British armor and artillery to Ballard's support. For the 101st, it was the tightest moment of the fighting. The 502nd was being pressed by several battalions of German troops. The greater part of the 501st was engaged in helping out down there, while the simultaneous drive of the German armor moved in upon a single battalion of ordinary paratroopers on the opposite side of the salient. And the salient had narrowed in width to less than a mile.

When the news of this occurrence reached Colonel Johnson, he and his men were in the midst of a debacle. In an hour the two battalions, under Ewell and Kinnard, had taken 250 prisoners, an additional 170 who were wounded, and had killed an uncounted number. The British tanks accompanying the parachute battalions had destroyed scores of German supply trucks which had tried to break away towards Eindhoven.

The news of the interruption annoyed Johnson. He was doing too well to stop. Let Ballard fight his own fight, he thought. But then, as further reports reached him, each one more serious than the last, he cut the battle off in mid-course and angrily ordered Ewell and Kinnard to pull back through Eerde to the larger town.

Kinnard, who was the last to withdraw, put the German medics in charge of their own wounded and left the group behind. There was nothing else he could do. As for the great number of enemy trucks, cars, and motorcycles which had been seized, he ordered that all of them (with the exception of a rolling kitchen complete with peeled potatoes and two sides of beef) be turned over to the Dutch underground. But the Dutchmen had been aiding the battalion all day, and when they heard that he was leaving they said, ''We've got to get out with you.'' So he armed them with German rifles and let them cover the prisoners during the march—eight Dutchmen and eight Americans guarding 250 German soldiers.

An entire Panzer regiment of armor had made the breakthrough to the outskirts of Veghel. Ballard's single battalion of infantrymen stopped them dead before the British artillery could reinforce the line. The men fought on open ground between Veghel and a village named Erp. Using infantry weapons—mortars, bazookas and rifle grenades—they held their ground with such heroism that even the Tiger Royals, the newest and best tanks of the *Wehrmacht*, were halted. Burning vehicles littered the fields outside Veghel. Although the fighting did not end for another eighteen hours, Ballard and his men had so clearly demonstrated their ability to hold Veghel that Johnson was able to halt the 1st and 3rd Battalions before they had moved out of their position. Deciding not to reoccupy Schijndel, he told them to outpost Eerde. He thought it was high time the men had a chance to rest.

22
Life in Eerde

The village of Eerde was only a small collection of houses set down in the pleasant rural countryside south of Veghel. It was not much larger than a whistle stop. Its sole claim to municipality was a church in the very center of the town, just above the schoolhouse command post of Colonel Ewell's 3rd Battalion. There was a windmill at the opposite end of town, overlooking a series of sand dunes, but the windmill had been abandoned for months. Behind Eerde was the Willemsvaardt Canal, while beyond it were the German lines.

Colonel Johnson had moved his forward command post from Veghel to a small brick farmhouse on the outskirts of Eerde, near a meadow marked by dead and stiffening cattle. The command post was an interesting and, in some respects, amusing place. A young Dutchman and his wife had been living in the building before the airborne invasion, and on the walls were photographs of old family groups and of the young couple themselves in their wedding costumes. Both had evacuated their place hastily when the lines approached Eerde, so the rooms still smelled—as did so many command posts in the combat area—of home.

Upstairs on the second floor was an attic filled with apples and old trunks. Because of the shellfire from the German lines (shells were falling on Eerde about one a minute) no one used the upstairs floor. Downstairs were two small living rooms, a bedroom about the size of a cabin on a sailing ship, a tiny kitchen with a fireplace, stone sink and hand pump, and, adjoining the kitchen, a barn.

The barn had windows of bright green glass. Quarters in there on the hay were assigned to the artillery liaison officers from division, who had to cook and keep company with an equally green and very hungry pig. Occasionally, the pig escaped from its enclosure and galloped noisily among the bedrolls of the liaison officers, and to see those men chasing the creature under the bright green light that illuminated the barn was a diverting spectacle.

But what was most remarkable about the command post at Eerde was the astounding number of people in it.

Lieutenant Colonel George M. Griswold of Jasper, Alabama, then the regimental executive officer, slept under a table in the dining room in company with the regimental adjutant, Captain Elvy B. Roberts. An enlisted telephone operator was in there, too. Four or five other enlisted men of the staff slept on the floor of the kitchen, where Private Butterworth, who cooked for the staff officers, stepped on them and cursed.

The living room was used for operations. Sergeant Suarez, Lieutenant Asman, Lieutenant Critchell, Private Hart and a couple of other men worked in there, catching what sleep they could by lying down under the tables at night, while British officers tramped in and out at all hours to study the situation map. Finally, Mr. Cughaneas, who was the Dutch interpreter, Lieutenant James Haslam of Salt Lake City, and two other men slept in a single bed in the shiplike cabin that adjoined the living room.

Since everyone slept irregularly on shifts, the problem was not so noticeable at night. It was during the day, when seventeen or eighteen men worked in three small rooms, while the shells whistled down onto the cobblestones outside that tempers became a little frayed.

A hundred yards down the street from the regimental command post, in the direction of the 3rd Battalion, was the regimental interrogation point for the German prisoners of war. They came in from the lines all the time. They had the haggard, unshaven faces and staring eyes of men who seemed to be suffering from shock. It was interesting to watch them.

They stumbled into the room like characters from a Nazi melodrama. There was always something a little artificial about German soldiers behind American lines; they reminded one of the demonstration troops for military intelligence teams. At the outset of the interview most of them, expecting to be shot very soon, sat quite erect on the edge of the chair, and, at every pause in the questioning, their sharp, dour eyes moved suspiciously from object to object in the room.

They seemed divided into four rather distinct classes. There were the elderly men, generally *Volksgrenadiers,* who were the most dispirited of all: they could remember two wars in their lifetime and not much happiness in between, and they had been reduced to that unsmiling animal state of which the highest aspirations were physical. There were the very young men, generally *Panzergrenadiers,* badly in need of a haircut; these fellows were rather stupid and one could see the frustrated bully under their thin veneer of respect. Finally there were the two officer types, one the ordinary officer and the other the SS.

The former were rather helpful to us. All the prisoners except the SS troops talked readily about their own positions as soon as they became convinced they were not going to be shot, but the ordinary officer class knew more about the German dispositions than did the enlisted men. The SS were the most difficult of all. Sometimes they were arrogant and tight-lipped; sometimes they were amused; always they were stiff and correct—and once in a rare while they were charming. All of them, enlisted and commissioned alike, were sorry when the questioning was done; and many of them, particularly the SS troops, made strenuous objections to the great room in Veghel (previously a barn for cattle) to which they were then committed.

They were sure our American salient would soon be cut in two.

2

It was then September 25th, eight days after the airborne troops had landed in Holland. The siege of Arnhem had ended in defeat, and the survivors were making their way down the highway with the haggard, staring expressions of men who had survived the almost unendurable. But although the tip had been knocked off, there still was hope of holding the salient. If General Dempsey's army, moving to Nijmegen along the highway that we were guarding, could break through beyond the second barrier of the Neder Rijn, much could still be accomplished. If the walls of the salient collapsed, the greater part of the British forces would be trapped to the north.

While our men guarded the lines outside Eerde, heavy motorized British traffic rumbled unceasingly along the main road (known as "Hell's Highway") to the north. It made us feel good to watch it go. Very seldom in a modern war can the ordinary soldier see with his own eyes the reason for his being there; mostly, he acts blindly, as some minute segment of a larger plan. There at Eerde and Veghel we could witness the plain results of our success: the traffic moved. It moved day and night with such unbroken monotony that after a while we wondered how on earth anybody would find room for it up north.

But we scarcely had a chance to rest from the dual threat against this all-important highway when the last and worst storm broke.

23
The Sand-Dune Fight

Lieutenant Bowser, up on the sand dunes outside Eerde, was the first to spot the figures of a few German soldiers. His men opened fire. In a few moments, Bowser sighted five tanks and what he estimated to be two hundred German soldiers approaching his position. When fire broke out over him, he withdrew while he still had a chance, and alerted the 1st Battalion lines behind him.

That left the sand dunes open to the enemy.

When Kinnard returned from the meeting at headquarters he found his entire battalion heavily engaged. Shellfire from the German tanks in defilade among the sand dunes was rocketing past the church steeple. Shells were beginning to crash into the windmill at the outskirts, a building that overlooked the dunes. Mortar fire was falling in the streets of the town. So confused was the entire situation that it took Kinnard more than twenty minutes to find out what had happened—that the dunes defense line had broken and the enemy was up there in force. He called regiment at once.

The 3rd Battalion was ordered to his support. Someone at regiment advised him that nine tanks from the 44th Royal Armored Tank Battalion were on their way to help.

Kinnard's command post was only a short distance from the lines. Not long after he had talked to regiment, a British artillery observer from the tank battalion arrived at the C.P. with a forward observer of the 907th Field Artillery, one of the units of the 101st Airborne Division. Kinnard pointed to the dunes and told them to lay fire directly into the face of the high ground. His own 88mm. mortars, positioned around the church, were already doing all they could.

To Kinnard's surprise, neither the British observer nor the man from the 907th Field Artillery Battalion would ascend the church steeple to observe. Kinnard considered the risk only an occupational hazard, and he got what he wanted when Lieutenant Howard of his own battalion volunteered for the job. Howard yelled down corrections both for the artillery and the mortar fire.

Johnson, in company with the British tank commander, arrived at Eerde at about eleven. The fight had become intense by that time: three or four rounds had struck the church just below the steeple. At the windmill, a private from the S-2 section was on duty. He came running back to the command post.

"I was driven out," he said, breathing heavily. "It's too hot."

Kinnard said: "Then get the hell back"—and he did.

To add to the misfortunes, a load of ammunition arrived near the command post of C Company. The battalion supply officer, his sergeant, and all of the company supply sergeants had just gone up to it when an artillery shell landed dead on the truck. This blew up the ammunition load and killed or wounded everyone in the immediate vicinity.

2

Kinnard made hasty plans for a pincers movement on the sand dunes. He wanted to crimp the Germans before they could move down out of their strong point. Calling a meeting of platoon leaders and tank men, he briefed them on the plan. "We'll put mortar and artillery on the dunes until you're ready to move into it," he said.

Colonel Johnson went outside the command post, talking to the British liaison officer. A shell burst only a few feet away, slicing off part of Colonel Johnson's ear and wounding the liaison officer. Kinnard, who was also in the group, escaped with nothing more than an earache.

Down at C Company, where the mishap with the ammunition truck had taken place, Captain Robert H. Phillips of Atlanta, Georgia, the company commander, was trying to jockey the British tanks into a better position. He told the tank commander that, if they moved forward quickly, their vehicles could get under cover close to the dune lines. The British commander, who was standing in the turret, refused. He said he would stay where he was. The next moment a shell from over the railroad tracks struck the turret of the tank, tore an ugly wound in the British officer's hip, and set fire to the tank.

Phillips and his men dragged the commander to safety. Bleeding hard, he lay on the ground and screamed: "My men! Get them out! They'll burn to death!"

As the second Sherman tank manned by the British came into position behind the flaming wreck of the first one, it was struck by another shell from the same German gun. The ammunition inside the tank blew up, pulverizing the crew and bursting the hull. A third tank, entering the adjacent lines of B Company, caught fire at once when it, too, was struck by artillery fire. That ended the tank participation; the British commander told Kinnard that he would not allow any more tanks forward until the battalion had cleared the line of the dunes and the railroad track.

Then A Company, under Captain Stach, deployed for the attack.

In forty-five minutes Stach had straightened away to the south of the dunes and begun to move north. His own example was an inspiration to the men; he moved recklessly from position to position on the front lines, heedless of the enemy fire. The latter was so accurate and intense that Stach had to give up the idea of keeping one platoon in reserve and had to use all three of them—two as a base of fire, while the third moved ahead, a dune at a time. Kinnard, who had promised to support Stach with artillery fire, could only guess at the position of the attack, but he tried to keep the artillery fire moving between 300 and 400 yards ahead of the paratroopers. Amid the heavy folds of sand the artillery bursts were muffled, and afterwards Kinnard estimated that he could have moved the range back two hundred yards without harming his own men—if only he had known where his men were moving.

The platoon leading off across the dunes was commanded by Lieutenant Cecil O. Fuquay of West Palm Beach, Florida. Following Fuquay was the 1st Platoon under Lieutenant Mosier, echeloned to the left rear to cover Fuquay's open flank. On line with Mosier's men was the section of light machine guns from Headquarters Company under the command of Lieutenant Murn, and in the rear of the guns was company headquarters and the 3rd Platoon under Lieutenant Harry J. Mier, Jr., of Uniontown, Pennsylvania. Every available man was firing into the enemy positions ahead.

The men were so tired and so hungry that, from the start of the attack, they fought savagely. What had begun as a tactical move became a soldier's fight. On Mosier's order, First Lieutenant James C. Murphy took a squad of men to clear a patch of woods on the west of the sand dunes. The group got through the first trees without incident, but as they emerged into a clearing on the other side they came under such a volume of rifle and machine gun fire that—with one exception—the line dropped. The exception was Private John A. Bleffer of Chicago, Illinois.

He set the example for the remainder of the battle. Disregarding the cracks of the enemy fire, he ran with his machine gun to an open position on the left of the squad line, brazenly flopped down, and opened fire at the Germans. His fire was so heavy that in a short while the German defense slackened off, and Mosier, coming to the aid of Murphy, was able to get the balance of the platoon up to the clearing in the woods and deploy his three machine guns on the line.

Bleffer's example had caught fire. The Americans—hungry and tired—were mad. As the three additional machine guns opened fire, Mosier and Murphy got up, yelling, "Let's go!" The entire platoon charged wildly across the hundred yards of open fields to the enemy positions in the dunes. Mortar fire was falling all around them; machine-gun bullets clipped the grasses; but they themselves were firing as they ran, and though some of the Americans dropped, the remainder burst into the German positions, scattered the terrified enemy, and charged upon the fortified positions. The paratroopers were beyond control: in twos and threes they jumped on the Germans in the foxholes, clubbing them, shooting them at point-blank range, diving for the next position. Lieutenant Murphy was almost galvanized by the spectacle.

"I saw them, in twos and threes, jump into machine-gun nests. I saw some of our men go individually at foxholes containing two or three Germans. What we did in those moments we could hardly remember afterwards, because we had not time to think. It was courage such as I'd never imagined possible—almost foolish courage—and I doubt if any group of men could have held their ground against it."

Murphy was right. Forty or fifty German soldiers dropped

their weapons and fled back into the dunes. Around their former positions, fifteen were dead, and five machine guns and one mortar had been overwhelmed. Of the seven German prisoners, all but one were wounded.

It was only a brief respite, however. Although Murn's machine gunners destroyed a great number of the enemy retreating from Mosier's and Murphy's positions, the German mortars and artillery to the westward increased their fire. The enemy still was in the dunes.

3

As the Americans crept into the heart of the sand, machine-gun, mortar, grenade and small-arms fire increased minute by minute. Advances had to be made painstakingly. As each group crawled around the base of a dune, they rushed on a few feet, took cover again, put fire ahead, watched for any move in the concealment of the scrub, concentrated on that movement, then moved ahead a little more. In this manner they gradually pushed the enemy back from the southern dunes. During this time the 60mm. mortars of their own battalion were putting shells directly ahead of them—good luck, since the artillery was firing too deeply into the dunes to be of much help.

All at once the men came to an area where the dunes leveled out. Ahead of them was a gigantic rise of sand. But between their own position and that fortified rise was a flat open stretch of ground. The men did not observe a German tank about a thousand yards to their left, and, while they were deliberating on the next move, the tank opened fire. In the first burst Lieutenant Fuquay was killed, and one of his sergeants, a squad leader, had his face blown away by the same explosion. Sergeant Kushner, the platoon sergeant, was terribly wounded.

Murphy got word from Stach to take command of the platoon. He reorganized the men, but decided that, at that stage, they were no longer in shape to spearhead the assault. He thought he would move into the company-support position.

Just then the enemy counter-attacked.

The enemy counter-attack infuriated the Americans. They were at that stage of blind anger where death was beside the point. The men of Company Headquarters had, on their own initiative, joined the assault as riflemen or become ammunition bearers. Soldiers and officers were mixed inextricably together; leaders were no longer needed. 1st Sergeant Frank Seymour of Beaumont, Texas, and one of the company runners took over two of the machine guns. The company didn't need a first sergeant just then. What it needed was fire support.

The movement through the dunes to counter the counterattack followed the same wild pattern of the day. Control was impossible. The soldiers moved on their own initiative. Groups of twos and threes moved off again, chose their own route of attack, went forward without orders. Here and there, above the splintering of rifle fire, were wild yells.

"I saw one man throwing rocks in the scrub to one side of him," said Lieutenant Blackmon. "The rocks hitting the scrub produced motion. The enemy fired at it. Our man got a line on the enemy position and knocked it out. I saw three men consult among themselves, then get their heads down and charge straight at an enemy machine-gun nest twenty-five yards away and take it without loss."

The climax came as the 3rd Platoon under Lieutenant Harry J. Mier was committed on the right flank with the mission of driving the enemy to the westward. If the Germans broke in that direction, the fire of the 2nd Platoon could get them as they crossed the open fields.

Mier moved his men to a copse of wood at the side, then left and ran forward. The men charged wildly into the Germans. There were a few moments of wild confusion, of shots and yells and hand-to-hand fighting. Then the Germans broke— and broke across the open fields, where the guns of the 2nd Platoon killed them as fast as they came.

The battle was over.

The 3rd Platoon alone had captured seventeen prisoners. The same number had been killed by that one platoon and the small group had flushed an estimated seventy more into the open fields of fire where the 2nd Platoon had taken them on the run. Almost none of the Germans had escaped. The 2nd Platoon, in its advance to the copse of woods and then to the dunes, had taken nine prisoners, killed fifteen of the enemy, and driven back approximately fifty more. For these achievements, A Company casualties had amounted to thirty-three percent of the company strength—seven men and one officer killed in action, thirteen men and ten officers seriously wounded in action, and eight men lightly wounded in action. The total casualties were eleven officers and twenty-eight men.

Stach went out among his group. He was a warmhearted officer and he liked his soldiers. As he commented later, they "were still with their chins up and ready to do what I asked of them."

4

A little later on that evening Sergeant Frank arrived at the command post with some incidental intelligence. One of the several German units which had opposed the regiment that day had been the same organization praised by Field Marshal Rommel after the fall of St. Come du Mont in Normandy—the one which had surrendered in part to Colonel Johnson at La Barquette and had attempted to hold the high ground of Hill 30 at Carentan in the face of Captain Stanley's assault. It was the 6th German Parachute Regiment.

The war had moved north for everybody.

24
Brief Interlude

It was autumn in Holland. The leaves of the poplar trees were turning yellow and drifting down on the roads. Mornings were brisk and clear and reminded us of the football season back home. As the weight of artillery shifted gradually from the Germans to the British, the sounds of war around Veghel and Eerde changed from the rolling "wops" of incoming shells to the short hollow "whooms" of tank guns firing the other way. Day by day, as time passed, it became safer to stroll through the lovely countryside. There was even talk of burying the dead cattle and horses, already bloated on the green meadows.

The rumor of going to Uden became current again. Some of the regimental staff—First Lieutenant Richard Engles of Madison, Wisconsin, and Master Sergeant (later Second Lieutenant) Paul Gordon—even set up offices in a great convent in that town.

Incidents on the line were trifling. Two German soldiers crossed over to our positions one day under a white flag to barter for the trade of two captured American chaplains for one captured German battalion commander. Some soldier made the mistake of taking the Germans to the regimental command post without a blindfold, and after that they could not be allowed to return. Sometimes Typhoons strafed the enemy lines with rockets and machine guns, and once, when the orange identification smoke drifted the wrong way, the planes strafed our own lines, too. But that was about all.

We had, by that time, learned to live out of the British Fourteen-in-One rations. These rations, which were somewhat similar to the American Ten-in-One, contained a variety of foodstuffs intended to serve one meal to fourteen men. Unfortunately, the food was British. The English cigarettes, called Players, tasted like warm wind and were hard to draw. The treacle pudding was better than it sounded, especially when it was served with a sauce of rice pudding. But some of the other delicacies—oxtail stew for instance—were unpalatable to our taste.

The seaborne luggage, which had been brought overland in trucks from the coast, was held in a forest encampment near Zon, under the charge of Lieutenant Jones. No mail had been received, but the division post office near Eindhoven was accepting letters to go out. Division "Forward" had moved to a tremendous factory building near the Willemsvaardt Canal at Veghel, where the Red Cross man attached to the regiment dispensed free tooth paste, cigarettes, razor blades, towels, candy, and magazines by the jeep load.

By October 1st Veghel had become almost British. Signs along the highway read, *"Keep off the Verge."* British motorcyclists, who wore leather coats, guided the traffic from the crossroads. Everywhere were the Royal Engineers, Royal Signals, Royal Armor, Royal Artillery, and Bren Carriers.

During this period the regiment lost its ablest tactician and best-loved commander, Lieutenant Colonel Kinnard. General Taylor, deciding that he was too good to waste on a single battalion, transferred him to the division staff as G-3—which put him in charge of the tactical operations of the entire division.

On October 2nd the men of the 327th Glider Infantry, looking fresh and clean from their recent showers in Veghel, filed down through the streets of Eerde to relieve the 501st men on the line. An air of suppressed excitement ran through the regiment. Relief! We were going to Uden; we were going to Belgium; we were going back to Hempstead Marshall. . . .

Hot food was served that evening in the courtyard of the school where the German prisoners had been temporarily housed. It was a blue, cold evening with the first promise of winter in the air; gusts of wind picked up the leaves and carried them here and there in tight whirls. High in the lonesome air British artillery shells scuttled by. A motion picture show had been arranged for that evening; as our men stood in line to wait for their portions of stew, they discussed the comparative merits of Betty Grable and Lana Turner. They grinned at the Dutch girls who were coming from evening prayers, and they obligingly relinquished portions of unused K rations to the worshipful little children. They wouldn't need the K rations any more, they were sure. They were going to the rear.

But when supper was over and the men had returned to their companies, they were told the news. After a day of rest and a chance to get a hot shower, they would move north into a sector along the Neder Rijn River at the extreme northern tip of the airborne salient just below Arnhem. For more fighting . . .

The soldiers were disappointed. But they had become accustomed to disappointments.

"So what? The line's better than garrison."

"Not so much chicken . . ."

"Infantry, though. Ordinary infantry. That's all we are."

"I got a kid brother in the 'ordinary infantry.' I bet he's seen more combat than you have."

"There goes Chuck. Hey, Chuck—"

"That guy had a foxhole so deep it took him five minutes to get out for chow."

"They say anything deeper than six feet is desertion—"

"Who said that? Give that man twelve silver dollars. . . ."

"Come on. Let's take in the show. . . ."
The voices trailed off down the cold, blue, ruined moonlit street—the ordinary voices of ordinary American soldiers.

2

Riding north along "Hell's Highway" on the morning of October 4th, we looked about us curiously. The pleasant Dutch land seemed empty of the enemy. The little children still waved madly as the trucks went by, or shook orange flags and jumped up and down for joy, and the older men and women still came out of their houses with smiles on their faces. But everywhere in the rural countryside was the evidence of battle. Around the road at Uden the fields were cluttered with burned and rusting vehicles, both British and German. A few dead cattle had not yet been removed. Though Uden seemed untouched, many of the previously neat homes along the way had become charred rubble.

The Dutch had nice homes. They were architecturally unimaginative, but practical; most of them were two stories high and built of red brick. The flatness of the land was not monotonous, because there were always windmills or trees in the far distance. There were many orchards, plenty of vegetable gardens, and a criss-cross network of neatly geometrical canals. It was hard not to like Holland.

To the American soldier, Holland seemed more like home than England or France. In England everything had seemed old and shoddy; in France everything had seemed old and primitive; but in Holland everything seemed new, clean and efficient. No one seemed very poor. And all the Hollanders (at least in that region) were cheerful. With the coming of the paratroopers and the retreat of the Germans they seemed to take up their lives where they had left off years before. There was no evidence of bitterness. The misfortune of the occupation had come and gone, like a plague of locusts; and already it was in the past.

Nijmegen, which the long regimental truck columns entered after a three-hour ride from Veghel, was a bustling, modern Dutch city. Although the old town had been bombed out of existence during the German occupation, the Dutch residents had cleaned the wreckage, stacked the bricks in neat piles along the sidewalks and actually swept the ground around the walls that still were standing—which left the ruins as clean and bare and well tended as those of Pompeii.

The yellow leaves were drifting down in all the streets. The wind scattered them willy-nilly, while the Dutch street cleaners chased them down and quickly got them out of sight. Sharp, brisk, wintry winds blew through the streets. Signs read—*"British Army Officers' Club"* and *"O.R.'s Club"* (which meant Other Ranks Club). Arrows pointed to British theaters and showers. Montgomery's men evidently liked Nijmegen, too.

The dominating feature of the town was the great steel bridge that spanned the Waal River at the northeastern end of town. There, the Eindhoven-Arnhem highway ran out onto an island of land between the Waal and the Neder Rijn. The bridge was the dividing point just then between "rear" and "forward." Behind it were the rest camps; beyond it were the British guns in the apple orchards and the narrow muddy roads leading to the command posts, the searchlights, the foxholes, and the Germans.

It was an interesting bridge. Along the railings at the traffic level the British had suspended large straw mats. Those mats concealed the nature of the bridge traffic from the German artillery observers a short distance to the north. The bridge was under observation from the German lines, so the British installed chemical smoke generators about half a mile upstream, and when the wind was right the smoke was an effective screen. Nevertheless, the Germans fired at the bridge periodically, and to cross it by motor was always a gamble. To the amusement of all of us, two prominent signs had been erected at the traffic level—one British, the other American. The British sign read, *"Don't dilly-dally on the bridge. Get mobile."* The American sign, as friendly as an advertisement for Coca-Cola, said flatly, *"Step on it!"*

According to rumor, Montgomery had selected his best anti-aircraft gunners to man the guns along the bridge. Whether this was true was a matter for conjecture, but at least the bridge was never wholly destroyed by enemy planes. The Germans had dropped one 500-pound bomb on the Nijmegen side of the bridge, canalizing the traffic over a narrow wood structure erected by the Royal Engineers and slowing vehicles on the "round-about" approach, which was under German

ARNHEM, HOLLAND
4 OCT – 29 NOV 1944

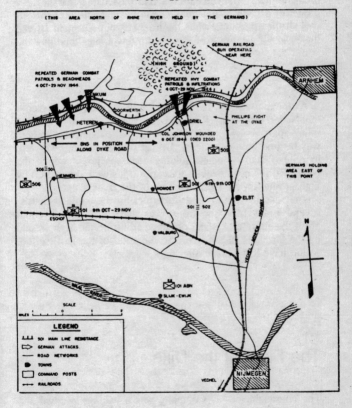

(THIS AREA NORTH OF RHINE RIVER HELD BY THE GERMANS)

GERMAN RAILROAD
GUN OPERATING
NEAR HERE

HIGH GROUND

ARNHEM

REPEATED GERMAN COMBAT
PATROLS & BEACHHEADS
4 OCT–29 NOV 1944

REPEATED HVY COMBAT
PATROLS & INFILTRATIONS
4 OCT–29 NOV 1944

RENKUM

DOORWERTH

PHILLIPS FIGHT
AT THE DYKE

HETEREN

DRIEL

COL JOHNSON WOUNDED
8 OCT 1944 (DIED 2200)

BNS IN POSITION
ALONG DYKE ROAD

502

GERMANS HOLDING
AREA EAST OF
THIS POINT

506 ≡ 501

506

HEMMEN

HOMOET

501 ≡ 9th OOT

ELST

501 ≡ 502

N

501 9th OCT – 29 NOV

ESCHOF

VALBURG

101 ABN

SLUK – EWIJK

SCALE
MILES

LEGEND

501 MAIN LINE RESISTANCE

GERMAN ATTACKS

ROAD NETWORKS

TOWNS

COMMAND POSTS

RAILROADS

NIJMEGEN

VECHEL

observation. From time to time German swimmers carrying high explosives tried to blow up the main span, but their attempts failed. They blew up the railroad bridge, however, and the British had erected a pontoon span between the two bridges.

On the opposite shore of the Waal the road ran out onto a broad highway flanked, after it had passed the marshes, by scores of British heavy guns emplaced in apple orchards. It was a little after noon when the trucks of our regiment arrived there, so we disembarked, grabbed a few apples, and dug in.

3

As the map shows, the two tributaries of the Rhine River— the Neder (or north) Rijn and the Waal—flowed about six miles apart at the extreme tip of the Allied salient. Arnhem was beyond both rivers. The British soldiers, whom we were to relieve, had occupied holding positions just south of the Neder Rijn. Unfortunately, these positions were dominated by high ground on the German shore of the river.

The reason why we had to detruck in the apple orchards, several miles from the front, was that the Germans could place the entire area under observed fire from the high ground on the far shore of the river. So the relief of the British lines would have to be made after dark.

25
The Fight at the Dike

The commander of C Company was a balding, shrewd and rather humorous captain by the name of Robert Phillips. He came from Atlanta, Georgia. His features crinkled up when he smiled. Because he disliked being too serious, his tone of voice was often mocking. There was something a little puck-ish in his nature. But his feelings were deeper than most people guessed, and he could be just as severe—or angry—as he could be friendly. He was a just and a courageous man, and was at his best under great pressure. He liked his men—which meant that his men liked him.

The situation on the afternoon of October 4th, when his troops detrucked in the apple orchard, seemed clear enough. At a few points along the river line the Germans had managed to establish bridgeheads, or salients, into the British ground. The British had not been able to counter-attack successfully; the Germans held these salients and obviously proposed to enlarge them. What we were supposed to do was to drive them out and make a front line of the unbroken edge of the river.

What happened when Phillips and his men attempted to do this on the night of October 4th was typical of the difficulties encountered by the other battalions. It also illustrated how a single company could sometimes fight a small war of its own, virtually alone.

During the afternoon, while the troops drowsed and ate apples in the orchard by the roadside, Phillips went forward with Major Bottomly, his battalion commander, to the British command post on the front line. Everything seemed quiet. With a British guide, Phillips reconnoitered the approaches for his company. Later he took his platoon leaders over the same ground. He did not return with them to the company on the road, but when the afternoon light began to fade out of the sky, he sent his operations sergeant on a bicycle to bring the soldiers forward. He thought it would be safe enough. The relief of the British seemed almost routine.

The company assembled at the battalion command post, half a mile from a large jam factory at the town of Driel.* Phillips met his men at that point. The soldiers seemed comparatively easy in mind; they knew their commander had been to the front ahead of them. Phillips himself remained unconcerned until, as darkness was coming on, he got a puzzling message from Bottomly:

"Hold up until I give you an all-clear on this. They're having a little difficulty along the line."

---

*This factory had been abandoned. Before the enemy bridgeheads were driven back across the Neder Rijn, our soldiers often stole into the factory at night, at the risk of their lives, to get jam for their rationed biscuits.

What a "little difficulty" might mean, Phillips could only guess. But his earlier reconnaissance had given him a pretty good idea of where it would be safe to hold up, so he moved his company forward until the men were a quarter mile from the north dike. That was as close as he dared go.

Darkness had fallen by then. To the south the flashes of the British guns looked like flickers of lightning against the low-lying clouds. A continued muffled sound of artillery—a sound difficult to describe: a concussion like the air-pressure of slamming doors—made some of the men nervous. But there seemed nothing to do except wait. Phillips contacted Bottomly by radio and gave him his new position.

"Stay where you are!" Bottomly shouted. "I don't feel good about this at all!"

Phillips, still uncertain of what had developed along the line, was not encouraged by knowing that Bottomly didn't feel good about it. But he stayed where he was, with the men lounging about in the open fields, until close to midnight. By that time the whole group had become impatient. Whatever they had to do, they wanted to get it over with. So Phillips contacted Bottomly again.

"Things sound quiet enough," he told his commander. "I'm moving up."

"All right," Bottomly assented. "Go ahead. But keep me advised."

When Phillips ordered his men to a slow advance through the darkness, it was that hour of the night when the artillery fire of both sides had slackened off. Except for nights of an attack, there were always a few hours in the combat zone when both sides had a chance to rest. In this comparative quiet the men's footsteps were clearly audible.

About 300 yards in front of the dike was an open country road paralleling the river. The road was empty. Phillips, in the lead of his company, turned along that way for a short distance. Finally, when he was sure of his own whereabouts, he broke the approach march to make a left turn across open country towards the German lines. He was not sure how far he would have to go before he encountered the British, so he moved slowly.

As quietly as possible the men crossed an open, watery meadow. At the north end, the lead scouts stumbled onto a group of prone but very much alive British soldiers.

"Down!" whispered the Tommies, waving the Americans flat.

Phillips realized from his afternoon reconnaissance that the British had somehow changed position. Crawling up to the lead scouts, he made contact with a British lieutenant.

"The beggars have got machine guns in those houses," whispered the officer, gesturing ahead. "Came right over the bloody dike."

"What are you doing about it?" asked Phillips.

"We're just a patrol. We're supposed to flush them out." The officer hesitated, evidently struggling with his pride. "Want to give us a hand?"

Phillips didn't like the idea of having his company where only a patrol was supposed to be, but he had to get up into position somehow. So he sent Lieutenant Richard Bonnell with the British lieutenant and a squad of his own men in a circling movement to approach and grenade the houses from the flank. While this was going on, he moved the remainder of his company out of the field into a small apple orchard about seventy-five yards wide and 150 yards long. He thought the men would have better concealment under the trees. The German artillerymen knew about that orchard, however.

2

The lead scout of Bonnell's squad had reached a point about forty yards from the dike when one of the German machine guns opened fire. The initial burst was followed an instant later by a heavy line of cross-fire from the other machine guns. Bonnell's lead scout was killed instantly and the squad leader behind him was shot through the leg, breaking the bone. Five minutes later a heavy artillery barrage thundered down in the tiny orchard. In less than a minute one man was killed by a shell that blew his hands off; another's jaw was broken by shrapnel; a third was literally blown apart.

Until the barrage lifted, there was nothing Phillips could do except hug the ground. But as soon as the firing slackened, he regained control of his company. He ordered Bonnell to get his squad back and bring up his platoon. He called to Lieutenant Bowser, who had the 2nd Platoon, and told him to take his squads to the platoon area designated that afternoon. And he directed the evacuation of the wounded, pulling them back into a small house beside the railroad embankment on the right flank of his position. Phillips' soldiers had seen him in action before, particularly during the sand-dune fight at Eerde, and they were not surprised to find no trace of the mocking, good-humored man who was their commander in garrison.

Relief of the British was Phillips' first concern. He signaled the third platoon to cross from their open position in the partially inundated meadow and gain the orchard. It was then about 0230 and very dark everywhere. As one soldier was climbing the fence that separated the open ground from the concealment of the orchard beyond, a German flare went off in the sky. The man on the fence was in plain sight of the machine gunners in the houses. But his training had been so thorough and his wits were so cool that he froze motionless on the fence, as he had been taught, and remained there for the ten seconds until the flare burned out. Because he was master of his instincts he lived to reach the orchard—and so did the rest of his platoon.

The British positions were mostly under the trees. Unluckily, there was no other place for an attacking force to be. In a few moments the orchard received another barrage. One man was killed leaping for his foxhole; another was wounded in the foot; a third died with a bullet in his chest as he was digging in; a fourth, though blown completely out of his foxhole by a shell burst, escaped uninjured. Three or four of the British soldiers were killed. And even when the barrage lifted again, and Phillips' men were ready to relieve the British soldiers, the fire from the German automatic weapons in the houses across the small field made it difficult for them to get away.

Accordingly, the British commander directed his men to leave by twos and threes and to reassemble at Nijmegen, six miles to the rear. When Phillips told the British officer that he would assume responsibility for the sector, the officer left, too, and after that the only British soldiers in the orchard were a few men and a non-com, left behind to bring out the British weapon-carriers as soon as the situation cleared up. They were not very happy.

3

Phillips and his men were also a little uneasy. The railroad embankment which bounded their right flank was twenty or thirty feet in height. On the opposite side of that embankment the Germans occupied positions in force, and though Phillips could prevent the enemy soldiers from dropping down the embankment into the orchard, he was unable to stop them from infiltrating over into positions at his rear. The Germans did this all night and by dawn Phillips' men were doing most of their firing in the direction of his original approach.

To the immediate front Phillips' company faced the dike. This was a heavy ridge of earth like a dam, broad at the base and tapering to the width of a country road at the summit. Most of the German infantry who had established the bridgehead were holding ground on the opposite, or river, side of the dike. Where the dike met the railroad embankment, forming a right angle junction, a cement archway opened through to the German side. Phillips could hear the motors of German tanks in that direction, so he guarded the approach with a machine gun and one of the British heavy guns.

The final factor in the situation was the enemy soldiers who had occupied gun positions in the houses to the left flank. By their addition, Phillips was virtually surrounded; having come into position by chance, under cover of darkness, his withdrawal was now impossible.

At daybreak he contacted Bottomly on the radio. Bottomly advised pulling out. A little of Phillips' dry humor came back to him. "There are two routes," he radioed. "Over the railroad into the Germans or over the dike into the river."

"All right," Bottomly said. "Hold on there. I'll send Company A to help you out."

Phillips settled down to a holding action. This was all he could do. In the early afternoon the Germans inside the houses across the small meadow hoisted a white flag. Under its protection an enemy party of three emissaries came forward—a German medical officer and two German noncommissioned officers. Phillips knew that one of the Tommies who had remained behind with the equipment spoke fair German, so he sent for him.

"They say they want to help us," the British soldier told Phillips. "He says he knows we have a lot of wounded men."

The American captain saw one of the German non-coms studying the orchard positions. "Give 'em two minutes to get back to their own lines," he said.

The outcome of their short good-will visit was that the mortar fire from the German lines became much more accurate. Phillips was furious. When the same white flag went up a short while later, he told the Tommy to shout over that he didn't want any more "friendly" visits.

Tom Rice, who was a mortar gunner in Phillips' company, found an abandoned British two-inch mortar. He used this weapon so effectively during the afternoon that later the bodies of German soldiers, killed by his fire, were found within a hundred yards of the American positions. Those who understand the looping fire of a mortar will appreciate what this marksmanship entailed.

Phillips employed the British soldiers to man two Bren guns and a Hotchkiss, firing east and west parallel to the dike. The Tommies had been scared during the hours of darkness, but their spirits rallied with daybreak; and one *Piett* gunner in particular did excellent work firing on the enemy emplacements in the houses across the way.

The men of Phillips' company had begun to believe that their own position was hopeless. Casualties had been heavy during the night and were mounting as the day passed. The operations sergeant had raised his head and gotten a bullet through his brain. To the horror of everyone, he lived for about two hours with the brains hanging out of the back of his skull. Periodically, the German artillery on the opposite shore of the Neder Rijn subjected the orchard to barrage. It was only a matter of hours, the men thought, before their defense would be destroyed by attrition, and the Germans would be able to close in.

At about this time Major Bottomly radioed to Phillips that Stach, with Company A, had started his attack. It would parallel the dike and sweep towards Phillips' area. This was just what Phillips wanted: it would bring pressure on the rear of the Germans at his left flank—those who were in and around the houses. He talked to Stach by radio and arranged to support him with the Hotchkiss and Bren guns.

4

Captain Stach was, by that time, one of the best loved company commanders in the regiment. Before combat his men had thought him too goodhearted to make a fighter. They were surprised to discover—particularly in the sand-dune fight at Eerde, where Stach had won a Silver Star—that under fire he was as warmhearted and concerned about his men as he had been in garrison.

Stach had a difficult time getting forward. The ground between his lines and those of Captain Phillips was open, offering no cover and very little concealment. As fast as his men moved across the open ground where the fire was heaviest, they were shot down; one platoon lost sixteen men almost immediately. The German small-arms and mortar fire was intense. Stach finally radioed Bottomly: "I'll have to have more help here. I can't get across."

He listened to Bottomly's reply and put down the receiver.

"What does he say?" asked one of his officers.

"He says he can't give us any more help. He says we're to get the men across."

"What'll we do?"

"Get them across."

Stach did. The climax of the fight came swiftly. Following Stach's example, the men got to their feet. After the first dozen yards those who still were alive began to go forward faster. The Germans who had infiltrated over the railroad embankment to the rear of Phillips' company started a withdrawal the way they had come. Phillips, who had put a machine gun to cover that embankment, had been waiting for this move all afternoon; and as fast as the Germans scrambled over the loose cinder embankment, his machine gunner knocked them off. The bodies rolled back to the shrubbery at the base.

Then the Company A men took the initiative. Getting to their feet, they went forward in a "goal-line" dash and forced the Germans into hand-to-hand fighting. A melee ensued. Phillips' machine gunner stripped the M-1 clips for more ammunition, pushed it into belts, and waited for the final move. In a short time the Germans broke. Groups of them in fours and fives dashed for the railroad embankment and the dike.

They were shot down. Some dashed directly towards Phillips' men, their hands behind their heads; presently, he had twenty prisoners. More surrendered to Stach. On the ground in the previous German lines were twenty-five or thirty dead, with dozens more in the woods to the south on the line of retreat to the railroad embankment.

At 1730 Stach and Phillips made contact with each other. The action had been so intense in the final half-hour that soldiers of both companies were shaken and trembling. Phillips' soldiers were surprised to realize that they still were alive.

But the end had not yet come. The Germans were in force on the other side of the railroad embankment. They had tanks over there.

5

Just as it was getting dark, the men heard the roar of the tank motors starting up. Phillips shouted for the men to watch the railroad embankment, especially the arch under the embankment by the dike where the tanks would have access into the area. He radioed Bottomly and, with Bottomly still in contact, took a covered position where he could report what developed. Private Wilfred F. Gray, of Madison, Wisconsin, was down at the archway with a bazooka.

The first tank started through. Gray came running back. "Damn bazooka won't fire!" he shouted as he grabbed another one.

The tank under the archway was by this time so close that the men were getting shaky again. They could see the nose and turret of the vehicle. Over the radio to Bottomly, Phillips gave a "blow-by-blow" description. Something seemed to be the matter with the set, and Phillips yelled for his radio operator. Where the hell *was* the man?

He saw him, then. The radio operator, turned gunner, was bore-sighting an abandoned British six-pounder. Phillips relayed this spectacle to Bottomly.

Next instant there were two terrific flashes. The tank had fired simultaneously with the six-pounder. The flashes seemed to meet in mid-air. Almost at the same instant, down by the bridge, Gray discharged his bazooka.

The tank went up in flames.

As six Germans with machine guns struggled out of the vehicle, Phillips, on the radio to Bottomly, became so excited he was almost incoherent. "We've got it!" he shouted. "No we didn't! Yes we did! There go the crew—two shot—five shot—they're all shot!"

Almost as one man, Phillips' group stood up in their foxholes and cheered. "BRING 'EM ON!!"

Somewhere on the wind of Holland in that late twilight of an autumn evening was the echo of a spirit that had begun in the shabby pine hills of Georgia, a long long time before. . . .

26

Sad Sack—Kraut Version

Though little was known of events behind the enemy lines, the captured diary of a German officer indicates that the enemy situation was not a happy one.

The officer was a Lieutenant Martin, who came from Jena and belonged to the 1st Company, Morhens Battalion, Raubenfeld Regiment, of the *Wehrmacht*.

The following are extracts from his diary* from the day of the parachute landings:

> *17 September 1944:* Enemy parachute landings in area around Eindhoven. Reading of proclamation by General Model. Incredibly large number of planes towing gliders overhead. Lasted two hours. I occupy the road-crossing, Breda-Tilburg, with three squads. Got one glider. Salvaged armored car. Inscription on glider: "IS THIS TRIP REALLY NECESSARY?" Slept five hours.

> *18 September:* Headquarters moved to Ramsdonk. Ordered to secure road-crossing with thirty men. An im-

*Translated by the prisoner of war interrogation team of the 501st.

mense amount of planes overhead again. Flying very low. Got one glider. New parachute landings between Eindhoven and Nijmegen reported. Trains move to Enengle. Night flights. Camp in flames.

19 September: Ordered to move to Ramsdonk. Seven houses on airport burned. Sent twelve boxes of ammunition to 69th Infantry Division. Begin demolition. Leave for Ramsdonk at 1030. Attached to 15th Army Headquarters. Stayed overnight. Changed clothing.

20 September: We leave for De Bilde near Utrecht. Ration truck ran over mine and was destroyed. Raining. Bottle of cognac with sergeants Reuter and Westenese.

21 September: Marching order at 1100. Everybody very nervous. Travelling through Zeist, Doorn, Amerenges, Rhenes and Grebbe, arriving at 1400. Division reserve; dug in. March order at 2000. "Immediately go to front," west of Arnhem. Went into position at night. Very dark.

22 September: Cold and foggy. The three majors are in the C.P. We're dug in towards the Rhine. Combat Team Marhmas in Heavendorp. Snipers working at night. Heavy rain. No idea of the situation. No mail. Very cold.

23 September: Day begins with an attack by lowflying airplanes. One killed and six wounded. Being hit by mortar and heavy machine-gun fire. Battalion arrives 1720. Hundreds of enemy transport planes drop colored parachutes. First really heavy aerial attack begins. Six planes knocked down. AA gun jams and drops out. Heavy machine gun is out. One killed and three wounded. We'll move into positions on the riverbank tonight. Factory across the river has been hit and is burning. Slept in the *Jaghuis*. Very restless.

24 September: Planes attack at 0900. We have to move into position on the Rhine by day by order of General Tettau (without consideration of the wounded).

Major Merkins inspects positions. Planes attack reserve positions. Our anti-tank gun is supposed to sink boats on the opposite side of river. Captain Schaarschmidt is sick.

25 September: Strafed by our fighters. One killed and six wounded. Got our 105mm. guns. Was at river at night. Received uninterrupted fire from 2100 to 0800. No casualties. Captured five prisoners.

26 September: Conference at C.P. Two wounded by mortar fire. Captain Schaarschmidt relieved.

27 September: Relieved from positions 0600. Reorganization of platoons. Mortar shell wounded two. Good dinner. Big field fortifications. Receive machine-gun fire on *Jaghuis*. Platoon Krumm on line. Infantry established bridgehead. No good news. Bridgehead lost again.

28 September: One man relieved from outpost. One man wounded in headquarters reserve. Moved to new positions. Men are very exhausted. Major Nuecking relieved.

29 September: We build reserve positions, using four squads. New regimental commander, Lieutenant Colonel Wagner (the man gripes a lot). Major Kermes is finished. Units remain on river during the night observing from tower. Received artillery fire all night. Many buildings hit. No casualties.

30 September: Received mortar fire at regular intervals. Received five direct hits in the building. Two wounded. Platoon Krumm still on line: No relief available. The men still are in their foxholes. Have forgotten the number of days. My vehicles are wrecked. Besvarmann and Sturne badly wounded while I was at the Battalion C.P. Plans for the Kasteel Doerweer crossing were postponed 24 hours. Observation post established in *Jaghuis*. At 0230 Major Stuks reported that crossings will be made. Twelve rubber boats behind house. First Lieutenant Nisdermayer made battalion commander of Hermann Goering Regiment.

1 October: Inspect positions at 0600. Receive mortar fire and artillery fire on positions. Then intermittent artillery fire and mortar fire on combat sector. Bombed and strafed at 1800. Americans attack from behind the factory. Very foggy. Platoon Krumm urgently requested. One man wounded. Many sick. Morale!!!!!

2 October: Received harassing fire throughout the night. Received heavy artillery fire at 1100. Our own artillery fires on us. Artillery barrage on C.P. in *Jaghuis* between 1245 and 1300. Bombed and strafed at 1430. Two hits on kitchen. No casualties. Heaviest mortar fire on *Jaghuis*. Twenty to thirty hits every ten minutes.

3 October: Jaghuis burns. Rubber boats brought in. We moved to block house. Men ready for embarking but boats not ready. Company becoming smaller and smaller.

4 October: We finally crossed at 0300. We're with naval units. Attack starts at 0630. First casualties. Second Company has withdrawn and I am left here alone. Many are left behind. We move to different positions tonight. There are only a few of us left. What's the purpose of all this? I am flank security. Am digging in. The night is cold and stormy.

5 October: Everybody is exhausted. I am a wreck. Received small amount of mortar shells on our positions. Have not had warm food for days. Nothing to drink. The war? Snipers have us pinned down. I have no idea of what is going on.

6 October: We have been in foxholes since early morning. The road to the factory is covered by enemy mortar and artillery fire. We are along this side of the Rhine. Major Stuks killed at 1700. There is no sense to this. We are all weak.

7 October: Freeze during the night. Still receiving strong mortar and artillery fire on factory and positions. Many men wounded. Situation hopeless. We just sit in our foxholes and wait. A house on the dam was burned during the night. Two men killed. Combat noises from the west. Bombers flying over.

8 October: Am digging my foxhole (deeper). Have not washed for five days. Receiving strong artillery fire. Situation very vague. Ration supply is messed up. Argument with Major Markens. 0115 hit by our own artillery.

9 October: Washed at medics. Situation restless. Received order to hold bridgehead under all conditions. Shell hit five meters from my foxhole.

When the diary was found, Lieutenant Martin was dead.

27
"Take Care of My Boys . . ."

The preponderance of artillery was on the Allied side. In other words, there were a lot of British guns. With their assistance, we were able to dispose of all the German bridgeheads on the island east of the Arnhem bridge and restore the lines to the river edge. In the north the Germans held considerable areas of land, but they were prevented from enlarging what they had gained.

On October 8th Colonel Johnson was making a routine inspection of his front lines. He felt he had every reason to be satisfied with us. Since the early morning of June 6th, when we had spearheaded the assault on the European continent and launched the battle that still was being waged, we had accomplished every mission assigned to us. The old men who had come to him at Toccoa from the induction centers were fewer in number than at the beginning; here and there among them were new faces. But the spirit of the regiment remained unchanged. He was confident that, if he ordered his companies to assault the German shore of the Neder Rijn and attack towards Arnhem, they would do so unhesitatingly. They were veteran soldiers.

During the sand-dune fight at Eerde Colonel Johnson had been wounded in the ear. The wound had almost healed, but a slight deafness remained.

On this morning, Johnson's inspection had taken him to Company D. He was standing outside the door of the command post with Major William Pelham, executive officer of the 2nd Battalion, and Captain Richard Snodgrass, the company commander. Enemy artillery fire had been comparatively light during the morning, and none of the three men was in a covered position. When a couple of shells exploded at a little distance from where they stood, they went on talking.

However, the enemy artillery observers on the high ground across the Neder Rijn had them under observation. The range was adjusted. Pelham and Snodgrass heard the next incoming shells in time to drop flat. Colonel Johnson, slightly deafened by his ear injury, was slower to react, and the burst caught him as he was falling. Shell fragments penetrated his neck and back, one of the pieces of steel narrowly missing his spine.

He was carried into the cellar of the command post. Captain Axelrod, the battalion surgeon, made the trip by jeep from the medical station in less than three minutes. Johnson recognized him.

Axelrod made the colonel lie still while he examined the wound in his neck. He had started to clean it when Colonel Johnson said, "My back . . ." After Axelrod had looked at the wound in his back, he went upstairs and telephoned for the ambulance.

At the regimental command post, on the way to the hospital at Nijmegen, Johnson saw Colonel Ewell and Major Allen. He talked for a minute about his wife and children. Like many gravely wounded men, he didn't believe he would survive. His last words to Colonel Ewell were: "Take care of my boys."

He died on the way to the hospital.

2

The news went through our regiment like an electric shock. Johnson dead—old "Jumpy Johnson"? It was impossible. He had been too alive, too vital, too much of a personality. Death was a commonplace on the front lines, but the death of Colonel Johnson was somehow unbelievable. He had been the personality of the regiment from the beginning. He had been a link with home and with everything we had left behind. We had known that many would die, but not old Johnson. We had been confident he would bring us through and to outlive him seemed strange.

Colonel Johnson had been one of those rare men, like General Patton, of whom it was possible to say that he had only one philosophy—to fight. He lived on a different level from most men: he possessed a higher degree of intensity and a greater concentration of flaming energy. He was a soldier's soldier—hard, impatient, demanding, furious—and all to one purpose: to destroy the enemy. In an age of faint ideals and quibbling uncertainties, he was like a steel knife.

Some men had disliked him. This was inevitable: he had been too strong an individualist. But the great majority, and especially those who had volunteered for the paratroops because they had too much energy for ordinary soldiering, wanted him as their commander. If occasionally he had been mistaken in his decisions, it made no difference to them; it was better to be wrong and advance, they believed, than to be right and retreat. Johnson's confidence in his own men was always felt. He was a power and a support, and with his death something vanished from the regiment that was never quite regained. Three-quarters of a year later, in Berchtesgaden, when the regiment was broken up, the old Toccoa men could be heard saying:

"Wonder what Johnson would do if he were here now?"

"Do? Hell—he'd be on his way to Washington by rocket. And if he couldn't talk Marshall into keeping the regiment, he'd see the President."

The colonel was buried with his own men in the division cemetery south of Nijmegen, on the road called "Hell's Highway," which went south to Eindhoven and Zon. It was a mild afternoon, slightly overcast. A porcelain-white sun was breaking through the clouds to the east. Along the railroad embankment in the distance—the same railroad which had been on the right flank of Phillips' company in its Johnsonian fight along the dike—a few tiny silhouettes of Dutchmen were making their way on foot. In the distance, to the north, British artillery was firing.

It was a time and a place that Johnson, if he had known he had to leave his regiment, would have liked—within sound of the firing, among his own men. Off to the left a group of German prisoners stood at attention, waiting. Close by were the commanders of the 101st Airborne Division, commanders of the British units, British and American chaplains, and a guard of honor from Colonel Johnson's regiment.

It was a simple ceremony, the same ceremony that Colonel Johnson had attended for many of his own men. The chaplain read a few brief words. The guard of honor fired a salute of three volleys. Somewhere, not far off, a bugler played taps. And then the men and the guards turned away, wondering which one among them would be next.

3

The officer who took command of our regiment after the death of Colonel Johnson was Lieutenant Colonel Julian J. Ewell. He was a brilliant tactician, a strong personality and—with Kinnard—the most universally admired officer in the regiment.

Ewell chose Colonel Ballard for his executive officer. Major Homan, a tight-lipped man of extraordinary military bearing, took command of the 2nd Battalion. Major Bottomly retained command of the 1st Battalion. Colonel Griswold, a mild-mannered individual who liked the military service but hated war, took command of the 3rd Battalion. With this shakeup, Ewell went on with the business at hand—which was not very much just then.

Montgomery's attempt to outflank the Siegfried Line had failed. With the collapse of the extreme northern tip, the salient rested on the south shore of the Neder Rijn. Since the bridge was down, the stream would have to be taken by assault. So supreme headquarters, rerouting the main impetus of supplies, resumed their slow drive to the eastward along the lines that had come through France.

The first large German town, Aachen, was soon to surrender to the Allies. But the going was slow and costly. Winter muds bogged the wheeled vehicles. *The Stars and Stripes* campaigned daily against trench foot. Newspaper accounts of bombing raids reported the first snows of the season. Soon it would be a winter war. The front in Italy was at a standstill; the front in Germany was at a standstill; the front in Holland was at a standstill. The high enthusiasm of late August and September had subsided.

During those slow weeks the front lines in Holland, in the neighborhood of Nijmegen and the "island," became almost as quiet as a rear area. Farther south the British 2nd Army pushed out and took s'Hertogenbosch, preliminary to a push that would clear the Scheldt River defenses and open Antwerp to shipping, and to buzz-bombs. But in the north the land was quiet.

It was much too quiet. Its very quietness gave rise to one of the great individual stories of the war.

28
The Incredible Patrol

The officer in charge of regimental intelligence was a youthful-looking, well-proportioned first lieutenant named Hugo Sims. Sims was married and came from Orangeburg, South Carolina, where he had been studying law before the war. He had a soft, slow, deliberate voice and a rather superior air, an air that sometimes annoyed other officers of the same grade. Nobody denied that Sims was competent, but everyone doubted whether he was as good as he thought he was.

Sims was worried. Since the lines had quieted down, his battalion patrols were doing poorly. A sense of injustice was evidently strong among the soldiers selected for the task: they felt they were risking their lives to no good purpose while their comrades slept safely in foxholes behind the line. So strong was this sense of injustice that some patrols went only as far as the German shore, rested for an hour or two in some place hidden from sight of our lines and then returned with a negative report.

Sims was in the dark concerning the nature of the German forces opposing the regiment on the other side of the river. For all he knew, the enemy was building up strength for an attack in force. If it came unexpectedly, the blame was his.

Turning these thoughts over in his mind one night, he conceived the idea of leading a classroom patrol into the enemy territory across the river: not an ordinary patrol—he expected ordinary patrols from the battalions. This should be a patrol that would shame the rest of the regiment. Studying one of the maps of the area, he thought of going inland five or six miles to the main Utrecht-Arnhem highway. There he could set up an observation post, stay hidden for twenty-four hours, report the traffic, take a few prisoners and return with them the following night.

He put the request in writing to Colonel Ewell. It came back with five letters scrawled across it: "O.K.—J.J.E."

Like a great many Southerners of old families, Sims had great self-assurance and a strong sense of what he thought the world ought to be. Given permission for the first time in his military career to devise an ambitious project entirely without supervision, he made preparations for what would be the perfect patrol.

From a group of aerial photographs he selected a house on the Arnhem-Utrecht highway, about six miles within the enemy lines. Plotting the coordinates of this house on the map, he could predetermine the azimuth line of march from the river.

The next step was to arrange for the British heavy guns to fire a single shell at regular intervals of time at a fixed and known point in the area. The explosions of these shells would give him a further check on the accuracy of his line of march. Finally, to deceive the enemy, he arranged for his own mortars to fire a flare half-hourly into the enemy lines. Flares were the usual indication that no patrols were out from lines firing them.

From S-4 he drew a 300 radio. From the regimental intelligence team and the prisoner of war interrogation group he got five volunteers: Private First Class Frederick J. Becker, Private Roland J. Wilbur, Private First Class Robert O. Nicholai, Corporal William R. Canfield and Master Sergeant Peter Frank. Frank spoke fluent German.

As such things usually happen, the rumor of this impossible patrol reached the soldiers of the regiment almost at once. Those who knew Sims, and especially those officers whose patrols had failed, grinned happily to themselves and settled down to watch the fun.

2

The night of the patrol was very dark.

"All of us were a little nervous in the last few hours," testified Private First Class Frederick J. Becker of Atlantic, Ohio.* "We all had blacked-out our faces and we began to look as if we were really going on this deal instead of planning it. I was stuck with one of the musette bags with half the radio in it. One of the other boys was to carry the other half, and I was a little griped because I was stuck with the heaviest part. But the other boys had their jobs, too. They had demolition blocks for blowing the railroad we planned to cross on the return trip.

"Instead of the steel helmets we had been wearing for the last month or two, we wore our soft overseas hats. Each of us had our pockets full of extra ammunition plus grenades and honed knives. We were really going prepared. In addition to our regular weapons we all carried .45 pistols. Wilbur was the only one of us taking an M-1 rifle, the rest of us chose the Tommy gun for more firepower. We tried to talk him out of the M-1, but we knew it would be nice to have him along with it. Wilbur has the reputation of being pretty accurate with that gun and is famous for never shooting at a man unless he can aim dead center for the head. He doesn't miss.

"After a dress rehearsal in front of headquarters, where Lieutenant Sims checked over our equipment, we decided we

*This interview, written by Corporal Russ Engel of the 101st Airborne Division public relations office, and copyrighted by Time Inc., 1945, appeared in LIFE for January 15, 1945, entitled "The Incredible Patrol." It is reprinted here by courtesy of the publishers. The interview, as given to Corporal Engel, included all members of the patrol except Lieutenant Sims.

were set. Now it was only a matter of waiting for darkness.
We sat around for a while and then went in for some hot
chow. The cooks seemed to know what was up, and the boys
in the mess line gave us a few pats on the back. Lots of our
buddies came up and wished us well and said they were sorry
they couldn't go along. They really were, too. We all tried to
act as if it meant nothing at all. After we washed our mess
kits one of the cooks came up and gave each of us three
K-ration chocolate bars and said when we came back he'd
have a swell hot meal waiting. It was getting dark now and
we all sat around the S-2 office getting fidgety.''

Here Pvt. Roland J. Wilbur, the M-1 rifle expert, took
over. He comes from Lansing, Michigan, where he used to
work for Nash Kelvinator. Now he almost looked like a
soldier in one of their magazine ads, sitting there with a grim
look on his face, cleaning the M-1 as he spoke.

''The S-2 office wasn't too far from the dike on the Neder
Rijn. We took off about 7:39. We rechecked all our stuff and
piled into two jeeps. In a few minutes we were up near the
area where we planned to cross. We stopped and got out of
the jeeps and began to wonder if the clothes we had on were
enough to keep us warm. It was overcast and cold and it had
begun to rain. We were wet before we had really gotten
started. A couple of hundred yards away we ran into the
group who had the boats ready to take us across.

''We were awfully careful about reaching the dike because
a lot depended on those first few minutes. We knew that a
couple of other patrols had been knocked off before they had
gotten to the water. Our main hope was that the Jerries
weren't on the alert because we were going over a little
earlier than the other patrols. We started to go down towards
the bank when a whisper from Lieutenant Sims halted us in
our tracks. He thought he had heard a sound from the other
side. After a couple of minutes of shaky waiting we decided
to take a chance. Edging down to the bank, we came to the
two rubber assault boats. Lieutenant Sims and two of the boys
carefully slid into one and the rest of us crouched low at the
bank and waited with our guns ready in case Jerry should
open fire as they crossed. It seemed to take them hours to get
across and we could hear every dip of the paddles in the
water. We were certain they would be heard and the whole

deal would be off, but they weren't. They made the opposite side and crouched low to wait for us.

"Finally we landed. Arrangements were made with the men with the boats so we could signal them by flashlight when we came back. They wondered if we had any idea when it would be and we told them that we hoped it wouldn't be until the next night. We hunched down and told the boatmen to be quiet going back. We could just barely see them as they hit the opposite shore."

Pfc. Robert O. Nicholai, a former member of the Merchant Marine who comes from Midlothian, Illinois, now broke into the story. He was given the Bronze Star for his part in the Normandy campaign and is the cocky member of the group.

"All of us started up the bank to the top of the dike, Lieutenant Sims in the lead. Nothing ahead looked like a Kraut, but there was something that we hadn't expected. A little way ahead there was a big pond directly across the route we had planned to take. We decided that it would be better to go around and change our route a little.

"We skirted the edge of the water but found we still had to do some wading in the dark. By the time we passed the pond our feet were slogging wet. Lieutenant Sims seemed to have on a pair of boots about ten sizes too large and they squished with every step he took. Someone said, 'Dammit, pick up your feet.'*

"Suddenly the first of our mortar flares lit up the sky and we were all flat on the ground. We cautiously looked around the countryside but there wasn't a Jerry in sight. It was now 8 p.m. and the flares were working just as we had planned. As soon as the flare died out we got up again. About 200 yards ahead we saw a light and a few shadows moving. We held a confab and decided that because we didn't want to take prisoners too early we would alter our course again. We bypassed the light and circled around to the right. Then we heard the unmistakable sound of Germans digging in for the night. It was the sound of folding shovels digging into the earth and the clunking noise they made as they were tapped

---

*This entire account minimizes Lieutenant Sims. In point of fact, the patrol would never have taken place without his initiative. It would never have succeeded without his inventiveness, and most of the decisions mentioned in the narrative were his own. From the introductory remarks in the LIFE story, here omitted, it seems evident that none of the patrol members understood what part Sims had played.

on the ground to loosen the mud. We now turned left again and as we did someone stumbled into the brush in the darkness. Immediately we stood still as statues and waited. Then we heard the zip of a German flare going up. We hit the ground and froze as more of the flares lit up the countryside. To either side of us we could hear Germans moving around. Now and then one of them shouted to ask what the flares were for. They had heard something and had whole batches of flares ready to shoot off. Each time a flare burned out we crept forward between the two enemy groups. In a half hour, when our own flare next went up, we had covered less than 300 yards.

"Then we crossed a road and found ourselves within twenty yards of a lighted tent. I was all for going in and taking whoever was there a prisoner. I thought it might be a Jerry officer and a good bag but once again we decided that it was best to skirt the area. We went one way and then the other through the fields. Every time we heard activity we edged in the other direction."

Corporal William R. Canfield of Selman, Oklahoma, now interrupted the story. "I was a little to one side of the group and suddenly I heard someone blowing his nose. I moved over to the left and saw a group of Jerries stopped for a minute on the road. I asked Lieutenant Sims if I might capture them and take them along but he said not now. I was sure feeling cocky.

"A little later I heard Becker make a noise and as I glanced at him he began to pull himself out of a slit trench he had slipped into. I walked over to him and saw a big, fat Jerry snoring away in the hole. For a moment we thought he might waken and looked down ready to pounce on him if he made a noise. When he remained asleep we went on and joined the rest up ahead. Now we were in a wooded area and we had to be careful of every step. At a clearing in the woods we came to a small road and not ten yards away we saw a couple of Jerries walking down the road with something on their shoulders. Nicholai sneaked along the road and looked more closely. He came back and reported that they were carrying a mattress. A little farther down the road we saw them walk into a house with their mattress. We waited but they didn't come out so we figured they must have turned in for the night.

"Farther on we crossed the road and stumbled right into an

ammunition dump. Sergeant* Frank, the interpreter, went over to check the writing on the boxes. He found they were shells for a heavy 150mm. infantry gun which Lieutenant Sims marked down in a little book he was carrying. He also marked the position of the ammo dump and the location of the mattress house. Just as we were starting to make a more thorough inspection around the ammo dump we heard the unmistakable sound of a German Schmeisser gun bolt being snapped back. In a second there came another. We stood rooted to the spot, afraid to breathe. The things seemed to come from just across the road. There wasn't much else for us to do but go sneaking back through the area of the sleeping men.''

Sergeant Frank now pointed out that he hadn't been too scared when the bolt snapped back. He had a story all ready for the situation. Every time they came to a new emergency he would review in his mind a story that might work the patrol out of it. This time he was ready to raise hell with the Jerries for making so much noise with their machine-gun bolts. Frank continued:

''Now we cut straight across the fields for about two miles. Nicholai was getting hungry and he simply reached down and grabbed a handful of carrots from a vegetable patch and began to eat them. Soon we had enough of the fields and decided that we were deep enough in the enemy territory to brazen it out on the road. When we came to a good paved road we walked right down the middle of it. Just ahead we heard the clank and rumble of a Jerry horse-drawn vehicle. We crawled into the ditch along the road and waited for it to pass. In a couple of minutes we were on the road again.

''Farther on we checked our compass course and started off to the right. We hadn't gone more than twenty yards when I saw Becker throw his hands in the air.** Right in front of us was a huge German gun emplacement. The gun and pits for the ammunition were there but there didn't seem to be any Jerries. About a hundred yards farther on we came to a strange collection of silhouettes. We couldn't be sure what they were and kept on going until we made them out. It was a Jerry motor pool with all types of vehicles parked for the

*Later lieutenant.
**This was the infantryman's hand signal for contact with the enemy.

night. We were all for taking one of the cars but Lieutenant Sims again turned thumbs down. He pulled out his map and noted the exact location. Soon we were on the edge of the town of Wolfheeze and decided that it would be best to work around it. As it later turned out, this was a good thing. The place was lousy with SS troops.

"We skirted the town pretty closely and could even smell the smoke from stinking German cigarets. We now crossed the railroad which we knew marked the two-thirds point on our trip. We were some distance behind the enemy lines and had the feeling we would be able to bluff our way out of almost any situation that might arise. The last three miles of rushing through the fields was pretty hard. The tall grass slowed us down but it also sheltered us from observation. Nicholai was in the lead, eating carrots again. When he heard the rush of a car going by he whispered to Sims that this must be the road we had crossed so much country to reach. Within a few hundred yards we came out on the road."*

Nicholai broke in again: "We all waited a few minutes at the side of the road while Lieutenant Sims brought out a map and checked our location. We were right behind a house that marked the exact spot where we had planned to hit the road. This was only luck** but it made us feel as if everything was going according to plan. Lieutenant Sims, looking over the house and the area, decided we might as well occupy the house for cover. We sneaked up carefully, listening for the slightest sound. Becker and Canfield now went through a window and a minute or so later came back to whisper that all was clear inside. But after a conference we decided that this was not so good after all. If Jerry were to see any activity around a house which he knew to be empty he would become suspicious. Becker and Canfield climbed back out and we headed down on the road again. In front Sergeant Frank was carrying on a monolog with Becker in German. This was funny because Becker didn't understand a word of it. We all fell into the spirit of it, feeling we could fool any Germans who came along. Soon one of the boys was singing *Lili Marlene* and we all joined in.

"After about a mile of walking along the road without

*The Arnheim-Utrecht highway.
**A mild understatement.

meeting a single German we came to a couple of houses. One of them had a Red Cross marking on the front. It was a small cross and the place hardly looked as if it were a hospital. At any rate it looked like the better of the two houses. As Sergeant Frank and myself edged close we could hear what sounded like snoring inside. We walked to the back door and found it open. In the front room of the house we found two Germans sleeping on piles of straw. They wore big shiny boots and I was sure they were officers. Sergeant Frank said they were cavalrymen. Leaving Frank on guard I went back outside and reported to Lieutenant Sims. He said we would take the men prisoner and stay at this house. I told Frank the plan and he began to shake the Germans. One of them finally began to rub his eyes. He stared at us and Frank kept telling him over and over that he was a prisoner. They just couldn't believe it."

After the dazed Germans had been thoroughly awakened they were questioned by Sergeant Frank. He got all the information he could from them and relayed it to Lieutenant Sims. Sims was now up in the attic setting up the radio with another man. In about ten minutes the men heard him saying into the radio, "This is Sims, Sims, Sims. We have two prisoners. We have two prisoners." They knew the radio was working and everyone felt swell. Soon Sims was sending information about the things he had noted along the way.

After questioning the prisoners Sergeant Frank told them to go back to sleep but they just sat up and stared. Frank asked them if they expected any more soldiers in the area. They said that another man was supposed to pick them up at about 5:30 in the morning.

After the radio had been set up everything was quiet until daybreak. The men took turns watching the road while the others tried to get a little sleep. At about 7 a.m., Nicholai reported the arrival of a young civilian at the front door. The civilian proved to be a boy of about sixteen in knee pants. He was both surprised and pleased to be taken captive by the "Tommies." The men took some time to explain to him that they were not Tommies but airborne GIs. When this had been taken care of, Sergeant Frank was allowed to go ahead with his questioning. The boy explained that the house belonged to some friends of his and he had just come over for some preserves. He knew the people had been evacuated and said they might not be back for some time.

The boy went on to say that his older brother, who was a member of the local underground, would also be along shortly. Almost immediately the brother was brought in by Nicholai. He was a slick-haired, effeminate young man and the patrol had doubts about him. He spoke a little English and produced papers to prove that he was a member of the Dutch underground. He began to tell the men about the various enemy installations in the area. He gave them artillery positions and unit numbers and all this was immediately relayed back over the radio.

In the following hour six more civilians were guests of the patrol. They all seemed to know that there was no one home and all wanted something from the house. They were told they would have to stay until after the patrol had left. The civilians were happy to see the men, but they didn't like the idea of having to stay. One of the captives, a very pretty Dutch girl accompanied by what appeared to be her boyfriend, wouldn't take no for an answer. The men said she was not averse to using all of her charms to get out, either, but they were firm.

At noon the traffic on the road began to increase. Convoys of big trucks appeared to be heading from the Utrecht area toward Arnhem. The men observed all kinds of vehicles and guns. Presently an unsuspecting Jerry entered the courtyard for a drink of water. Opening the front door a little, one of the men pointed his Tommy gun at the German and commanded him to come in. The German came in laughing, apparently not quite convinced that the whole thing wasn't a joke. He turned out to be a mail orderly who had lost his way after taking mail to a near-by town. He seemed to be an intellectual type and was very philosophical about being captured.

Shortly afterwards the idea of food occurred to everyone in the house. The men in the patrol got out their K-ration chocolate and the civilians began to dig into the little bags they all carried. It began to look as if the civilians had been going on a picnic. They brought out bread and cheese and shared it with the Americans. An hour or so later the German who was supposed to meet the first two prisoners at 5:30 finally showed up with two horses and a cart. The men let him enter the courtyard and water the horses. Then they called out to him, "Put up your hands, you are a prisoner." He didn't seem to understand and it was necessary to repeat the order. Then he answered calmly, "I must feed my horses." Finally he raised one hand and came toward the house, muttering that it just couldn't be true. Now the civilians helped in the questioning, because the Germans were not too sure about the names of towns where their units were stationed.

Once the men watching from the windows were tempted to whistle at a passing car. It was driven by a pretty German WAC. The men said that the only thing that restrained them was the fact that their lives depended on it. Because everything had gone so smoothly the men were feeling pretty cocky. They wanted to capture a truck, a couple of staff cars with German WACs and drive back to Renkum.

Two more Germans entered the courtyard and were immediately taken prisoner. They were very sore, mainly because they had come along the road just to goldbrick away a little time. By this time a big fire had been built up in the front room where the prisoners were kept. The prisoners kept the fire going and the men argued to see who would stand guard in the warm room.

As darkness approached the men began to assemble their equipment. Becker was left on guard in the house with the prisoners and civilians while Lieutenant Sims and the others went out to look for a truck. The German mail orderly, who seemed the happiest to be captured, was chosen to help them. He agreed that as soon as Sergeant Frank told him, he would help stop the truck by shouting, *"Halt Kamerad!"* As they waited the German said to Frank, "I am happy because the war is over for us." Frank replied that it would all depend on the next few hours and that he would be able to say with more certainty the next day.

Becker reported that when the lieutenant and the others left the house the remaining prisoners looked a little scared. Finally one man came and asked Becker in pantomime if they would be shot. Becker told them that such things aren't done in the American Army. All of the Germans in the house wore the Iron Cross and had seen service against the Russians.

While the men were waiting along the road a whole German company passed on bicycles. As each German rode by he would shout, *"Guten Abend"* to the men along the road and they shouted back the same. One man stopped and asked Sergeant Frank if this were the right road to the next town. Rather than become engaged in conversation, Frank told him he didn't know.

Getting impatient after an hour and a half, the men decided they would stop the next truck that came along, no matter what kind it was. In the meantime a motorcyclist stopped by the road and went into the courtyard of the house. Nicholai rushed across the road and grabbed him. It developed that he was checking up on the absence of the other men. When Nicholai brought him across the road he saw the mail orderly and rushed up to shake his hand. They were old friends and had served together for years.

A few minutes later the men heard a truck coming down the road and told the two Germans to step out and shout, *"Halt Kamerad!"* When the truck came, all the men shouted at once and the truck stopped. It turned out to be a big five-tonner carrying 15 SS men. Nicholai jumped on the back and herded the Germans off, taking their weapons as they got down. They were all very surprised. At first the driver refused to leave his seat but after a number of strong threats, namely shooting, he finally got off. He was a tall man and very cocky. When asked to put up his hands he said, "Who says so?" When he was told that he was a prisoner of war he looked astonished and said that it was impossible. As he spoke he put one hand up and with the other drew a pistol, but only to hide it in his pocket. Sergeant Frank took it away.

The driver was told to get back in the truck and pull it off the road. He seemed reluctant and Frank had to hold a gun against his ear while he started the motor. He seemed unable to keep the motor from stalling every few seconds and when he moved into the courtyard he had trouble turning. It was obvious that he was stalling for time. He kept looking at Frank and saying in German, "This can't happen to me." He told Frank he was on his way to meet the captain of his battalion. When he was told he was to drive the truck and the men to the Neder Rijn he said there wasn't enough gas. He was told that if that were true then he would be shot, so he said there was enough gas for twenty miles.

Now Becker and the prisoners in the house came out and piled into the truck with the SS men. The Americans spaced themselves around inside the truck so they could keep guard.

Lieutenant Sims and Sergeant Frank sat in front with the driver. When they were on the road the truck stalled again. As the driver tried to start the motor an amphibious jeep pulled up and a tall SS officer began to bawl him out for blocking the road. Canfield was off the truck in an instant and had brought the officer inside. As it turned out, this was the captain the truck driver had been going to meet.

Again the sergeant concentrated on getting the driver to start the truck. He worked hard at stalling the motor and had to be threatened before he would drive at all. Finally he got the truck under way and they set out on the return route they had mapped out before the patrol. Every now and then the driver would get temperamental, folding his arms and saying, *"Hab' ich eine Wut!"* ("Am I mad!"). After a prod or two with the gun muzzle he would go back to safer driving. Farther along the road toward Arnhem he was told to turn off to the right. Shortly the truck came to a muddy place in the woods and bogged down hub-deep. No amount of trying by the SS driver was able to move it. It was now 10 p.m. and the patrol decided they might as well try to make it back on foot.

Now the men regretted having so many prisoners. As they piled down from the truck the SS captain bolted to the side of the road in the darkness. In a flash he was in the woods. Nicholai shouted for him to stop and ran after. In a moment the others heard two shots and Nicholai's only two words of German, *"Hände hoch*, you son of a bitch!"* followed by a great crashing in the underbrush. Becker also ran into the woods to see if he might help. Following the noise he found Nicholai and the captain. Nicholai was still shouting. *"Hände hoch"* and with every shout he would kick the captain in the seat of the pants. When they came back to the truck the captain was cowed and willing to go quietly.

Lining the Germans up in two columns, Sergeant Frank now gave them a little lecture. He said they could just as easily be shot as taken back and that all six Americans were risking their lives to get them back safely. He told them that if anyone tried to escape or made an unnecessary noise he would be shot immediately. Starting out again with the SS captain and Sergeant Frank in front, the column made its way along the road toward the river. As they walked the SS captain told Frank that it was useless to try to cross the Rijn with the prisoners. He said the Americans might as well turn over their guns because they would surely be caught by the Germans.

The captain also asked if he might have a cigarette. He was told he couldn't have one now, but that later he would have more and better cigarettes than there were in all of Germany. The captain said the Germans had nothing against the Americans and he couldn't see personally why the Germans and Americans didn't get together to fight the Russians and Japanese. We are both white races, he said. Sergeant Frank answered that the Russians were also white. Yes, replied the captain, but they are inferior. Finally the captain asked if it were not possible for them to rest a while, or at least to slow down. He was told that he had the misfortune to be a captive of American paratroopers, who just didn't walk any slower. Now as they walked along they constantly heard German voices.

Arriving at the railroad crossing the patrol decided finally that they didn't dare blow up the tracks with the two and a half minute fuse they carried. Reluctantly they crossed the tracks and ditched their demolition charges in bushes by the road. Along this last stretch of the road they passed countless houses with Germans inside.

When they came to the town of Renkum the patrol marched boldly down the center of the main street with a great clicking of German hobnailed shoes. It was obvious from the sound alone that they could be nothing but a group of marching Germans. They went through the town without incident and headed straight for the near-by dike. Everyone was feeling wonderfully light-headed. Arriving at the dike they had marched right down to the water when they saw a squad of Germans at a river outpost. As they came close Sergeant Frank called out to them in German that there was nothing to worry about. When they stopped two of the men rushed over and told the Jerries to put up their hands. The column moved on, cleaning out two more posts along the river. The six-man patrol now had a total of 32 prisoners.

On the dike Lieutenant Sims gave the prearranged flashlight signal to the other side. Soon the answer came—three blinks. The SS captain*, his truck driver and one of the patrol were the first to get to the other side. Part of the patrol stayed

---

*Who remarked: "I congratulate you. I didn't believe it was possible."

behind to cover the crossing while the rest of the prisoners were ferried over. Finally the last three men touched the Allied side of the Rijn. The incredible patrol was over.

Shortly afterwards the soldiers were awarded Silver Stars. Lieutenant Sims, who received the Distinguished Service Cross, had dinner with General Taylor and was promoted to captain. The story of the patrol went the rounds of the European Theater, and the battalion intelligence officers of the 501st Parachute Infantry tightened their belts and sighed.

29
Home Life in Holland

On November 4th, in Paris, General Brereton, commander of the 1st Allied Airborne Army, wrote in his diary: "Supreme headquarters is continuing to put pressure on Field Marshal Montgomery to force the release of the 82nd and the 101st. Keeping airborne soldiers in the front lines as infantry is a violation of the cardinal rules of airborne employment. The big difficulty is airborne replacements. They have to be especially trained. Ordinary infantrymen cannot be used as replacements. They should come out quickly, otherwise their morale will be seriously dented. They think they are better than ordinary foot soldiers and prove it by their vicious fighting. They resent remaining in the line after their initial job is finished."

General Brereton was right. And if we had been any other place except Holland, we would have agreed with him wholeheartedly. It just happened that in Holland most of us were having a pretty good time.

East along the island the Germans still held bridgeheads, including several dikes which they could open to flood our area. But the water was not yet high enough in the rivers for this, so both sides limited themselves to a polite and more or less sporadic duel of artillery. The Germans held the high ground across the river and, from that vantage point, could

place all of the American lines under observation, so travel
along the forward roads within our positions was restricted to
the hours of darkness. Before that restriction took effect, it
was not unusual for a jeep to arrive at a battalion command
post trailing—or being led by—a string of gray explosions.

Something should be said here about motoring in the black-
out. Accustomed as we were to flaring headlights, this was a
unique and rather eerie experience. After dark in our particular neighborhood of Holland, two British searchlights, their
beams directed at the sky, flooded the black sodden land with
a queer luminous blue glow, known among the soldiers as
"artificial moonlight." A jeep being driven along the roads
near the front lines could be kept to its path by this faint
luminosity, but that was about all. No one ever exceeded five
or ten miles an hour. Drivers put their windshields down and
strained their eyes to see where they were going. The blackness and silence of the surrounding land gave rise to a foolish
sense of expectancy, as though an ambush lay ahead, and it
was always a shock to realize that you had passed without
knowing it into a silent, pitch-black, apparently abandoned
town.

We were dug in along the landward side of the dike. We
deepened our foxholes or made them into small dugouts lined
with boards. Regularly, battalions on the line were relieved
and sent back to a reserve area (much more dangerous than
the front) for brief periods of rest.

The graves registration officer and his crew, who lived at a
peaceful little village called Valbourg were busy from time to
time recovering the bodies of those killed by artillery fire. It
was not a pleasant job. Even less agreeable was the task of
retrieving the British paratroopers who had died by the edge
of the river during the early days of Arnhem. Those bodies
were in a bad state of decomposition. Once, one of the
G.R.O. crew, as they were called, lifted a man by his shoulders, only to have his head come off. One truckload of such
bodies was a pulpy mass of green flesh and dried blood, with
maggots oozing out between the cracks in the truck. That load
was left overnight in the yard at Valbourg and, next morning,
to the horror of the villagers, scores of small and very curious
little Dutch children had surrounded the vehicle.

The children of the island were all spic and span. Their
clothes were neat, their faces were polished like apples, and

most of them, to the amusement of the soldiers, wore wooden shoes. They liked American candy. But they never acquired the British children's habit of asking for "goom." None of them was very poor, and it seemed evident that Holland had no "lower class." The farmhouses were all of stone, well constructed. Produce seemed ample, and though meat was scarce, fruit was so plentiful—including the celebrated jam of Driel—that after a while the soldiers had more than they could eat.

We still were living off British rations, however.

In the days before looting became a major scandal, Colonel Ewell was walking with Major Bottomly in the fields behind regimental headquarters when he saw a few of the soldiers hunting a steak dinner, at that moment still on the hoof. When the bewildered cow clumped in a wide circle and unexpectedly ran square into her pursuers, Ewell reportedly drawled, "Bottomly, that cow is attacking our men. . . ."

However, two 101st soldiers with bazookas shot open the safe of a church near Driel and that of a bank in Nijmegen, and when the repercussions of those major forays had died down, even a souvenir postcard was considered to be loot.

The heavy military traffic on the island turned the country roads to seas of mud. We had never seen so much mud. The roads were narrow, which made it difficult for wide vehicles to pass each other, and the commonest sight on the island in those days was a heavy British lorry on its side in the ditch. There were so many of them in this situation that after a while we decided we were better drivers than the British.

The English soldier came to battle prepared to do a slow and thorough job. He preferred deliberateness to the sudden dash, the savage gamble. In that difference of temperament lay the gulf between him and the American soldier. Where the American went to the line lightly equipped and prepared to get the dirty work over with in a hurry—or die in the attempt—the British Tommy carried his pots and pans and stoves and tents along with him, reconciled to an interterminable siege in the field and determined, while he was about it, to be as comfortable as possible.

All over the island between the Waal and the Rhine the British encampments were more elaborate than our own. Tents sprang up under the orchards. In the evenings little groups of Tommies could be seen cooking heavy dinners over their own specially constructed kerosene burners, which were three times the size of the American "squad cooker." The Bren carriers that came up through Veghel and Uden to Nijmegen were packed tight with every conceivable need of life in the field—sometimes even chairs and tables.

The paratroopers were the only Americans in the British sector. When we drove to Nijmegen for a shower, we used the British "ablutions." We obeyed British traffic rules, answered to British guards at the Waal river bridges, were guided along the highway by British military police. The Dutch, the British and the Americans were all mixed in together, and on the whole they got along very well with each other—especially the Dutch and the Americans.

2

Then one day it began to rain. It rained and it rained. The rivers rose until the Waal began to flood the lower streets of Nijmegen and press against the dikes. The waters were muddied and turbulent. We began to realize that we had been in combat for more than two months. Secretly, division notified Colonel Ewell that the Germans might open the dikes to the north.

We wanted to be relieved.

30
Mean High Water

It was after supper. The men were sitting around the kitchen table of an abandoned Dutch house in Valbourg, a mile or so from the front lines. The house, which had once been a Dutch "pub," was one of the few buildings in the village that had not been struck by shellfire. Since the rains started, mud had steadily accumulated around the outside, until even the wooden shoes the men had collected for souvenirs were too low to keep it out. The mud had a soupy consistency. Night after night and day after day for twenty days the storm clouds had rolled over the village, and steadily the river had risen.

"It don't matter which way you look at it," Private Campoli was saying. "If the shell's got your number on it, you're finished, no matter how deep you dig."

"It ain't the one that has your number on it," objected Biffle, the cook. "It's the one that says, 'To Whom It May Concern.' "

"Nobody's gonna die by a bullet around here," said Simione. He was playing solitaire by the stove. "What I hear today, we're gonna die by drowning."

"Who says?" Campoli demanded.

"Message center. They're ready to pull out."

"The whole regiment?"

Simione nodded. Biffle pulled the coffee pot onto the fire. "What for?"

"The dike's gonna bust."

"Them dikes is a coupla hundred years old," said Campoli comfortably. "You think maybe they're gonna bust just because there's a war on?"

"I'm telling ya. The Germans are gonna open the dikes. Up north."

"What latrine did you get that out of?"

"Everybody knows about it at regiment. Even the Dutchmen."

"I don't believe it," Campoli announced definitely. He had been through the African invasion. "They'd have told us about it before this."

"Go ask the lieutenant," Biffle suggested.

The lieutenant was alone in the next room, writing a letter home. He had just finished censoring the men's mail and he wanted to include his own letter with the others.

"Lootenant," said Campoli entering the room, "What's this about the Germans opening the dikes up north of here?"

"It's supposed to be a secret," said the lieutenant cheerfully.

"What'd happen to us?"

The officer shrugged. "We'd have to get back twenty miles or so. To high ground."

Campoli spat on the hot stove. "Just when we were getting settled." He went back into the kitchen. "The lootenant says it's the straight dope."

"Marshall here can't swim," said Simione.

"That's one way of getting rid of him."

"You can swim all right if they throw you in, can't you, Marshall?" Biffle asked.

"They tried that when I was a kid," said Marshall. "They had to call the Portland Fire Department."

"S-4 better issue water wings, that's all I can say," Simione declared, dealing the cards again.

"Why don't we pack up?" worried little Marshall. "Maybe the regiment'll pull out and leave us here."

"So what?" Campoli demanded. "Ain't you fed up with the army?"

"It's the swimming—"

"Float, that's what I always say," announced Campoli, helping himself to another cup of coffee. "If you can't swim, float."

"What'll we do with all our Dutch stuff?" Simione asked.

"Not so loud," warned Marshall nervously. He quoted a familiar British road sign: *"Scrounging Is Looting. Penalty—Death."*

"I'd like to see 'em shoot me for what *I* got," added Simione. "Shut up while I finish this game."

"Maybe we ought to get packed," Biffle ventured, looking at his pots and pans.

"Hell, no," Campoli said. "The Lootenant knows when to get ready. Lootenants know everything."

"He'll hear you," whispered Marshall.

"Yeah," put in Simione loudly. "Who does Campoli think he is, anyway—a civilian?"

Writing alone in the next room, the officer grinned. He liked his men. He was the only officer in a group of eight of them, so he ate with them, slept with them, and worked with them. Not much attention was paid to his rank, but he got all the cooperation he needed, and that was what he was there for. Occasionally, the two chaplains spent the night at the house, but neither was conscious of his rank. They liked the tranquil atmosphere of the Valbourg; that, and Biffle's pancakes for breakfast.

"Anyway," Campoli went on, "it's a change from shelling."

"I don't care what you guys say," said Marshall. "I'm going to pack."

There was silence for a while. Somewhere not far off the

lieutenant could hear the *"wop-wop"* of incoming shells. Presently there was a succession of *"wop-wop-wops"* closer to the house. He sighed.

2

The Protestant chaplain bundled in, his trench coat black with water. Behind him was his driver, Private Le June.

"Your phone is out," said Chaplain Engels, as he stripped off his coat. "They've been trying to reach you from regiment."

"What for?"

Le June broke in. "You have to be ready to clear out, sir," he said. "The Germans are going to blow the dikes tonight."

"Just what I was saying," said Simione, entering.

"You can tell the men to get their stuff together," said the lieutenant.

"You oughta see that river," volunteered the driver. "The water's up to the windows of the houses on the other side."

"Hell!" said Campoli, entering the room. "I'm for staying right here. What's the sense of getting scared by a little high water? In Africa—"

"Sure," interrupted Simione. "There's plenty of high places around here. What about the church steeple?"

"Now, now," frowned the chaplain, warming his hands at the stove. "You know who has priority on *that*, don't you?"

"It's a Catholic church," said Le June. "It's reserved for Father Sampson."

"Can you take care of Marshall, Chaplain?" asked Simione. "He can't swim. He says he can't even float."

"He missed church last Sunday," said the chaplain severely. "Let him sink."

"Hey, Marshall!" shouted Simione promptly, "The chaplain says it's all because you didn't go to church last Sunday!"

Marshall put his head in the door. "Couldn't you have a quick service for me, Chaplain Engels? I sure do hate to miss those hot cakes. And Biffle might drown. . . ."

"Biffle will be rewarded in Heaven," said the chaplain solemnly. He turned to the lieutenant. "You and I had better pack."

The lieutenant and the chaplain slept in a whitewashed

wine cellar underneath the house. The chaplain moved in there the first night.

"Don't you want a small foxhole in the floor, Chaplain?" Green had said to him at the time. "Say about ten feet deep?"

"Christianity began in the catacombs," the chaplain answered with dignity. "What was good enough for the early martyrs is good enough for me."

"I agree with the chaplain," said Cavanaugh, who slept in the attic.

"All I can say," Marshall had remarked gloomily, climbing back up the ladder, "is that it ain't very good for the morale of us guys upstairs."

Just now the lieutenant began folding his blankets. Simione sat in the corner trying to decide what to do with four pairs of wooden shoes and two German helmets. The lieutenant looked up thoughtfully. "What do you think I ought to do with this German carbide lamp?"

"I'll trade you for it, Lootenant," offered Simione. "I'll give you this Dutch ash tray. And a pair of wooden shoes."

"You can't keep the ash tray," said the officer. "That belongs to the house."

"Lootenant," called Private Le June from upstairs, "can we take Jenny with us?"

Jenny was a highly odorous little shell-shocked dog that the men had adopted. The lieutenant said "No."

"But she'll drown."

"Rot," said Green's voice. "Dogs can swim. A dog is a Highly Developed Creature. Higher even than a Marshall."

"Lootenant," persisted the driver. "If you was to see this here dog walkin' around the place where we're going, what'd you think?"

"That she swam there, I guess."

"That's all I wanted to know, Lootenant," said Le June cheerfully. "Jenny's mother thanks you. Jenny's father thanks you. Even Marshall thanks you."

"I think I'll stay here and drown," said Marshall.

Campoli put his head in at the top of the stairs. "What'll we do with the kitchen stuff? Can we take all those plates with the swastikas on them?"

"Leave everything here that belongs to the house," said the lieutenant firmly.

"The kitchen stuff should come with us," said Chaplain Engels. "Especially the pancake griddle." He called up to Campoli. "Tell Biffle I hold him personally responsible for the pancake griddle. He'll have to sign for it."

"Who's going to sign for Biffle?" asked Green upstairs.

"Biffle knows what kind of a Hereafter he can look for if the chaplain starves," said the chaplain. "Tell him his only hope of Heaven is to stick by me."

"I'll tell him, sir," said Green. "But I believe he's a Holy Roller."

"In matters of pancakes," stated the chaplain, "I am non-denominational."

The group had almost finished packing when the shelling started again. Father Sampson, the Catholic chaplain, came heavily down the stairs to the cellar.

"Are you all packed, Father?" asked Marshall excitedly. "The dike's gonna bust. Straight dope."

"Don't talk to me," said Father Sampson. "Don't anybody talk to me."

"I know what's the matter with him," offered Campoli. "Notre Dame lost to Army."

"No fooling, Father?" Simione asked.

"Fifty-nine to nothing," he groaned. "Fifty-nine to nothing!"

The telephone rang for the first time. They heard the subdued voice of Green. "The line's in now," he called down. "Regiment says we have to be ready to move out in thirty minutes."

"We'll be ready," said the lieutenant. "Tell everybody to have the house policed up before we go."

"What's the sense of policing up the house if it's going to get washed away?" asked Father Sampson.

"You're just discouraged," said Chaplain Engels.

"I think I'll go into Retreat," he said. " 'The father hath eaten sour grapes and the teeth of the children are set on edge.' "

"Maybe the Pope will annul the game," suggested Simione.

The priest glowered at him. "For that you can pack my bags," he said.

3

When everybody in the house was ready to leave, and Green had driven the ton-and-a-half truck around to the side entrance, the lieutenant inspected the rooms. While he was upstairs the Germans started shelling the area again. He could hear the descending whistle of the shells.

"Lots of duds tonight," commented Campoli expertly. "Hope they don't shell the road while we're getting out."

"You think you couldn't be killed by a dud?" asked Marshall, hesitating at the top of the stairs. "If one of those hit you, you'd be deader'n a dead dud."

"I don't like that," scowled Campoli.

"The African Corpse!" shouted Marshall, running down the stairs. The lieutenant heard him enter the kitchen. "Nobody loves me," he said plaintively.

"The chaplain loves you," put in Biffle.

"That's because he's kind to dumb animals," remarked Cavanaugh.

"Not when they're that dumb," Green denied.

The lieutenant finished inspecting the upstairs rooms as quickly as he could. The house had a bare and desolate look; all its life seemed gone. When he got back to the kitchen he found the men dressed in webbing, with steel helmets and weapons. They looked different.

"Have a cup of coffee, Lootenant," offered Cavanaugh nervously.

"Have a chair, Lootenant," suggested Simione.

The lieutenant looked at Cavanaugh. "Who took that silver coffee set out of your room, Cavanaugh?" he asked.

"Sugar and cream, Lootenant," the man suggested hopefully.

"Answer the question."

"There's some pretty big mice upstairs, Lootenant," he suggested.

"I'll give you three minutes to get the set," said the officer. "And the same goes for the rest of you. Three minutes to get everything you took out of the house and put it on the table here."

"Even them plates with the swastikas on them?" asked Simione.

"The kitchen is under my charge," interposed Chaplain Engels. "Leave that to me."

"Three minutes," the lieutenant warned, looking at his watch.

The men moved off unhappily. No sound reached the kitchen except the whistle and explosion of the shells outside. Father Sampson wrote something on a scrap of paper. Chaplain Engels helped himself to a cup of coffee. The lieutenant smoked a cigarette.

Presently the men began coming back. Cavanaugh put the coffee set on the table. With it he put a porcelain plate with a painted windmill. Simione brought two bottles of Dutch wine, three silver spoons and a crucifix. The driver reluctantly laid a pair of ice skates on the table. Biffle added four blue spice jars, a pot of Dutch jam and a kitchen knife. Green put down a set of silver hair brushes. To the entire collection, little Marshall added Jenny, who looked at everyone curiously for a while and then curled up by the wine and went to sleep. Outside, the shelling stopped.

Everybody looked at the lieutenant.

The lieutenant in turn looked at the two chaplains. "Loot," he said loudly. There was silence in the kitchen.

"Regiment says to stand by," called Green from the telephone.

Everybody waited for the lieutenant to say something.

4

"Well," said Chaplain Engels at last, "I guess it's up to me." He paused. "Father Sampson, you'd better pay attention."

The priest sighed.

"Either this collection is all wrong or it's all right or it's partly right," said Chaplain Engels. "Bless me, Critch, you ought to be left to squirm out of this yourself."

The lieutenant grinned. "Put it back," he said. "Orders are orders."

"My own interest in the matter is purely impersonal, of course," said the chaplain. He spread his hands on the table. "Let's all vote on the ethical aspects of this problem. How many of you agree that stealing is wrong? Raise your hands."

"Aw nuts," said Simione. But everybody raised his hand.

"Now let's suppose that a cow was killed by a German 88, and the men in the front lines wanted a steak dinner. Bear in mind that even a dead cow is not their property. Is it wrong to take the meat? Father Sampson, will you please listen to this? Hands please, everybody?"

Nobody raised his hand. "You must have been a revivalist, Chaplain," remarked Green.

"Now we have a situation," he continued, "in which it has suddenly become all right to take someone else's meat. Give me a reason for the difference."

"The meat'd spoil," said Biffle. "The owner won't come out where the shooting is and cart it away."

"Besides, he left the cow out there in the first place," offered Marshall, who was always concerned about animals.

"A very good point," said the chaplain. "One more."

"We came here to liberate 'em," said Campoli aggressively. "Lots of us get killed doing it. Don't they owe us a steak once in a while?"

"Very good," agreed the chaplain pontifically. "I leave the subject of steaks with reluctance. Let us now consider these household objects. Since there is not much difference between cows and dogs, except where Biffle is concerned, you may remove the dog."

Jenny was taken out by Marshall.

"We can divide the remaining objects into the useful and the purely decorative. That will make the moral problem simpler. What are you writing, Father Sampson?"

"My resignation," announced the priest. "The staff will never forget this day."

"In the useful pile," went on Chaplain Engels, "we can put the hair brushes, the Dutch wine, the jar of preserves, and the kitchen knife. We now come to the difficult part. What is the moral justification for taking these fine objects?"

"If we leave 'em here they'll be underwater," said Cavanaugh.

"Quite so," acknowledged the chaplain. "But Father Sampson will agree with me, I believe, that in this delicate decision we can no longer ignore the moral fact of looting. I leave out Lieutenant Critchell; he has military prejudices. We are taking someone else's property. Am I right?"

"We're fighting for 'em," protested Campoli.

"And they left the stuff here," added Green.

"But they might come back," interpolated the chaplain, "in a boat."

Everybody agreed reluctantly that he was right. Cavanaugh and Simione looked baffled. Marshall looked worried. "That dike must've busted by now," he said to Green. "Go see if the phone is still working."

"I want to watch this," said Green. "Go do it yourself." So Marshall went out.

"We are all agreed," said Chaplain Engels rhetorically, "that the Lord commanded, 'Thou shalt not steal.' Correct me, Father Sampson, if I misquote. It is also true that he did not carefully define stealing. There is no particular record of what Noah took into the ark with him, and I am not sure who owned the animals. However, we have already disposed of the cow, the dog and the fruit. The question now before us is: will the inevitable loss of these articles in the future justify our taking them from their absent owner in the present?"

"That's not the question at all," put in the lieutenant. "The question is one of military discipline."

"Now don't exchange gold for brass," soothed the chaplain. He waited for an answer. Nobody said anything.

"Father Sampson," said Chaplain Engels, "I have narrowed this problem down to a simple moral decision between right and wrong. I leave the answer to you. Speak in words of wisdom to your flock."

Everybody looked at Father Sampson. There was silence in the room.

"Come on, Father," Simione urged.

"Yeah," said Campoli. "There must be another side to this somewhere."

The priest shifted slowly. "I'm not in good form tonight," he said at last. "I would rather leave this to Chaplain Engels. It seems more of a Methodist's problem."

"I've done all the spade work already," said the other.

Father Sampson looked thoughtful. He frowned at the objects on the table. At length, "It seems to me . . ." But then he paused again.

"Go on," they all urged.

The telephone rang in the next room. "Never mind that," said Cavanaugh hastily. "Marshall's in there."

Another silence ensued. The priest rubbed his face painfully. He frowned. At last, with a gesture of finality, he spread his hands out on the table. "All right," he said. "Here is my decision. . . ."

"Hey!" interrupted Marshall, shouting from the next room. "It's all off!"

Everybody looked up.

"We can unpack," clarified Marshall, entering. "Regiment says they aren't going to open the dikes. Not tonight."

"How the hell can they tell?" asked Cavanaugh.

"Beats me. But that's what they say."

"Damn!" said Simione. "All that wasted work."

"Let's clear this stuff off," suggested Biffle.

"Just by chance," said Green happily, "I happen to have in my pocket three small shells and a pea. . . ."

"Pancakes for breakfast, Biffle?" asked Chaplain Engels.

"Yes, *sir*."

"What about a friendly little game of poker?" asked Simione.

"Suits me," said Cavanaugh. "Move over a minute, Father Sampson, while I clean off the table?"

"Certainly, certainly," he said. He moved over to the stove, rubbing his face thoughtfully. "I can't understand it," he said. "I can't understand it." He paused a few moments, still thinking. Then, decisively, "There must have been a Protestant on the team."

Outside, the rain and the shelling both started again.

31
Good-bye

Winter had come when we were relieved. In Nijmegen the trees were bare, the river high. It was November 24, 1944, and the 101st Airborne Division had been on the front lines continuously for two months and thirteen days.

The Dutch had not forgotten us. At the first word that the American paratroopers were leaving Holland, the people lined the roads once again with orange flags and the little children came out to scream and wave. Everywhere in the towns were the smiles of grateful people. Much of their land had been ruined, yet still they were grateful—grateful for freedom. The paratroopers were their "liberators," and not all the weight of the British forces could persuade them otherwise.

In Veghel old friends—the doctor and his family, the maids in the house, the underground men, the young girls—stood on the streets to wave a last good-bye. The regimental interpreters, who had accompanied us from the beginning, had been dismissed with gratitude and letters of commendation; they, too, were in the crowds. And the crowds were the same at St. Oedenrode, Eindhoven, and Zon. "September 17th!" they shouted. "September 17th!"—while the tiny children, not quite certain what it was all about, jumped up and down for joy.

The towns had been repaired. Veghel looked neat and orderly. The foxholes in the lawn of the doctor's house had been refilled and turfed with sod. Inside the house, on the wall of the dining room, was a framed "Geronimo Certificate" bordered with parachute silk—the last of such certificates of commendation that Colonel Johnson had signed. The doctor said there had been no shelling in Veghel for more than a month.

It was a bright, sunny day. Holland seemed cheery and free. Even the military cemeteries, where so many of our men had been left behind, seemed more cheerful than anywhere else in Europe. Holland was a land where military success had brought the right kind of peace.

Of all the countries we were to know in Europe, we liked Holland best. It was a land like home. The people were friendly, the homes were clean, the children were honest and gay, and the girls were warm. Holland was a place where there had been peace of mind even in the midst of war. The Dutch were not exclamatory and emotional, like the French; they were not slow and stand-offish, like the British; they were not dour and severe, like the Germans. They were clean, industrious and content. They seemed at peace among themselves, and their land was wholesome and good.

So the American soldiers waved good-bye; the Dutch interpreters went off to join the Dutch Army; and the airborne invasion of Holland was at an end.

PART III

". . . there has been a break-through . . ."

32
The Lonely Camp

About sixteen miles below Reims, and eighty miles north of Paris, was a French cantonment named Camp Mourmelon. It was situated in the heart of that limestone countryside where, in World War I, the Allies had wintered along the static line of the Meuse, a countryside of rather somber aspect, channeled by the weather-softened trenches and caved-in dugouts of twenty-five years ago. It was a land that had never been reclaimed from destruction; and though a few poplar and linden trees lined the road to Reims, and pines had grown back over many of the chalky mounds, the general air was one of desolation.

Camp Mourmelon itself was a formal military post. The houses were built of stone. Around each of them were deep air-raid shelters. During the occupation of France, the Germans had constructed the necessities of permanent garrison life: at the main crossroads by the entrance was a fine motion-picture theater. There were hot showers in separate buildings, a hospital, leak-proof quarters, and well-built offices; if the cots in the barracks had straw ticks for mattresses, at least they were real cots.

In spite of these facilities, however, Camp Mourmelon was somehow as mournful as the desolated countryside in which it was islanded. The stone houses were tinted pastel hues, but they had no air of cheer. They were damp all the time; the stoves were absurdly inadequate; and the bare electric lights, though more efficient than the candles everyone had used in Holland, had a depressing effect on the spirit. Not since its activation at Camp Toccoa had the regiment occupied more adequate quarters—nor had it ever occupied drearier ones.

Winter and wartime had much to do with this. Since late October the skies of Europe had been clouded over. Rain or

snow had fallen periodically. In Mourmelon the streets were
as deep in mud as the soupy roads of Holland had been. The
rain often fell at night, and then the sounds of water running
down the cold stone gave the hours of darkness that mood of
eternity familiar to all men who have known the long winter
of a war.

The quarters for junior officers were situated at the extreme
end of the post, a mile from regimental headquarters, and
bounded by a small sign that read, "To the dump." Inside,
the houses were freezing cold. Downstairs in each one was a
large, bare room with a fireplace, adjoining a kitchen without
a stove. Upstairs were two large double bedrooms and a
single room, each chamber papered in nauseating colors.
There was never much to do at night except keep warm by
drinking cognac or champagne (the latter—late 1944 vintage—
selling in Reims for about $1.50 a bottle).

A close study of the airborne situation in Europe, as made
by those soldiers who were most interested in survival, indicated that the next reasonable mission would be a jump across
the Rhine. With the Allied lines temporarily stalemated by the
winter, it was certain that nothing would be attempted in this
direction before the spring. This supposition gave everyone at
least three more months to live. Rumors of the arrival in
England of the 17th Airborne Division strengthened the general conviction among our own men that the 101st would get a
rest for a while. So they were not too discouraged by the very
small numbers who were allowed to go on pass to Paris each
week. Everyone settled down to await his turn.

It was December 1, 1944—sixteen days before the break-
through in the Ardennes.

2

Our ways of life and our habits of thinking had changed a
great deal from our early days in England. Most of us were
greatly sobered. We still joked a great deal, but beneath this
surface-play was a tacit understanding of what DeQuincey
termed "elder truths." Though many of us still were very
young, we had experienced certain ultimates of existence
which, in moments of solitude, were not good company.
There was no record of any soldier waking up in the night and

screaming, as some of the men of World War I are supposed to have done, but in a score of little ways we had changed.

We no longer feared the unknown. What we feared was battle. Battle was like parachuting; it was impossible to get used to it. Experience only made the terror greater. There were those who would admit no fear of battle, just as there were those who would admit no fear of parachuting, but such men either lacked the capacity to examine their souls or else lived only for the moment. It was the man who could look farthest into the future who was likely to have the greatest misgivings. And he was the man who was most likely to know that there could be no courage without fear.

Many things which had become almost second nature to us would have caused much complaint if they had been introduced into our earlier training. Our sleeping bags were one example. They were issued by the army so enthusiastically that most of the blankets had been recalled. The new bags were neat, economical—and exasperating. Their inner lining was made of army blanket material with a seam on one side and a zipper on the other. The outer lining was of a waterproofed material similar to the light cloth used in the shelter-half. Once a man was inside (a matter of considerable struggle), he had almost no room to turn over. He was snug enough, but he was trapped. A device on the zipper was supposed to release the entire side when the metal tab was pulled to the top, but this arrangement either opened the bag completely at the very moment when a man had at last worked himself into a position to sleep, or else it locked tight on him. If the latter happened, there was nothing he could do but struggle to his feet like a participant in a sack race and hobble off for help. A cartoon by Dave Breger in *The Stars and Stripes* showed a man in this predicament being carried off by his buddies to the blacksmith.

Our thinking was largely colored by *The Stars and Stripes*. This was a tabloid-size, four-page newspaper, distinguished for its tart editorial outlook on the commissioned officer. For comic strips it offered Dick Tracy, Dagwood, Li'l Abner, and Terry and the Pirates. Nobody seemed to miss Superman.

The cartoons were fine. They had a sharp edge of satire. In a world of much blundering and very human weaknesses, it was not surprising that bright young men like Mauldin could find so much to make them famous. Opinion about Mauldin differed considerably, but though his work was admired it was not loved. Men who object to human nature have a suicidal touch; given the opportunity to clean house, they would probably include themselves. Much warmer was a character known as Hubert, whose creator came a little closer to Chesterton's maxim that no man should be superior to the things that are common to all men. Warmest of all was the Sad Sack, but he belonged to *Yank.*

The best column in *The Stars and Stripes,* as far as the enlisted men were concerned, was a letter column called "The B Bag." The good officers liked it, too, although the wisdom of letting the men blow off steam against their necessary leaders was somewhat problematical when the stakes of the war were so high. Most men forget injuries to their pride rather quickly, and in "The B Bag" they were reminded of them all the time. That was why the column was so entertaining. In it the commissioned officer was disassembled daily and his malfunctions pointed out in detail. The sorrier aspects of life in every corner of the European Theatre were thus given the dignity of print, where the rest of us could read and nod our heads.

Without "The B Bag" we might never have known that Lieutenant M—— used the enlisted men's latrine but forbade them to use his own; that Major Mc—— ordered eleven enlisted men to carry his personal loot of French brandy and wine to his château on the outskirts of Nancy; that Colonel B—— and Lieutenant Colonel O'—— had furnished their officers' club with chairs and billiard tables intended by the Salvation Army for the enlisted men, because Private W——, minding his own business, had failed to salute the colonel when he was out with a local prostitute.

Perhaps the smallest item of our lives overseas was one which often seemed the greatest. This was the ubiquitous K ration. Each box was supposed to make a full meal for a soldier on the line.

The outer cardboard covering was difficult to open without an instrument. Inside was a second box, thickly coated with paraffine and evidently designed to withstand every kind of shock known to man. Once the soldier had opened this second cover, he had a choice of three staples in small tins—chopped ham and eggs, pork loaf, or processed American cheese—depending upon whether he had been given a breakfast, dinner, or supper ration. Of the three staples, chopped ham and eggs was the most popular.

There were two types of biscuits. These biscuits, jocularly known as the K-2 and the K-9, were on a par with hard tack and no one ever understood why they were included, unless they were for use as spoons. The cellophane package containing them was, like everything else in the K ration, almost impossible to tear apart, and the great numbers of such packages discarded intact in the remoter parts of the European Theater are probably still in the open air, still resisting the changes of climate, still in the state they were made. Nothing could destroy the K ration, not even digestion.

Also included in the ration was an envelope of Nescafe or lemon powder. The lemon powder was disliked. Some woman dietitian, writing in "The B Bag" of *The Stars and Stripes*, once explained that its use was to supply a dietary deficiency necessary to wounded men, but this explanation only aroused derision. Since the American soldiers' firm attitude towards food they did not like was to ignore it or throw it away, it was sometimes difficult to understand why the Quartermaster Corps never hired a psychologist.

Finally, the K ration contained some sugar, a few pieces of candy, a few cigarettes and a roll of toilet paper. The presence of the last-named among the units of the menu revealed, more eloquently than words, the elemental nature of our lives.

The Stars and Stripes and the mail from home were the two bright spots of each day. Otherwise we lived rather meagerly, going to Reims once or twice a week, going to the movies, or getting drunk. There was not much to look forward to in the future, and the war seemed to have come to a dead stop. So oppressive was the atmosphere at this turning point of the war, and the queer, cold, rainy little stone camp was so many miles from anywhere, that two soldiers—a master sergeant and the division chief of staff—shot themselves.

THE ARDENNES

What had been learned in Normandy and put to work in Holland had fused the organization into a single weapon of war. With Bastogne, the regiment came of age.

"Of all the fine accomplishments of the 501st, north of Carentan, in the Veghel area, and at other places, I think the attack east from Bastogne was the greatest. I shall never forget it. This attack disrupted the enemy avalanche and gave us time to organize a defense position with the rest of the Division. Lieutenant General Fritz Hermann Bayerleine, who commanded the opposing German troops, said: 'The movement of the infantry regiment which came out of Bastogne to attack me reacted decisively on my thinking. Their fire superiority at Neffe was something I witnessed with my own eyes.'"

ANTHONY C. McAULIFFE
Major General
Commander of the defense
of Bastogne

33

Deutschland über Alles

Winter had come and all of Europe was cold. At the front, along the Siegfried Line, the soldiers lived in foxholes sodden with inches of water. Feet and wheels bogged down. The freezing winds that crossed the battlegrounds stiffened the dead before they could be moved and froze live fingers, curled around steel triggers. Day after day the skies were sullen, bringing long snows. The few soldiers who were lucky enough to be on pass in Paris walked through a city free but stricken, where some of the little children were bundled in clothing made from window curtains. And there were no fragrances of things cooking.

Unknown to the Allied army at that time, the Germans were secretly building up their forces behind a sector of the line facing the Ardennes. This had been going on since the middle of November, and by the first week or two in December the peak strength of twenty-five divisions had approached. With the attention of the Allies on the northern sector around Aachen, American reconnaissance in the Ardennes was negligible, and the Germans on the front lines in that area indulgently let the American patrols have their way—to a point. The main strength was building up in the rear.

Both General Eisenhower and General Bradley had discussed the possibility of a German push in this region. Their discussion had taken place much earlier in the winter, and, when the decision was made to keep those lines only lightly defended, it was a deliberate risk. Aachen was the gamble—Aachen and the Ruhr.

So in December of that winter the Ardennes line was held by the VIII Corps of the 1st U. S. Army under the command of Major General Troy H. Middleton. Eighty-eight miles long, the line extended from Remich, Luxembourg, to

Losheimergraben, Belgium. And by December it had become so quiet that old and battle-worn divisions were rotated into that sector for a rest, while divisions newly arrived in the European Theater of Operations were sent there to get a mild battle indoctrination. The front there was like the later front for the 101st Airborne Division along the Moder River in the Hagenau sector of Alsace-Lorraine: a region of snow and cold and spare artillery shells in the night.

In their discussion, Eisenhower and Bradley had outlined on a map the maximum penetration they believed the Germans could achieve in the event a breakthrough was attempted. Their sketched outline differed, that day, only by three or four miles from the actual limits of the German push.

Meanwhile, at Camp Mourmelon, the soldiers who were not lucky enough to be on pass in Paris got ready, indifferently, for a French Christmas. The atmosphere was doleful. The shabby little village of Mourmelon-le-Grand was no fit subject for a Christmas card and, though the great Reims cathedral had a beauty that two wars had not seriously touched, it was sandbagged to the height of its entrances and seemed gloomily waiting for a third conflict. The soldiers were glad to be out of the lines, but they missed Holland. Many of them still were corresponding with the friends they had left up there.

Home seemed further away that Christmas than ever before.

"On 12 December and thereafter," Colonel Marshall recorded, "the American outposts along the VIII Corps front heard sounds indicative of a great volume of vehicular motion coming from behind the enemy positions immediately confronting them. At 1st Army Headquarters these reports were interpreted as signifying enemy forces detraining for action in the Aachen area. A G-2 periodic report from the 1st Army warned of a large-scale concentration of German armor building up against this part of the general front, but there were other situation reports which lowered the emphasis of the warning. The 1st Army tried to keep some of the German strength from moving north by a deception maneuver which simulated the arrival of the 75th Division in the VIII Corps area."

On December 15th the VIII Corps line was held, in part, by the 4th and 28th infantry divisions. Both units had been under fire in other sectors for a long time and were in the

Ardennes region for a rest. The 4th Division was 2,400 men below strength.

At another part of the sector was the very green 106th Infantry Division, the soldiers of which had marched off the boat from the United States only ten days before. They had been in the Ardennes sector four days—scarcely time for many of them to have heard a shot fired. Completing the sector was the 9th Armored Division, up to strength except for Combat Command B, then with the V Corps.

2

Early in the morning of December 16, 1944, the blow fell. Von Rundstedt's divisions, pushing forward with heavy armor and mobile artillery, and accompanied by overwhelming forces of infantrymen, hit almost squarely on the lines of the inexperienced 106th Division. Those men, who had been lulled to a false sense of security by the earlier quiet, dropped back after short clashes and, before they could reorganize, were overrun. The 28th Division received a blow that was almost as severe, but those men, who had been longer under fire, managed to regroup and then fought savagely.

Higher headquarters ordered a defense in place. The inadequacy of this order became apparent when, a few hours after the fighting started, there was no place left to defend. Plan Number Two, from the same source, was a defense along a line roughly paralleling the Belgian border. This also failed.

On December 19th, at 12th Army Group Headquarters, Eisenhower, who had called a meeting of field commanders and chiefs of staff, listened for a moment to the gloomy talk. "I want only cheerful faces around here," he said. "We'll deal with this attack and make capital out of it."

"Let him get through!" Patton said gleefully. "All the way to Paris if he wants. Then we'll cut him off at the base."

Meanwhile, at Mourmelon, everything had changed.

"At 0800 on 17 December, the 101st Airborne Division . . . was told from Headquarters of the XVIII Corps Airborne that it was to go to Bastogne. At about the same hour, Combat Command B of the 10th Armored Division, which was enjoying a period of rest after combat at Remeling, France, was ordered to move to the vicinity of the city of

Luxembourg. The order came from the Third U. S. Army. On the following night—18th of December—the 705th Tank Destroyer Battalion, then in position at Kolilshield, Germany, was ordered by the Ninth United States Army to march to Bastogne and report to the VIII Corps.

"In this manner, by different routes and under separate authority, three battle-tested organizations began their moves towards the small town in the Belgian Ardennes with which their own fame was to be thereafter inseparably linked. Bastogne was at that hour still the Headquarters of the VIII Corps. It was made the point of rendezvous, however, because of the unusual importance of its military position. It is the nodal point of the highway system in the eastern Ardennes, a countryside that is naturally forbidding to the movement of mechanized forces and becomes fully accessible to motorized armies only when the roads are under their control. A force holding at Bastogne unhinges the communications of an enemy striking south and west towards the line of the river Meuse.

"At Mourmelon the 101st Division was short many of its soldiers, who were on leave in Paris. The Division Commander was in the United States. The Assistant Division Commander was giving a lecture in England. The artillery commander, Brigadier General Anthony J. McAuliffe, got the Division staff together at 2100 on 17 December and outlined the prospect in these words:

"All I know of the situation is that there has been a breakthrough and we have to get up there. . . ."*

*From preparatory accounts by Colonel Marshall for *Bastogne—The First Eight Days.*

34

The SHAEF Reserve Is Committed

"In less than twenty-four hours both the 82nd and the 101st were in position 125 to 150 miles away. It was one of the swiftest and most efficient moves ever made in the war."—Lieutenant General Lewis Brereton.

At Mourmelon the night was cold, rainy and black. At the motion-picture theater the second show had almost ended. In the barracks, men polished their boots, or played crap, or dozed. Down at the officers' club, the bar was just getting noisy, while in Mourmelon and Reims the men on pass had half an hour before they would meet the truck convoy taking them back to the post.

It was ten o'clock. Ewell walked up through the chilly blackness to a staff meeting at division headquarters, wondering what it was all about. To the south a few French searchlights probed at the low-hanging clouds. The night was quiet.

When he returned, it was after midnight. At that hour all of the officers and most of the non-commissioned officers were routed out of bed. Blinking, astonished, they heard the words, "another mission," with disbelief. Another mission! The regiment was only three weeks out of the front lines in Holland! There had been no preparation—no chance to train the new men! At least half the combat equipment had been turned in for salvage. And more than a hundred officers and men were in Paris on leave. . . .

One officer, shaken out of a sound sleep with the news, crossed groggily to his footlocker, drew out a bottle of cognac and, drinking a quarter of it in a few gulps, sat down to unwrap his presents.

The majority of the enlisted men were allowed to sleep until daybreak. However, the officers and key non-coms worked while the men slept, to make up for the more serious deficiencies in supply. On Major Butler, the regimental supply officer, a stolid, kindly officer, fell the heaviest responsibility: he had less than twelve hours to compensate for every supply shortage in the regiment. Part of the task was impossible, for many of the critical items had already gone forward to quartermaster depots for exchange.

Ten percent of the troops that left for Belgium the next day had no arms. A few supplied themselves with German weapons. Some of the men had no helmets; others, no basic load of ammunition; almost no one had a winter overcoat. For food, the only thing which could be issued, following a hot breakfast and lunch (the last two hot meals for some time), was a K ration.

So vague was the enemy situation on December 18th that the majority of the troops who climbed into the trucks at 1400 had no idea of what they were supposed to do or where they were going. They knew they were going north; they knew it was to fight. But that was all.

A hurry-up call to the transportation corps at Oise Base in Reims had resulted in the emergency withdrawal of 380 carrier trucks from the main supply routes throughout the rear area. How those trucks were overtaken, rerouted to Mourmelon, unloaded, and delivered to the 101st Airborne Division in a period of less than twenty-four hours is a story for the history of Oise Base Section. It is sufficient to note here that the majority of the drivers had been on the road for long hours when they were overtaken and turned around. Their trucks were what are called *portes* in the cavalry—an engine and a cab hauling a long, open trailer, similar to a railroad boxcar, though without a roof. Practically speaking, they were ideal for the emergency, but so many troops were loaded into each one at Mourmelon that the men were comfortable only when they were standing up. When darkness fell and they tried to lie down, many of them had to lie on top of one another.

Long after the Bastogne operation was over, we were to remember that truck ride to the Ardennes—remember it more vividly than most of the incidents of the siege. We had gone to battle by air and on foot, but never like this. The tremendous convoy of trucks—companies, battalions, regiments—rolled out through Mourmelon-le-Grand (where the French villagers, waving from the streets, must have wondered what it was all about) and up through rolling, bare countryside pock-marked with the excavations of World War I. The day was overcast. The air was still. Up and down the shaven hills of northern France went the long trucks, and wherever the road made a sharp turn the vehicles could be seen for miles ahead and miles behind. It was tremendous. On the way, incidentally, we passed the monument at Waterloo.

During those hours, the men of the 28th Infantry Division were struggling to hold back the overwhelming waves of German divisions. They fought on commanding ground around Wiltz. And because of their tenacity, courage, and unwillingness to admit complete defeat, the 101st Airborne Division met no opposition on its twelve-hour journey up to Belgium and Bastogne.

2

Ewell had preceded his regiment. He found Kinnard and McAuliffe making a brief reconnaissance of the area to the immediate west of Bastogne, where they had tentatively decided to place at least one element of the division. In the confusion the advance party for the unit had gone astray, and Kinnard, acting in the emergency as a complete division staff, had only an M.P. private to guide the regiments and battalions to their assembly areas. Helpless, he sent that man down to the crossroads to await the first trucks.

Bastogne in those early hours was a spectacle. All over town units of VIII Corps headquarters were moving out. The hospital staff packed in such haste that all manner of personal belongings were left behind. Long after the building had been torn apart by subsequent bombings, curious soldiers scrounging in the cracked rooms found nurses' undergarments, fatigue dresses, French-English dictionaries and broken bottles of perfume. On the streets, little bands of wild-eyed soldiers followed the armored columns in retreat to the east. The streets echoed with the clank of heavy armor, mobile artillery, tank destroyers—all moving away from the fight.

Fortunately, many of the disorganized and retreating soldiers discarded their equipment in Bastogne. Systematically retrieved later on, this equipment made a considerable addition to the basic supplies. And among the last things given to Kinnard by VIII Corps was an administrative order showing the location of the ammunition dumps, water points, and evacuation hospitals.

Colonel Ewell, talking with General McAuliffe at the rapidly emptying VIII Corps headquarters, agreed with the general that nobody could be certain of anything just then. Nevertheless, Ewell wanted some definite assignment for his men. McAuliffe believed it was impossible to give anybody a definite assignment before the Germans materialized. But he agreed on the importance of occupying strong defensive positions prior to the first engagement, so on a chance he picked up one of Kinnard's maps, gestured to the road that led out of Bastogne towards a small town named Longvilly, and said to Ewell, "Move out on this road at six o'clock, make contact, attack and clean up the situation. . . ."

McAuliffe's words may have been ironical. But Ewell did just as he was directed. And his initial moves that night and the next morning determined the scheme of defense which was to save Bastogne.

3

Night had fallen and the trucks ran on. Despite the risk, headlights blazed along the whole convoy—a deliberate gamble for the sake of speed. Colonel Marshall's account remarks that if the Luftwaffe had come that night—as it was to come to Bastogne a few nights later—the story of the Belgian town might have taken a very different turn. But the Luftwaffe missed its opportunity, and the night was prickled only with silent stars.

In the towns and villages along the way, soldiers on pass who were walking with their French girls turned to stare. The airborne men shook their heads. French girls, unescorted, shouted—"*Arrêtez! Restez ici!*" But the trucks, their headlights flaring, rolled on: up through crowded streets, over bridges, and out into countryside again, where the air had a wintry cold. Then at Bouillon, in Belgium, the lights were extinguished. As the columns ran darkly through tunnels of trees, where only hand flashlights illuminated the way, the men experienced again that curious dividing point of combat, where ordinary life was left behind.

Speed dropped only slightly. In the clear, away from the

trees, a small moon illuminated the way. The land became hilly. Some of the men slept; others stood with their faces to the wind. None guessed that Ewell and McAuliffe had already decided their immediate future.

Ewell expected his vehicles to be delayed by the choked traffic on the road and thought they would arrive in Bastogne around 2300. The lead elements anticipated that time by half an hour, making our regiment the first unit of the division to arrive at its destination. While the battalions bivouacked on the open ground for the night, and the men of the staff sat around dim kerosene lanterns in a little Belgian home converted to a temporary command post (where Dave Hart and Suarez slept with the cows), and while parts of the 3rd Battalion and Headquarters Company tramped for hours trying to find their proper place—Ewell went forward through Bastogne to reconnoiter the morning advance. His regiment would be the first out of Bastogne.

Of his responsibility McAuliffe afterwards remarked: "There were many men and commanders in my operation who did outstanding things. But Ewell's was the greatest gamble of all. It was dark. He had no knowledge of the enemy. I couldn't tell him what he was likely to meet. But he has a fine eye for ground and no man has more courage. He was the right man for the spot I put him in."

35
Ewell "Develops the Situation"

It was foggy and damp at six o'clock in the morning. The 1st Battalion had been selected to lead off on the push out the Longvilly road. The coatless men moved through the streets of Bastogne, sloshing in mud and dirty water. Between their double lines, on the road itself, heavy armor still was moving eastward, away from the oncoming enemy. It was a ludicrous sight to see a few of the airborne troops wave at the retreating armor—fire power much stronger than any of them could have. One paratrooper, still without a weapon, picked up a stick and, for the benefit of the demoralized columns, shook it in the direction of the enemy. Here and there unhelmeted men were wearing wool caps or were bareheaded. Few wore overcoats. But they pushed forward out of the town with a sense of confidence, and in a little while they were in the silent, foggy countryside.

Following the 1st Battalion as it moved out of Bastogne was B Battery of the 81st Anti-Aircraft with eight 57mm. guns. Behind that unit in turn—considerably behind it, as a matter of fact—were the 2nd and 3rd Battalions of the 501st. The latter was getting itself badly tangled in the snarl of traffic within the town, and since Ewell was not yet certain of how and where he would employ those battalions, he contented himself with the advance of the 1st Battalion and its supporting unit along the Longvilly road. On one occasion the men turned off by mistake towards Marvie, due east. But Ewell was able to set them right, and by 0730 in the morning, with the light just breaking, the situation looked fair enough.

In that region the Bastogne-Longvilly highway ran along a valley dominated on each side by gently sloping hills. Those hills were partially covered with sparse vegetation, but the overgrowth offered little concealment. On this morning, however, the fog was dense. It was so thick that the left flank guards of the 1st Battalion by-passed two platoons of enemy infantrymen dug in on a hill in the vicinity of Bizory; though slight sounds carried distinctly on the damp air, neither the Germans nor the Americans became aware of each other's presence. Unsuspecting, the 1st Battalion marched straight towards the main body of the enemy.

The Germans, of course, were equally unsuspecting. Until that moment they had forced back the stubborn 28th Division, and the less stubborn, badly fragmented 9th Armored Division, without meeting heavily organized resistance. This had given the ordinary German soldiers new confidence; their morale was higher on the morning of December 19th than it had been since the invasion of the Normandy coast. In documents and letters later taken from German prisoners or from German dead, the enemy soldiers were writing home, "At last the war has become fun again."* They described the

---

*From a document taken by a 501st prisoner of war interrogation team.

slaughter of armored and infantry divisions along the way as "a glorious blood bath" and prophesied to their families in the clean little towns of Germany that the European struggle would soon be at an end. Once again, evidently, it was *Deutschland über Alles*.

The first encounter with the deployed 1st Battalion of the 501st parachute Infantry in the early hours of December 19th must have been a shock to them.

2

Contact was made at what seemed to be an enemy road block near the village of Neffe. The division reconnaissance platoon, which had somehow gone astray at the beginning of the advance, was on the point of overtaking the lead scouts of the battalion when, from the fog directly ahead, there was the unmistakable fast rattle of a German machine gun.

Almost to a man, the battalion went flat. With the first sounds of fire the two German platoons which had been by-passed in the fog discovered their enemy in front and behind them. The confusion was so great that the German guns were quickly disposed of. However, the machine gun that had opened up at the crossroads and given the first alarm of the Bastogne siege, evidently outposted a lead element of considerable weight.

The valley road at that point did not pass through the center of the valley, but ran close to the rising ground on the left flank. Thus it was only on the right, where the valley sloped away to a small stream, that it was possible to deploy the men adequately. In keeping with McAuliffe's words, Ewell drily told the commander of the 1st Battalion, Lieutenant Colonel (then Major) Bottomly to "develop the situation." He himself found a stone house in a pocket of the hillside and established a temporary command post. Within a short time Bottomly reported to Ewell by radio that he was opposed by approximately two platoons of infantry and two Mark IV tanks. Ewell, to whom the report was put in the form of a question, told him to go ahead and fight his own fight.

The Mark IV tanks were firing, from a defiladed position near Neffe, straight down the highway. Consequently, the 57mm. guns of the anti-aircraft company could not be brought to bear on them. And by ten o'clock in the morning, with no advance having been made on either side, the situation became a deadlock. Little more could be done just then; in Bastogne the 2nd and 3rd battalions still were struggling to get through the choked traffic of the VIII Corps, fleeing to the rear.

Off on the left flank of Ewell's position was a group of large farm houses in a broad valley. The valley ran down towards Neffe, but before it reached that village (held, Ewell judged, by the enemy) the ground rose up again to conceal the two villages from sight of each other. It occurred to Ewell that if the 2nd Battalion were to seize the town of Bizory, which lay in that direction, his men would be well situated to move onto the high ground adjacent.

Lieutenant Colonel Homan was in command of the 2nd Battalion. Implementing Colonel Ewell's orders as soon as he got free of Bastogne, he seized Bizory with no opposition and only a little fire from the direction of the deadlock at Neffe. During this time the 3rd Battalion, still in Bastogne, was trying to get out of town by an auxiliary side route. Ewell ordered the commander, Lieutenant Colonel Griswold, to strike for Mont, farther to the right of the forward positions then held by Bottomly and Homan. Ewell eventually intended to use Griswold's battalion in a flanking attack on Neffe, but he kept these intentions to himself. What chiefly concerned him was getting the battalion out of town.

3

Bastogne at that hour still was crowded with drifting and staring men. So great was the shock they had received that many of them were inarticulate. They trickled through the German lines in twos and threes, making no attempt to organize themselves, refusing to be organized by anyone else. When they asked the paratroopers what they were doing, and the paratroopers replied, "Fighting Germans," they only stared. To them, at least temporarily, the war seemed lost.

Not all were like that, however. Some of the haggard, beaten men accepted a K ration, ate it silently, and then asked for a rifle. They were ready to go back and fight. Some of the armor was in good shape, and the morale of the armored men

BASTOGNE, BELGIUM
19 DEC 1944 - 10 JAN 45

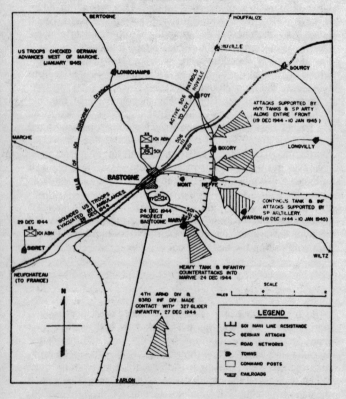

who elected to remain at Bastogne and fight it out was high. Among them, seven tanks and three tank destroyer crews organized themselves into a combat team and voluntarily attached themselves to the 2nd Battalion, while another platoon of armored infantry stuck it out with the regiment until the siege was lifted.

By noon of the 19th the situation was clearer. The 1st Battalion was halted at Neffe, fighting what Ewell thought was only a difficult road block. The 2nd Battalion had seized Bizory and was deployed on favorable high ground. The 3rd Battalion had reached Mont, but because the ground between there and Neffe was flat, and the enemy fire heavy, the soldiers had been unable to carry out the second phase of the order and sweep down on the road block at Neffe. By these three operations, however, a line had been stretched along commanding ground outside of Bastogne to the northeast. This was the critical and—as events later proved—decisive deployment.

Ewell decided to move his 2nd Battalion to Magaret, which would still further improve their position. He sent Colonel Homan with one company of men to secure the approaches to that town by seizing a small patch of woods on a long ridge above it. Homan did so, but was presently engaged along his entire front.

Company I had been separated from the 3rd Battalion and was making a reconnaissance of wooded areas to the front. It was ordered into the town of Wardin to investigate the reported existence there of an armored road block. The ill-fated company encountered the enemy in the town, but at 1500 radioed that its men were doing all right. When a company of volunteer tank destroyers arrived at Ewell's command post, however, he sent them to the 3rd Battalion to help out in case the group at Wardin needed support.

It was then 1600. Ewell had formed three battalions approximately abreast and in contact with the enemy all along his front. For the first time since the German break-through, the enemy was meeting a line of troops which refused to give ground.

At dark Ewell ordered the battalions to break contact and form to defend a general line along the high ground to the west of Bizory-Neffe and roughly parallel to this line to the southward. Taking his plan back to the red stone buildings where division headquarters had been established, he got McAuliffe's approval. On the way he assured himself, for the first time since daybreak, that Bastogne had not been seized.

Walking along the main street of the town, he met a sergeant of Company I.

"Have you heard about Company I?" asked the sergeant. "It's been wiped out."

Ewell, hurrying back to his radio, didn't believe it.

The town of Wardin lay on the extreme right flank of the Bizory-Neffe-Wardin line, which Ewell had formed on the commanding terrain northeast of Bastogne. Wardin was a small place of a dozen-odd houses, set at a little distance from one of the main roads entering Bastogne. Captain Wallace had taken his men of Company I into the village as part of the general reconnaissance ordered by Homan in compliance with Ewell's instructions. What ensued there was tragic.

When Wallace and his men entered the town, they encountered only a few Germans. Without much difficulty, they drove those men from the dreary Belgian houses and took possession. Wardin had strategic value and, though it was closer to the enemy than Bizory and Neffe, Wallace believed he could hold his place.

He and his men had been in the town only a short while, however, when a force of German armor appeared unexpectedly on the outskirts. As the tanks—they were Tiger Royals—spread out to prevent Wallace's force from escaping, the tank gunners opened fire point-blank. Under cover of this fire, a whole battalion of German infantrymen, who had all the ardor of their late successes, closed in to the streets. Wallace hastily withdrew part of his force to fight at the flanks of his command post and to keep one avenue of retreat open. The remainder of the Americans held out in the concealment of the houses.

The din was soon terrific—the fast rocketing *"whisht-bang!"* of heavy-caliber shells at close range, the clattering of fallen rock, the explosions of bazooka shells, the rattle of small arms and the queer vibrating *"brrrrrrrrp!"* of German automatic pistols. Bazooka gunners deliberately squatted in the open where they were plainly visible to the Germans and fired point-blank on the tanks. Soldiers in the houses held their positions until shells burst through the rooms and demolished the lower floors. Other soldiers snatched up the bazookas of men who had died.

House by house, fighting in a blaze of fire, the Americans retreated. The smoke of explosions from the tank guns clouded vision from one side of the street to the other. The Germans were systematically demolishing every house. Everywhere was the ammoniac stink of cordite; in the rubble of the demolished buildings hands, heads, legs protruded. Those paratroopers who still were alive fought their way towards Wallace and the command post. One youngster, running out into the center of the street, deliberately knelt in a furious rattle of small-arms fire and discharged a bazooka shell squarely into the lead tank. The tank was halted and, though the boy was dead an instant later, the rest of the oncoming armor was momentarily canalized.

Wallace, giving the infantryman's equivalent of "abandon ship," ordered the remainder of the men to split up—to get back to Bastogne singly or in pairs—anyway they could.

On the street before the command post the men threw up a hasty tank obstacle. As the armor and the swarms of German infantrymen approached this final point, Wallace directed all the fire power at his disposal to cover the withdrawal of the men who were left. One by one, as the small-arms and heavy-caliber fire grew heavier, they passed through the barricade, Wallace urging them on. Then the officer ordered the men at the barricade, too, to fall back. A few of them refused. The final survivors of the trap of Wardin saw, as they looked back, the figure of their captain, still at the barricade, still fighting—the last they were ever to see of him.

4

All that afternoon and night the survivors trickled into Bastogne. At the regimental command post, a great room which had once been a school study hall was set aside for them, where they cleaned their weapons on the children's desks. They were very silent. A few of them sat against the wall, under a statue of the Crucifixion, with their heads in their hands.

Wallace, like many of his men, left a wife and child behind him. Of approximately 200 of his soldiers who had gone into Wardin eighty-three survived.

36
The Second Day

Undertones of tragedy marked the evening of the first day at Bastogne. As the light dimmed in the sky, the streets of town became deserted. The inhabitants disappeared into their cellars. In the great dark rooms of the regimental command post the only illumination came from the flicker of the squad cookers as the survivors of Company I heated their K rations. Nothing had been heard of a truck column bringing ammunition and other supplies to the town. Father Sampson was missing. And there were rumors that our division hospital, set up to the rear of Bastogne, had been captured.

The 501st Command post was plainly visible from the enemy lines. With the exception of the church across the street, it was the most prominent building in Bastogne. Downstairs on the main floor were a dining hall, an immense cloister with Doric columns, a skylight, and an adjacent chapel. The chapel was used for a temporary aid station, while the cloister was designated for use by the company and regimental kitchens (if the equipment got through). The dining room, which occupied a wing of its own, was left to the Franciscan nuns, who were taking care of twenty or thirty very young, very curious children. It was interesting to note that, when the German artillery began to fall on Bastogne, those children disappeared underground with the nuns and did not reappear until three weeks later.

Upstairs in the seminary were dozens of connecting rooms, each of them piously decorated. Above the second floor were dormitories for the former pupils, while on the fourth floor was a vast chamber which had been occupied before the Ardennes break-through by VIII Corps military police. The haste with which the M.P.s had abandoned their quarters was evident in the discarded material strewn about the floors: paper-bound books, magazines, pin-ups, galoshes, webbing, blankets, even uniforms. The few of us who explored this room felt a little satisfaction in the debacle of the withdrawal— mute testimony of that upheaval of life which had come to a rear echelon when it had suddenly become a forward area.

By morning of the next day, December 20th, the temperature had dropped below freezing. There was little wind before dawn, and the unmoving blanket of clouds limited visibility in the darkness. The 501st men were in the same positions they had taken up at nightfall and not much had been done to extend the flanks. Though other units had been brought up to either side, the 501st still was squarely in the line of the German advance.

One of the first moves made by McAuliffe, as an artillery commander, was to dispose his airborne artillery and tank guns in such a manner as to bring coordinated fire from all of the pieces on any one point of the line which he intended to "develop," or which was attacked by the enemy. Subsequently, when Bastogne was encircled, he was able to deliver the same concentration of fire on any point of the 360° defense. On the morning of the 20th, however, his main concern was the sector occupied by Ewell's regiment. And the honors of the day were about evenly divided between Ewell's men and McAuliffe's artillery.

The night had been reasonably quiet. From the Americans captured at Wardin the Germans had identified the division opposing them, and they evidently spent the hours of darkness massing their forces for a major drive. The much criticized G-2 of the Allied armies at the time of the Ardennes break-through was not the only one to be surprised in those days; documents later captured from the German staff revealed the enemy's astonishment at finding the 101st Airborne Division (which their intelligence had reported to be at Mourmelon, France) directly in the path of their advance at a key focal point of communications, a hundred miles from where they were supposed to be.

2

The first troubles on the 20th began at 0530, before there was light in the wintry sky.

East of Bizory, where Homan's 2nd Battalion men were

deployed, was a rise of high ground. Between that high
ground and the American front line was a clear field of fire,
extending more than 3,000 yards. On that expanse, the only
cover for an attacking enemy was the natural defilades where
the farmland rose and fell. Homan's position was ideal for
defense—so ideal, as a matter of fact, that, when an ob-
servation-post spotter who had field glasses reported that
six enemy tanks were starting across the fields, accompanied
by what he estimated to be a battalion of German infantrymen,
the event took place at such a distance that the Americans,
though alerted, could only sit by their guns and wait.

A scratch force of American tank destroyers had attached
itself to Homan's battalion during the night. At word of the
impending attack, the crews disposed their vehicles north of
the village of Bizory on either side of a small road that was a
key approach to the American lines. Meanwhile, Homan had
notified Ewell about the approaching enemy; Ewell had notified Kinnard, and Kinnard, through McAuliffe, the artillery.
One by one the guns within Bastogne were brought to bear on
a predetermined coordinate—where, when the signal came to
fire, their shells would drop in a screen across the oncoming
Germans.

The expanse of ground in front of Homan was so great that
the Germans advanced for a whole hour before they were
close to the coordinate for the artillery barrage. During part of
this time the men of the 2nd Battalion could keep them in
sight, and, the nearer they approached, the brighter grew the
morning. When the American machine gunners suddenly opened
fire, the tank destroyers fired simultaneously, and, within an
instant or two, in a curtain of artillery bursts, the German
lines were struck squarely by hundreds of shells from
McAuliffe's guns.

From full silence to the blaze of fire took only a few
moments. The Germans still were at such a distance from
Homan's men that the automatic weapons' fire had little
visible effect. But so intense was the coordinated artillery fire
from within Bastogne that the paratroopers, who had a grand-
stand view of the entire episode, witnessed the Germans
begin to falter. Here and there, among the mushrooming
clouds of artillery smoke, the tiny black figures stumbled and
fell. Behind them one of the heavy tanks turned back towards

its own lines—then rolled and halted. Two of the tanks were destroyed, and a third disabled.

The tiny figures of the Germans began to run. More and more of them fell. For twenty minutes the rolling barrage continued to pursue them. When it lifted, the only Germans who remained on the open fields were the scores of still bodies.

The shock of that first repulse must have been a severe one to the German troops. Until that morning they had met other pockets of stubborn resistance—the 7th Armored Division, whose soldiers had made a gallant stand at St. Vith, and the elements of the 28th Division already mentioned. But when the Germans, filled with confidence, attacked Bastogne on the morning of the 20th, they were repulsed not only with heavy casualties, but also by a group of organized soldiers who obviously intended to deny—to twenty-five enemy divisions—a critical road-net in the heart of the salient.

3

Towards midmorning of the 20th it started to snow. The German forces, under cover of thick woods to the northeast, began to shell Bastogne, devoting particular attention to the huge building by the church steeple.

This was the building which we had selected for a regimental command post. It was the largest command post any regiment could have had. It was five stories high and perhaps a quarter of a mile in circumference. The walls were about three feet thick. This was thick enough to withstand shellfire, but, unfortunately, the operations offices had been selected in the very first hours, before anyone knew the direction of the enemy. When the lines were consolidated outside Bastogne, it was found that the Germans could—with good luck in their marksmanship—put artillery through the windows.

The snow came down steadily, gently. Soon it blanketed the bodies of the dead Germans at Neffe and those beyond Homan's positions outside of Bizory. The paratroopers were seeing the last bare earth they were to see for two months. Meanwhile, the shelling of Bastogne continued. The Germans regrouped for a concerted attack in force, and the fateful day was quiet.

The 1st Battalion, which had fired the first shots of the Bastogne siege, had been unable to seize Neffe beyond the turn of the valley road. Company B had successfully taken a house on the side of the critical Neffe road, and, from the windows of that house, the soldiers were able to command all the approaches to the battalion front. Machine guns were set up in there, while the infantrymen of the other companies dug foxholes and, where they could, lined the interiors with straw.

In Homan's area at Bizory, where the first enemy attack in force had been repulsed, there was no change. But at Griswold's 3rd Battalion, which had taken up positions at Mont, the 1st Platoon of Company B of the 705th Tank Destroyer Battalion had attached itself during the night. This was a valuable reinforcement. Griswold posted one of the vehicles at a bend in the Neffe road, where it commanded the stretch leading to that enemy-occupied town, and where it also commanded a draw leading off to the south. Another destroyer was placed to complement the fire of the first, while the second section of the platoon, from concealed positions, guarded the approach directly across the valley.

The countryside outside of Bastogne was ideally suited to a strong defense. As Colonel Marshall noted:

"The country around Neffe and Bizory, except for the small but well grown tree plantations and the clusters of farmhouses which appear as villages on the map, is absolutely barren and appears for the most part to be grazing country. The dominant terrain features are the long and quite regular ridges which run generally in a north-south line. These hills are gently undulated and the hillsides are quite smooth. From the top of the commanding ridges one may see great distances on a clear day, and the ridges fall away in gently sloping draws which provide imposing fields of fire to the flank and enable an easy coverage of the main lines of communication. The reverse slopes are almost smooth and accessible from either end of the hill, making them useful to artillery and armor. The roads are close enough together so that one may move on to the ridges from either direction. When the country is covered with snow, as it was after the first day . . . nothing obtrudes on the landscape except the small black patches of forest. Neffe is on low ground next to the railroad tracks. From the ridge where Ewell's 2nd Battalion was deployed, one may see into Bizory, Mont, Neffe. . . ."

Everywhere there was silence. The skies were leaden; the snow came down steadily, almost audibly. No planes were in the air anywhere. At division headquarters, McAuliffe, in contact with General Middleton by radio, happened to remark that Bastogne would probably be surrounded.

The soldiers blew on their stiffening fingers and waited.

37

The Worst Night

At seven o'clock a few shells fell in Bizory and Mont. These were followed by a few more and, shortly, by a great number. Finally, a heavy barrage dropped on all the critical points along the defensive line. So intense was the artillery fire from the German positions that within a few minutes every telephone wire connecting the battalions to regimental headquarters was severed.

When the firing slackened off, the German forces struck simultaneously in a two-pronged offensive against the 1st and 3rd Battalions.

Bottomly, at the 1st Battalion, radioed Ewell that the enemy troops were charging straight down the highway. They came with the shouts and high morale of men convinced they were going through. Not even in Normandy had the paratroopers encountered such high morale. Bottomly reported to Ewell that it was too dark to see much, but that he could hear tanks coming along with the troops.

It was a bad hour for the regimental staff at Bastogne. On orders from someone, the records were packed, the equipment readied, the men dressed for retreat. If the two flanks collapsed . . .

The snow had ceased. The night was bitter cold.

There were eleven battalions of guns at McAuliffe's disposal within Bastogne. All eleven battalions dropped a "dam of fire" across the Neffe road, approximately 200 yards ahead of the town. It was the most effective American defensive fire during the siege. Three German tanks—two Panthers and a Tiger Royal—were struck almost at once; they had drawn up beyond the last houses in the village when they were hit, and there they stayed.

The short delay before the artillery barrage, however, had enabled a considerable number of German infantrymen to approach so close to the American lines that the greater number of shells fell behind them. Those men charged wildly towards the Americans, firing and shouting. Company B, posted in and around the house, on commanding ground at the side of the road, took the shock without yielding an inch of ground. The automatic weapons in the windows controlled the approaches so effectively that not a single German soldier got within bayonet distance of the American lines. Everywhere in the darkness the enemy troops stiffened and fell and died, and their blood spotted the snow. Weeks afterward they were still there, grotesque and stiff, the foremost bodies 300 yards in advance of the wrecked German armor.

The action in this area continued with intensity for some time. The soldiers were fighting in that bitter fume of smoke and sweat and cold where each man seemed hopelessly alone. There was no consciousness of cold or snow or wet clothes or hunger. When men are fighting each other, and the issue remains in doubt, there are only the simplest and most basic elements of human experience.

Meanwhile, the men of the 3rd Battalion were struggling to hold back a simultaneous enemy attack from a different quarter. It was evident that the Germans had abandoned their attempt to enter Bastogne across the wide field of fire opening down from Homan's positions, where they had failed that morning. The dual attack by dark left Homan's forces alone and evidently had the object of bending the two flanks of the 501st until those flanks collapsed and Homan was trapped in the middle.

The Germans attacking Griswold's forces also had supporting armor. But the enemy tank commander must have observed the tank destroyers behind the American lines, for his armor did not leave the concealment of a little wood just west of a château at Neffe. From that position the tanks could put down a base of fire for their advancing and—as events shortly proved—suicidal infantrymen.

The open and comparatively smooth slope which separated
Mont and Neffe afforded a field of fire for Griswold's battalion almost as extensive as that which fronted the 2nd Battalion under Colonel Homan. In addition to this wide field of
fire, the slope was crisscrossed with man-made obstacles—a
checkerboard of barbed-wire fences erected by the Belgians to
make feeder pens for cattle. The fences were in rows about
thirty yards apart. Each fence was five or six strands high.
Because of the manner of their construction, it was almost
impossible to crawl underneath the fences: a man approaching
Griswold's forces at Mont had to halt at each obstacle and
climb through.

Whether the German commanders knew of the existence of
these obstacles and decided to risk the attack anyway, or
whether the leading enemy soldiers just stumbled onto them
by accident in the darkness, will probably not be known. But
the attack, once launched, had to be carried on. The German
infantrymen ran forward with the same enthusiasm, the same
wild yells and eagerness which had characterized all their
offensive actions since the break-through. When they reached
the fences, they simply climbed through. But it broke them.

As fast as they reached the obstacles, Griswold's machine
gunners swept them down. The Germans were in great strength,
and the forces behind, pressing upon the forces ahead, made a
massacre inevitable. Bodies of the dead piled up around the
wire fences, and the attackers who followed, climbing over
those bodies, became bodies themselves a few steps beyond.
The volume of tracer fire from Griswold's gunners was spec-
tacularly intense; prisoners questioned later said that its visible effect, as much as the holocaust around the fences, was to
them the terrifying element of the night attack.

What Griswold's men were facing was a whole German
regiment—the 901st *Panzergrenadiers*, better soldiers than
the *Volksgrenadiers* who had attacked Homan to no effect in
the early morning. These Germans rushed towards the 3rd
Battalion of the 501st with such high spirit that, despite the
wire fences and the field of fire, Griswold was forced to
regroup part of his battalion to reinforce his left flank. By the
time he accomplished this, the action had become intense and
the German casualties terrible. The total destruction of one
side or the other was so imminent that the American tank-
destroyer men, having no targets for their guns, fired the

.50-caliber weapons from their vehicles, jumped out, and joined the infantrymen on the line.

By the time the German fire began to slacken off, the insane double attack of divisional strength had lasted four hours. It was close to midnight. Enemy dead were piled up in such numbers around the wire fences that even the German withdrawal was difficult. Around Neffe, where the other attack had taken place, the situation was much the same, and, though the casualties on the American side had been very heavy, the *Panzergrenadiers* had been decimated. Ewell's eye for ground had given the paratroopers an advantage they were never afterwards to lose.

As he remarked later: "I think that, as of that night, the 901st had 'had it.' They no longer had enough men to be an effective offensive force. They had been pretty well chewed up before they got to us, and we completed the job."

At the regimental command post, the staff unpacked to stay.

38
Home Station—
The Screaming Eagles

As everyone knows, the newspapers in the United States did not announce that the 101st Airborne Division had been cut off and surrounded by the enemy until a day or two before the relief of the besieged city. Oddly enough, most of us at Bastogne were almost as slow in getting the news.

Newspaper maps of front lines in a war usually show a salient in clear black, like a pool of spilled ink. The impression is that within that pool the land is thick with soldiers, that every square inch of terrestrial space has its allotted guardian. Nothing of the sort is true, of course. The break-through of the German tanks in Holland and their advance on Veghel through the heart of the enemy country were more typical than unique. Where the vehicles crossed the highway, and where they approached Veghel—both being guarded areas— they were engaged. But the remainder of their movements was through virtually deserted countryside, like the land on the road from Addeville to La Barquette.

Something of the sort was just as true at Bastogne. The first evidence of enemy forces to the rear of Bastogne came when a reconnaissance patrol engaged a small force of Germans on the road leading back to the hospital. In a few hours the enemy forces had moved elsewhere; but, as time passed, engagements on the roads to the rear became more frequent. McAuliffe at division headquarters knew that Bastogne would be ringed by the enemy, but at the respective regimental headquarters, and especially on the battalion lines, only rumors of the engagements to the rear reached the men. On the night of the 20th and the morning of the 21st the whole situation was in doubt. Yet the front lines of the German drive had already gone beyond Bastogne.

Von Rundstedt was aiming for Liége, where the largest supply dumps behind the Allied lines were situated. His plan was to seize those dumps and thus equip his army for the drive on Antwerp. Once Antwerp had been reached, the Allied forces would be split in half.

Nothing of this was known, however, on the morning of the 21st in Bastogne. After the Germans had fallen back, all was still and cold. The gentle descent of the snowflakes by the old church on the main street gave Bastogne the picturesque air of an old-fashioned Christmas card. By morning the snow had made the whole town clean and white—dangerously white for patrols; so Captain Phillips, with Lieutenant Frank as interpreter, ransacked the houses of Bastogne for bed sheets to use as camouflage.

That day—for the first and last time of the war—the operations offices of regimental headquarters moved underground.

A narrow corridor about ten feet below the surface of the earth, reached by a flight of stone steps, admitted to a series of cement-walled chambers underneath the convent command post. Each room was about ten by fifteen feet. When desks and chairs were put in, there was not much room to move around. The regimental commander, his executive officer, the adjutant, the intelligence officer, the operations officer, and their enlisted staffs were all crowded together into the connecting rooms. With the exception of the apartment in a private house across the street, occupied by the prisoner of war interrogation team, and with the further exception of a few aid stations, those underground chambers were the only warm rooms in Bastogne during the siege. They were not only warm, they were also safe. And consequently very crowded.*

One of the last convoys to get through to Bastogne from outside brought the regimental kitchens. For lack of space in the forward positions the mobile stoves were set up—with nothing to cook—along the sides of the glass-ceiled cloister upstairs and beneath a huge statue.

The wounded who came from the lines were put temporarily in the cold chapel adjacent to the cloister. Major Carrel, the regimental surgeon, was ill, but Captain W. J. Waldmann of Bakersfield, California, a man with a high forehead and a grave manner, took his place. Operations and transfusions were performed by the yellow light of two gas lamps. The wounded men, wrapped in the few blankets on hand, were laid on the freezing floor of the chapel. As new casualties were brought from the lines, aisles were made between the litter cases. Soon the floor was covered with wounded men, who lay where they could see the crazy shadows dancing on the plasma tubes and the gas bottles for the lamps.

Presently, the enlisted men of the staff realized that no wounded were being evacuated. And that was how the word of the encirclement finally spread.

2

Four German divisions and elements of three others faced the 101st Airborne Division when Bastogne was finally surrounded. Each of our men was outnumbered four to one. No one felt heroic about this, and no one made any speeches about it, written or otherwise. The troops were never called upon—as democratic statesmen are so fond of doing, especially after lunch—to give no inch of their embattled ground.

---

*For emergency lighting, the Sisters of Saint Francis donated almost all of the religious candles in the seminary. Literally hundreds of those candles were burned during the siege.

Nor were they ever told that what they were doing was important, significant, or destined by any combination of circumstances to go down in military history. It was even doubtful that General McAuliffe's mimeographed Christmas message to the troops reached every foxhole.

But as soon as the word spread among the troops, both in town and on the lines, that the roads out of Bastogne had been cut off and the division surrounded, a curious, very subtle change took place in the atmosphere. It was difficult to understand. Perhaps it was this:

A certain good-natured rivalry had existed from the beginning among the various units of the division—the 501st, the 502nd, the 506th, the 327th Glider Infantry, the airborne artillery, and the others. In England, in Normandy, in Holland, in France the good-natured conviction of each unit that its own soldiers were the best had persisted. However, the various units as a whole considered themselves head and shoulders above the other divisions in the E.T.O.

So when Bastogne was surrounded, and the circle of the defense was manned, not by strangers, but by the "old gang"—the "Hell Raisers" of Newbury and Lambourne and Chilton Foliat and Littlecote and Greenham Common and Carentan and Eindhoven and Nijmegen—and we knew that the rear was protected and the flanks secured by what we considered the only kind of soldiers worth fighting with, the atmosphere in Bastogne became much as it would have been if someone had erected a sign on the highest point of town—
HOME STATION—SCREAMING EAGLES.

No matter where the Germans attacked around the circle, the men of the other units could say to themselves: "The Five-O-Deuce is getting it right now," or "Poor Sink. He's having a bad night." They could trust the 502nd or the 506th or any of the others. Those were not regiments a self-respecting 501st man would want to join, naturally (on account of Sink or Michaelis or too much "chicken," or any one of a dozen reasons), but they were a damned sight better regiments than any others in the E.T.O.

The stray units and fragments of units which had stayed to fight with us were not accepted just as additional fire power. By their free decision to remain and fight they were raised to the level of the airborne troops; were given, so to speak, honorary membership in the division. There were no strangers in Bastogne during the siege. Only after the siege had been lifted, and sad-faced, weary infantrymen of the relieving units filed by the hundreds through the ruined streets, did our men, and those who had fought with us, realize what had come to us for a little while and gone, and would never come again.

39
"Nuts!"

The day of the 21st was quiet for our regiment. The Germans had decided to abandon the attempt to gain Bastogne through the positions chosen by Colonel Ewell around Bizory, Mont, and Neffe, and were spreading around the town.

McAuliffe, worried by the dwindling supply of ammunition, and still in contact with higher headquarters by radio, asked for air resupply as soon as the weather cleared. He was promised it—*if* the weather cleared. But with the leaden skies over the town, as they had been closed over all of Europe almost without break since early November, there seemed little hope.

Captain Waldmann, working in the chapel hospital, knew that his supply of plasma would last only another day or two. Even by then, in spite of everything that he, Captain Axelrod, Captain Jacobs, and the other medical officers could do, some of the wounded had died. Outside in the courtyard, piled in the trailer of a jeep, were dead soldiers from the line, their bare legs, yellow in color, sticking out from under a frozen canvas cover. Everywhere, things were half-completed or not done at all. As the German shelling grew heavier and heavier, and the third night fell, the American artillerymen within the town counted their ammunition. On the lines the inadequately clothed men fought back strong, continual, probing attacks and counted their own ammunition. The situation at Bastogne that night and the morning of the 22nd was at its lowest ebb.

2

Around 11:30 in the morning of a dirty gray day—the 22nd—four tiny German figures waded up through the snow on the road from Remoifosse to the American lines. The soldiers of the artillery unit who had dug themselves into fortified positions along that sector drew a bead on the target. But they held their fire. The Germans were carrying a large white flag.

Word passed down through the front lines like an electric shock: the Germans wanted to surrender!

The road from Remoifosse happened to lead to Colonel Harper's medical station. There, to the astounded medics, the German group—a major, a captain, and two enlisted men—reported themselves in crude English and demanded to be taken to the commander of troops in Bastogne. Both officers were arrogant, and it annoyed them to be blindfolded. So Colonel Harper left them at his command post.

On the line many soldiers crawled out of their foxholes, stretched upright in full sight of the Germans across the way, and, for the first time since their arrival, took time to shave. Men of the other sectors were more cautious, but Colonel Harper's men knew they were safe as long as the German emissaries were inside Bastogne. So they relaxed and ate their K rations with legs dangling over the edges of foxholes.

Division headquarters had been set up above and below ground in a series of red-brick storehouses, not unlike garages, where the VIII Corps had had its own headquarters. German artillery shells had been falling on the brick houses at least once an hour. But during the presence of the German intermediaries the morning was still.

Colonel Harper and Major Jones took the surrender message to General McAuliffe. The note read as follows:

"The fortune of war is changing. This time the USA forces in and near Bastogne have been encircled by strong German armored units. More German armored units have crossed the river Ourthe near Ourtheville, have taken Marche and reached St. Hubert by passing through Hompres-Libret-Tillet. Libramont is in German hands.

"There is only one possibility to save the encircled USA troops from total annihilation: that is the honorable surrender of the encircled town. In order to think it over, a term of two hours will be granted beginning with the presentation of this note.

"If this proposal should be rejected, one German artillery corps and six heavy AA Battalions are ready to annihilate the USA troops in and near Bastogne. The order for firing will be given immediately after this two hours' term.

"All the serious civilian losses caused by this artillery fire would not correspond with the well-known American humanity."

And now let Colonel Marshall tell what happened:

McAuliffe asked someone what the paper contained and was told that it requested a surrender.

The General laughed and said, "Aw, nuts!" It really seemed funny to him at the time. He figured he was giving the Germans "one hell of a beating" and that all of his men knew it. The demand was all out of line with the existing situation.

But McAuliffe realized that some kind of reply had to be made and he sat down to think it over. Pencil in hand, he sat there pondering a few minutes and then he remarked, "Well, I don't know what to tell them." He asked the staff what they thought, and Colonel Kinnard, his G-3, replied, "That first remark of yours would be hard to beat."

General McAuliffe didn't understand immediately what Kinnard was referring to. Kinnard reminded him, "You said 'Nuts!' " That drew applause all around. All members of the staff agreed with much enthusiasm and because of their approval McAuliffe decided to send that message back to the Germans.

Then he called Colonel Harper in and asked him how he would reply to the message. Harper thought for a minute but before he could compose anything, General McAuliffe gave him the paper on which he had written his one-word reply and asked, "Will you see that it's delivered?"

"I will deliver it myself," answered Harper. "It will be a lot of fun." McAuliffe told him not to go into the German lines.

Colonel Harper returned to the command post of Company F. The two Germans were standing in the wood blindfolded and under guard. Harper said, "I have the American commander's reply."

The German captain asked, "Is it written or verbal?"

"It is written," said Harper. And then he said to the German major, "I will stick it in your hand."

The German captain translated the message. The major then asked: "Is the reply negative or affirmative? If it is the latter I will negotiate further."

All of this time the Germans were acting in an upstage and patronizing manner. Colonel Harper was beginning to lose his temper. He said, "The reply is decidedly not affirmative." Then he added, "If you continue this foolish attack your losses will be tremendous." The major nodded his head.

Harper put the two officers in the jeep and took them back to the main road where the German privates were waiting with the white flag.

He then removed the blindfold and said to them, speaking through the German captain: "If you don't understand what 'nuts' means, in plain English it is the same as 'Go to Hell.' And I will tell you something else—if you continue to attack, we will kill every goddam German that tries to break into this city."

The German major and captain saluted very stiffly. The captain said, "We will kill many Americans. This is war."

"On your way, bud," said Colonel Harper.*

The small party of the enemy, carrying their white flag, disappeared down the snowy road in the direction of their own lines. The USA troops climbed back into their foxholes.

And the threatened artillery barrage failed to materialize.

3

Shortage of ammunition, especially for the artillery, was McAuliffe's chief concern. That day the 463rd Field Artillery Battalion had only 200 rounds of ammunition.

McAuliffe passed the word to ration the firing to ten rounds per gun per day. He clarified his order for one artillery

*From *Bastogne—The First Eight Days*, by Colonel S. L. A. Marshall.

commander just before an enemy attack: "If you see 400 Germans in a 100-yard area, and they have their heads up, you can fire artillery on them—but not more than two rounds."

There was food—two boxes of K rations a day per man—but not for long. And the snow was blanketing the lines deeper. Already trench foot had set in.

Not enough maps, not enough ammunition, not enough clothing, not enough plasma, not enough food . . . What *was* there enough of?

Well, there was enough spirit.

And the next morning, after a night of heavy fighting in other sectors, the miracle happened. It was a simple miracle. Yet for a continent where months of winter had already grayed the skies day after day without change and would gray them again solidly for months and months afterwards, leaving only that one small patch of good weather in the dead center of a crisis, it *was* a miracle.

For the skies cleared and the sun came out.

And up from England by the hundreds roared the C-47 supply planes and the fighters—throttles open—destination: Bastogne.

40
Aerial Delivery

"The fortunes of war are changing. . . ." It was a double-edged phrase.

The sun had not been up an hour before our first American fighter planes appeared. They were cheered by the frozen paratroopers at Mont and Bizory and Neffe and all along the lines—small silver planes which came swiftly from very high up and in a few moments were roaring in circles around the town, a thousand feet above the foxholes. Men who had gone to sleep in covered positions underground were awakened by the familiar thunderous buffetings of air pressure caused by exploding bombs. Within Bastogne the few windows still unshattered shook and rattled and subsided and then shook again.

Those men who had a good view of the German lines—like Major Pelham, who occupied an observation post in a private farmhouse clearly visible to both sides—could watch the planes dive on some object behind the German positions, then pull up in a fine curve a few hundred feet off the ground, leaving behind, where the bomb struck, a perfectly-formed balloon of orange flame and black smoke which expanded soundlessly, brilliantly, and with spectacular beauty over the dazzling, snow-white hills. Moments later the sound would come.

The noise continued all day. Between the concussions of the exploding bombs we could hear the occasional *"whiff-fisssssss!"* of rockets from the Typhoons—a sound that brought to mind, all in a piece, the golden lines at Eerde and along the Neder Rijn. Close liaison was maintained by radio with the air support around Bastogne, and one infantryman, who reported five German tanks bearing down on his position, had six P-47s darting upon the tanks within a few minutes.

Close to the red-brick buildings which housed division headquarters was a gentle slope of hillside clear of shrubbery or trees. It was concealed from the lines by a higher rise of land beyond. This bare slope, dazzling white with snow in the sun, was selected as the drop zone for the C-47 supply ships. Division S-4, Colonel Kohls, placed Captain Matheson of the 506th and Major Butler of the 501st in charge of the bundle recovery, and notified each regiment to send five jeeps with trailers. Distribution of the parachuted supplies would be made directly from the field.

No hour had been given McAuliffe for the expected arrival of the C-47s. So from the break of dawn on a freezing crystal morning, December 23rd, Butler, Matheson, and the supply officers of the other units, each with a jeep of his own, stamped their feet, blew on their fingers—and waited. The rumor of an air resupply had reached the men on the lines, and, with the Germans virtually immobilized by the daylight bombing, they were having a quiet, cheerful morning. In straw-filled foxholes, dugout command posts, and farmhouses the American soldiers waited.

The first C-47s to reach Bastogne dropped parachutists. They were pathfinders out of England—men who had been called from classes at school several days before, and who had been waiting all this time for clear weather. They landed safely, set up radar sets—refinements of those which had been used in Normandy—and guided the resupply ships to the drop zone.

At 11:50 the planes roared in—241 of them.

What ought to be said is difficult to say. A tribute is an awkward thing. Even the men who felt like waving their arms and yelling did nothing at all except stare up in silence at the roaring planes. Bastogne vibrated with the thunder of American engines. These were the pilots, many of them, who had flown the division to the invasion of Normandy half a year before. They were the men who had been criticized or scorned by the parachutists for taking evasive action under fire—and who had then flown them to Eindhoven and Zon and Eerde and Veghel without mistake.

And now here they were again, the other half of the airborne equation, our young fellow countrymen, the youngest of all soldiers, sweeping in with their olive planes through the clear, blue December sky of Belgium, and low over the snow-covered hills, to resupply—in a town the world was watching—the same old gang.

Crowds of Belgian townspeople emerged from their catacombs under the houses to stare. It was difficult for us not to feel a sentimental pride of country. The equipment parachutes, blossoming over the white field where Butler and the other men waited to receive them, were green and blue and yellow and red—ammunition, plasma, food, gasoline, clothing. . . .

The planes made a circle of the besieged town and then turned away to the north, flying at an altitude of about a thousand feet. Flak had become heavy, but not a single plane took evasive action. The controls of one ship were shot away just as it swept, empty of its parachuted supplies, over the German lines. Its pilot had been gaining altitude. As the bullets struck it, a little wisp of brown smoke gusted out in a faint streak from its tail. Slowly the plane curled upon one wing and nosed down into a vertical dive. The airborne troops who watched, and who had ridden so often in the familiar C-47 cabin, could imagine the scene inside: the two American youngsters struggling with the controls, the cockpit windows showing nothing but uprushing earth, the instinctive start backwards towards the cabin, and then . . .

A balloon of smoke and fire went up from the earth where the plane fell.

2

The drop zone was only a mile square. Yet 95 percent of the 1,446 parachuted bundles were recovered. One hundred and forty-four tons of fresh supplies had come to Bastogne.

So speedily did the supply crews make distribution and load the bundles into jeeps (without stopping to detach the parachutes) that the artillery units were firing the new ammunition before all the bundles on the field had been recovered.

When the second aerial resupply was made, the ammunition shortage was no longer a problem. Gasoline had the lowest priority; since the division was not going anywhere, only 445 gallons were delivered. But food supplies, which had the second highest priority, remained far below the margin for safety, even after the deliveries had been made; the 26,406 K rations that had been dropped were, though impressive in figure, enough to feed the division personnel for only a little more than a day.

McAuliffe authorized foraging.

Troops like to forage, and nobody is better at it than the American soldier. An abandoned corps warehouse yielded 450 pounds of coffee, 600 pounds of sugar, and an equally large amount of Ovaltine. Most of those items were delivered to the aid stations for the use of the wounded. In an abandoned corps bakery, flour, lard, and salt were uncovered, while from a Belgian warehouse came margarine, jam and additional supplies of flour. Also found in the latter storehouse were 2,000 burlap bags. These were sent out to the front lines for the soldiers to use as padding for their feet.

The farms at the outskirts of town yielded potatoes, poultry and cattle, the staples most needed for the men. Because discipline and selflessness were at the highest during the siege, the soldiers who commandeered such items took them back to the kitchens at the regimental command post, instead of roasting or cooking them makeshift on the spot. As a result, the butchered farm animals were skinned and cleaned properly, and the meat was divided evenly among each of the battalion kitchens. It was not uncommon, in those uncommon days, to see the skinned, bloody carcass of a whole cow or a gigantic hog being hosed down by the cooks on the stone floor of the cloister at the regimental C.P., under a blue and gold statue of the Virgin Mary.

Oddly enough, the cooks themselves worked under intermittent shellfire. The glass ceiling of the cloister was also the roof of the building, and shells from the German guns to the northeast sometimes burst among the stone cornices. The KPs were kept busy sweeping away the broken glass. It is a statement of fact that no place in Bastogne could be termed a rear area. After the first German bombing, the town was sometimes more dangerous than the lines.

3

The fighting that took place on the 23rd and 24th, in different sectors of the all-around defense, was intense. The lines of the 501st parachute Infantry underwent continual probing attacks by the Germans, especially each nightfall, but after the first two days the Germans had clearly abandoned the costly effort to enter Bastogne over the wide fields of fire which opened from the regimental positions. Division headquarters had no such respite, however, and for every six-hour period in Bastogne there were one or more attempts by the enemy to break through in force. Those who liveed within the town seldom guessed how many men were dying in the suburbs to keep the streets empty of all but Americans.

McAuliffe had conceived the expedient of drawing a small reserve from each of the organizations on the line. These reserves were formed into a task force, with armor and tank destroyers, and were used as a mobile support, capable of moving to any sector of the line seriously threatened by an enemy attack. Ewell, copying the plan, created Task Force X, under Captain Frank McKaig and Lieutenant Ernest Fisher, to support his own battalions. For some reason, the Germans never attacked simultaneously on all sectors of the perimeter defense, so the mobile task forces were an effective device.

Approximately 2,000 civilian inhabitants of Bastogne remained in the town during the siege. They lived underground in mass shelters, one beneath a convent in the center of the town, another beneath the regimental command post. A few lived under their own houses. Those who lived in the great cellars of the two convents dwelt in conditions of indescribable filth. Old men, too crippled to move, sat in chairs at the side and stared into the darkness; young children crawled about the cement floors; men and women lay together on rough blankets or piles of burlap. At the regimental command post, this condition became such a threat to the health of the soldiers that at length certain male civilians were assigned the task of policing their own shelters and, under shellfire, of emptying the refuse outside.

An interesting, though rather ugly sidelight of life in Bastogne during the siege was the impossibility of digging slit trenches or making other arrangements for field sanitation. A large privy was dug in the courtyard outside the regimental command post, but because that area was under constant shellfire, few of the men would use it. In the beginning they utilized a large indoor latrine obviously built for school children. However, the plumbing froze after the first day; so in time the place was boarded up. From then on, at all hours of the day and night, soldiers could be found searching for unused toilets through the smaller rooms upstairs in the seminary.

The days and nights were bitter cold. Ewell authorized his men to wear whatever would keep them warm. That no loss of discipline occurred during the resultant individualism was a tribute to the discipline already ingrained in the troops. A few hours after the word had gone around, many soldiers appeared in civilian wool sweaters, crude blouses of parachute silk, and Belgian winter caps. One officer wore a Canadian combat jacket which he had saved from Holland. An enlisted man appeared at the command post in an army blanket, with holes cut for his arms and a rope binding it about his waist. He was the personification of the Sad Sack, but no one seeing the stubble of beard on his chin, the lines of weariness around his eyes, the tight, humorless slit of his mouth and the dirty hands cracked from exposure, gripping the one clean thing in his possession—his rifle—could have smiled.

The parachutes recovered from the equipment bundles were used to cover the wounded men. The command post personnel donated their blankets to the men on the line. Every

civilian sheet and blanket in town had already been collected
and put to use. Also every bottle of liquor.

On the afternoon of December 23rd, word came to Bastogne
that Patton's armor was fighting its way to the besieged town.
If luck held, Patton—with the division commander, General
Taylor, in the vanguard—would reach Bastogne by Christmas
Day.

41
"Oh, Little Town of Bethlehem . . ."

Early in the evening of December 23rd, just after the winter
darkness had fallen and a brilliant three-quarter moon lighted
the snowbound little town with a blue glare, Chaplain Engels,
Lieutenant Peter Frank, Sergeant Schwartz and Sergeant Harvey were having a premature Christmas dinner in the second-
floor apartment of the prisoner-of-war team, across the street
from the regimental command post.

The chaplain had just come in from the lines, where the
night was almost as quiet as it was in town. In the blacked-
out, rickety apartment there were light and warmth. Lieutenant Frank, a Viennese by birth and an American by choice,
had a flair for entertainment. He had set the supper table with
linen, silver, wine glasses, plates, and candles—all (except
the seminary candles) borrowed from the abandoned supplies
of the house. Three bottles of looted wine were open on the
sideboard; a stock of good Belgian cigars had been set out,
and in the frying pan on the stove was steak, a gift from
Chaplain Engels.

In half an hour the party had become merry and mellow. It
is traditional with soldiers to feel more and more immortal as
the wine is drained, and, the more immortal they feel, the
more they toast each other's imminent death: this must be the
root of that brooding melancholy which characterizes so many
drinking songs. The officers and men toasted one another's
distant wives and sweethearts, departed friends, and one an-

other's lives and imminent deaths; they all toasted, in the old, old manner, confusion to their enemies.

"Gentlemen," announced Lieutenant Frank, "the Queen." Everyone rose.

"Stalin," proposed Sergeant Schwartz.

"General Ike."

Glasses clinked.

"Benes . . ."

"McAuliffe . . ."

"Lady Macbeth . . ."

When the dinner was over and cigars had been handed around, the group, with Lieutenant Frank at the piano, sang Christmas carols.

They were midway through *Silent Night* when a buffeting of air pressure shook the floors and rattled the windows.

"Somebody's getting bombed," said Frank, pausing.

"Go on, Lootenant," said Harvey, " 'sh probably Berlin."

But a moment later a soldier put his head in the door. "German planes," he announced. "They're bombing the town."

There was a little silence. Then Frank said: "The hell with it. I'm staying here."

"Of course," said the chaplain, lighting a cigar.

But the next bomb exploded with such violence that one of the windows burst inward. The floors wobbled and shook. Plaster fell. Rushing to the door, the chaplain shouted the time-honored battle-cry of the infantry school—"FOLLOW ME!"—and fell head-over-heels downstairs.

The first bombs were dropped uptown in the vicinity of a railroad overpass near division headquarters. An aid station was hit, killing most of the men and, with them, a Belgian girl who had volunteered to work as a nurse. Other bombs then struck the houses on the square below division headquarters, bracketing the group of shelters where the Belgian citizens had taken refuge and demolishing a memorial statue to the Belgian dead of World War I. One bomb had struck only fifty feet from the command post.

Another bomb tore through two floors of the command post itself and lodged—unexploded—in the ceiling of a potato cellar.

The force of aerial-bomb explosions defies description. Soldiers in Bastogne that night could tell by the rattle of anti-aircraft fire whenever the planes were coming to dive down. The small-arms fire always grew heavier as the plane reached the bomb-release point of its dive: this crescendo of noise had the same effect on the nervous system as a crescendo of drums. When the plane had swept by, the firing ceased, and then everyone knew that the bomb was on its way. Conversation ceased. Sometimes we could hear the high, whistling flutter of the descending projectile, and then death was very close.

Fires burned late in the town that night. Out on the lines, one or two of the battalion command posts had had near misses, but no one had been injured. Desolation gripped the upper regions of the town, however, and when the fires burned themselves out, only the charred skeleton of buildings remained around the main square. Bastogne, which had been untouched when the troops moved in, wore that ghastly air of desolation which had come to so many European towns in the war. In the still night a man walking past the ruins could smell the sickly-sweet odor of the untended dead.

This was Christmas, 1944.

2

Christmas Eve was bright moonlight. Out at Neffe, where the enemy had repeatedly and vainly attacked, day after day, the 1st Battalion men still occupied the house they had seized the first day. At Mont across the way, and at Bizory further on, Homan's 2nd Battalion and Griswold's 3rd Battalion settled down in the snow for a Christmas-eve dinner of K rations. Since the rumor of Patton's armor fighting towards Bastogne, nothing further had been heard, and an atmosphere of fatalism ran through the lines. Old friends, shaking hands with each other, said good-bye. Christmas, they thought, would bring the end.

Tom Rice had been wounded. He lay with the other wounded men in the chapel adjoining the seminary at the regimental command post. The great vaulted room was cold—so cold that the wounded men's breath frosted in the air. The aid men had covered the broken stained-glass windows with canvas, but snow drifted in through the cracks.

On Christmas Eve, Chaplain Engels and a group of men

and officers from the regimental staff formed a choir to sing
to the wounded. Colonel Ewell came in for a few minutes to
talk to the men. The soldiers and officers of the amateur
group took their places silently, in a transept high above the
floor of the chapel. It was a quiet, blue, frozen evening. The
little town was blanketed under moonlit snow. The soldiers
who had been dozing were awakened by the choir of men's
voices singing:

> Oh, little town of Bethlehem,
>   How still we see thee lie;
> Above thy deep and dreamless sleep,
>   The silent stars go by. . . .

One by one the soldiers opened their eyes, their pale faces
turned up to the men who were singing. . . .

> Yet in thy dark streets shineth
>   The everlasting Light;
> The hopes and fears of all the years,
>   Are met in thee tonight.

Here and there in the cold darkness a few men wiped their
eyes with their sleeves. Outside, the ruined little town was
silent. The gas lamps in the archways hissed; the operating,
the blood transfusions continued. There was a pause. Then
the men sang again—

> Silent night! Holy night!
> All is calm, all is bright. . . .

Softly the wounded men began to sing. Wind gusted the
tarpaulins on the windows. Thoughts were far away . . . back
home . . . carols on other and happier Christmas Eves.
  When the singing ended, a soldier in the transept, whose
throat was not entirely clear, began to read:

> And she brought forth her first born son and wrapped
> him in swaddling clothes and laid him in a manger;
> because there was no room for him in the inn. And there
> were in the same country, shepherds abiding in the field,
> keeping watch over their flock by night. And lo, the

angel of the Lord came upon them, and the glory of the
Lord shone round them: and they were sore afraid. And
the angel said unto them, Fear not; for, behold, I bring
you tidings of great joy, which shall be to all people.
For unto you is born this day in the city of David a
Saviour, which is Christ the Lord. And this shall be a
sign unto you; Ye shall find the babe wrapped in swad-
dling clothes lying in a manger. And suddenly there
was with the angel a multitude of the heavenly host
praising God and saying, Glory to God in the highest
and on earth peace, good will towards men. . . .

The choir and the wounded men sang together—

Oh come all ye faithful, joyful and triumphant—
Oh come ye, oh come ye to Bethlehem. . . .

Uptown there was sudden bombing. In half an hour the
flames of a dozen houses licked over the snowy blue silence.
At headquarters of Combat Command B, a bomb that fell
nearby knocked over a makeshift Christmas tree which the
men had decorated. They righted the tree and, when the plane
had gone, pinned a Purple Heart medal to a small, battered
doll.

42
The Siege Is Lifted

At 1650 on the afternoon of December 26th, a lieutenant of
the 4th Armored Division named Boggess drove the first
vehicle of his division into the lines of the Bastogne forces.
The siege was lifted.

In the seven days during which the 4th Armored Division
moved to the relief of Bastogne, the division had lost over a
thousand men. Its total medium tank strength at the end of the
period was equal to the tank strength of a single battalion.

As to what this victory—won by the defenders of Bastogne and confirmed by the force that relieved them—availed the Allied cause, and as to how it influenced the emergency of December 1944, there is an official estimate from the command of 12th Army Group.

Preoccupation with the key position of Bastogne dominated enemy strategy to such an extent that it cost him the advantage of the initiative. The German High Command evidently considered further extension to the west or north as both logistically and strategically unsound without possession of Bastogne, as that town overlooks the main roads and concentration areas of the spearheads. By the end of the month, the all-out effort in the north had become temporarily defensive; in the west there was a limited withdrawal, and the array of German forces around Bastogne clearly exposed the enemy's anxiety over that position. Until the Bastogne situation is resolved one way or the other, no change in strategy can be expected.

How well these words were sustained by the passage of events is now history.*

Bastogne was on the front line, however. And evidently the Allied reserves were shaky, for the 101st Airborne Division was not relieved. It formed the lip of a funnel, so to speak, through which a new weight of artillery and infantry units were being poured. Von Rundstedt's advance had been halted somewhere to the east of us, but there remained the task of cutting up his salient, destroying his matériel and restoring the lines to their old uniformity along the border of Germany.

Someone even started the preposterous rumor that the 101st would have to help. To this, the soldiers turned a deaf ear. And for a few days life went on as before.

*From *Bastogne—The First Eight Days,* by Colonel S. L. A. Marshall.

43

Come You Home a Hero*

> *Come you home a hero*
> *Or come not home at all . . .*
> THE SHROPSHIRE LAD

"No!" shouted the voice on the telephone. "I want it tonight. Bring it over now."

"Damn," said the lieutenant under his breath. He clicked off the receiver. Tired, wet, the snow thick on his boots, he had just come in from the lines. Glumly he stood in the underground operations office of the regimental command post and stared at the wall.

"What's up?" grinned the operations sergeant. "Have to go out again?"

"No," he said, buttoning his coat, "Yes," he said.

The sergeant folded *The Stars and Stripes*. "Did you read this about the 'heroes of Bastogne'?" he asked, accenting the inverted commas. "Somebody says we said, 'They got us surrounded—the poor bastards.'"

"Did you say that?" asked the officer.

"No."

"Neither did I," he said. "Especially not when they bombed." He went out.

Since nightfall the blizzard had become severe. Artillery had set fire to a house in the main part of town, and the glow—whitened by the storm—looked like flares. He stood at the gate of the command post, watching. It was a fire, all right. The shelling had stopped for a while. Cursing the captain who had called for him, he shoved his hands deep in his pockets

---

*This story, written by the author in Bastogne, appeared in the *Atlantic Monthly* for July 1945, and was named by Martha Foley as one of the distinguished short stories of the year.

and turned left past the frozen sentry toward the gate of town. No one was abroad. Half-tracks and tanks were parked along the sidewalk by the prisoner-of-war enclosure. They had not been moved since the last attack two days before and were banked high with snow. He blew the storm out of his face and tramped down to the shelter of the city gate.

Bastogne had changed greatly since that first foggy daybreak when he and the other men had marched into it. Until then the war had passed through the Belgian town twice without harming it—once during the German advance and again during their retreat. Most of the buildings still showed evidence of German occupancy. The walls of the convent at the northeastern side of town were slotted with loopholes for machine guns.

But since the airborne units had held the town, ruin had come to it. Unlike the neat Holland towns the lieutenant remembered, where the Dutch people had come out as soon as the shellings were over and begun piling the bricks in neat stacks against the sidewalks, Bastogne had had no repairs. Water spilled out of the broken water mains unattended, then froze and made icicles on the charred stone. Stores stood burned and wrecked, their wares abandoned. Not a window in town except those on the outskirts was unbroken. Night bombings by solitary German planes had torn up the streets, caved in the houses, left wreckage in which, for six days, no one had had the time to dig out the dead.

Few shells had fallen by the city gate. But out beyond it, for a stretch of several hundred yards, the road led across a black misty stream and up onto the hillslope of the opposite side. There, heavy artillery shells had been falling all day. The lieutenant hesitated a moment. It was a gamble. If he waited, they might begin afterwards; if he went now they might start at once. He shrugged his shoulders and walked forward across the open stretch, keeping close to the snow-filled ditch. The storm blinded him. He tried to listen for the first whistle of the shells.

Back home, imagining the war, fear had been something he had overlooked. He had overlooked other things, but fear had been the greatest. It colored everything most men did in combat. All of them felt it in varying degrees. For some it was incapacitating. They lasted a little while on the line—long enough, as a rule, to realize that the fear was not subsiding. Then a near shell-burst or some violent shock ended thtir usefulness under fire. Like men who fainted when they were inoculated, one could never tell beforehand which ones it would be—the steel workers or the public accountants.

He wondered what a hero was. He supposed a hero was something you became after it was all over, when you could think about it by a hot log fire. Or wear the campaign stars to a dance at Fort Benning. It made him snort. He turned up the slope of the hill towards the lines, getting the snow at his back. A series of houses, almost levelled by the earlier German bombs, flanked the street at one side. They looked queerly skeletonlike against the storm. He tried to remember which way the shells had come during the day. Diagonally over the hill from the northeast—that was it. He kept to the shelter of the ruins. Somewhere along this hill was the command post that he was looking for, the basement headquarters of Task Force O'Hara.* The captain had said the place was marked by a stack of wood. Stack of wood! Even the fences were deep in snow.

On the other side of the hill, shortly before nightfall, the enemy had begun an attack. It was only a probing effort, but the volume of small-arms fire audible through the storm was impressive. Once a 40mm. tracer shell ricocheted over the rooftops where he walked, whirling end on end musically. Beyond where it fell, the flames of the burning house in the main part of town where whipped up in a fresh wind. He remembered what Bastogne had looked like on Christmas night. Bombs had set part of the southern limits of the city burning. He and the Protestant chaplain had stood by a church near the prisoner-of-war enclosure and watched it—a curtain of luminous orange smoke over the moonlit rooftops, the whole city blue and silent and snowy while its houses burned.

He saw a pile of wood. But the house next to it was on the wrong side of the road. Seeing a cellar door at the bottom of the steps, he climbed down and tried the handle. The darkness inside was cold. It had a sickly-sweet odor. He recognized that odor at once and closed the door again. Some dead civilian, he thought. Lots of them had taken refuge in abandoned cellars during the bombings. If any of them were killed, they were found afterwards only by accident.

*Not strictly true; it was really Task Force X.

"Halt!" shouted a voice. He stopped dead.

"Lieutenant Foley," he said. "Artillery liaison."

"The password, sir."

"Brassie." The guard let him approach; the lieutenant heard the little click of the safety being put back on. "You can ask in the C.P., sir," said the guard in answer to the question. He gestured back towards the house. The lieutenant opened a door into a room warm with gaslight and armored force officers. A major, working on the situation map with a grease pencil, was a thin young man with black hair, about twenty-five. He shook his head. "Better try in the main part of town," he said. "Nobody ought to go wandering around getting lost out here."

The lieutenant said nothing. He persisted up the hill road another quarter of a mile. The wind had grown stronger. The snow still was fine and dry. It was the kind of snow that back home would last all night. If it had not been for the constant explosions over the hillcrest and the occasional *"wop-wop"* of incoming shells on the open space in the valley, he would have enjoyed the walk. But a man felt naked outdoors in a country here shelling was heavy.

Eventually he found the second woodpile. This time the cellar door opened into a dim, warm room under the abandoned house.

2

"Twenty-*four!*" Captain McKaig was shouting over the phone. "Twenty-four galoshes short . . . That's right. Find out from Jenkins what the hell happened. Tell him I need those things tonight. Got it? . . ." He twisted the lever of the telephone. "Sit down, Foley. . . . Give me Red again, Klondike. . . . Red, give me . . ."

Someone said to the lieutenant as he came in, "Hello, Jess." It was Captain Lunin, the surgeon of the 1st Battalion, a small, round, cheery man with a dark face like an eclipsed moon.

"Any news about Father Sampson?" asked the lieutenant, looking for a good chair.

"Still missing," said an enlisted man in the corner.

"Coffee coming up," announced Captain Lunin briskly.

"Sugar on the table. And tea." He rubbed his hands. "Over here, we *live*. . . ."

"Except that Lunin's never here," said Captain McKaig, still at the telephone. "Operator, what the hell has happened to this line? I got Kangaroo—I wanted Red. . . ."

"Give us the low-down, Jess," said Captain Lunin, pouring the coffee. "You get all the inside poop."

The lieutenant leaned back and drank the coffee gratefully. Now that he was safely inside, he was glad he had come. The shabby little room was comfortable. Task Force O'Hara had been formed of several small units taken variously from the whole division. During the first days in Bastogne, when the pressure from the German forces had been too heavy to spare reserves from the line, it had served as a mobile support. Now that the armored columns had relieved the town, its future was uncertain.

"All I want," shouted Captain McKaig to Lunin, "is to stay indoors tonight. After tonight they can send me anywhere."

The lieutenant tried to remember the news he had heard during the day. "Division says our oak-leaf cluster for Holland was approved. For the unit citation. I don't know who approved it—corps or army. And they say Roosevelt mentioned Bastogne. That's all I know."

"We're famous," said the enlisted man.

"Don't I know it," agreed Captain Lunin. "I expect to make a fortune lecturing to women's clubs. The Battered Bastards of the Bastion of Bastogne—that should be a drawing card. But tell me more about the oak-leaf cluster. Is it definite?"

"So they say at division." The lieutenant poured himself another cup of coffee.

"That makes *three* for us. Normandy, Holland, Bastogne," said the enlisted man in the corner.

"Carnegie Hall is another possibility," Lunin mused. "To accommodate the crowds."

"We were in *The Stars and Stripes* again today," added the enlisted man. "A big article. Says this place was like Gettysburg. Valley Forge. The Alamo."

Lunin rubbed his face. "Maybe I ought to go in for the big time."

The lieutenant leaned back towards the fire and let the warmth burn into him. He recognized the familiar banter of

the group. It made him think of something he had written
home after the Normandy invasion—that in the midst of death
they were in life. It was true. He looked at the shabby, warm,
comfortable room that Task Force O'Hara had made for itself
out of the abandoned cellar—the pictures of girls from home,
the opened packages, the letters. Since the siege, the whole
town of Bastogne was undermined with hidden places like
this. Almost all of them were underground. Walking through
the streets of town at night you saw nothing, only the ruins,
the snow, the lemon flares of outgoing artillery. Yet warmth
and congeniality and hot coffee were all there, behind the
blacked-out doors of the wrecked Belgian homes, underneath
the desolated shops.

"Foley is here," shouted Captain McKaig over the telephone. "I can't talk all night. . . . All right, all right, we've
got the galoshes. Twenty-four short." He went on talking.

"You're putting me in for a Medal of Honor, aren't you
Jess?" asked Captain Lunin.

"That's right," said the lieutenant. "That night you dug an
underground station single-handed."

"A Medal of Honor," Lunin mused. "I'd get to go home.
And it would help the publicity for my lecture tour."

"I was all set to go home once," put in the enlisted man.
"But the doc said it was scabies. I thought I had leprosy."

"That wasn't me," said Lunin. "We always cooperate in
matters like that."

"I'd give a lot to be on Hollywood and Vine right now,"
continued the enlisted man. "Even with leprosy." He moved
over to the light; the lieutenant saw that he was Sergeant Selz,
the 1st Battalion supply sergeant. "My wife says it's kind of
dull at home right now. Imagine that! I told her that what I
wanted was to be bored stiff with her, right in the middle of
North Hollywood." He laughed. "She thinks I'm having a
good time with those French girls."

"Louisiana for me," clarified Lunin. "I'd settle for a
newsstand on Canal Street."

"And tell that driver," shouted Captain McKaig over the
telephone, "that he'll have to go out to the Red C.P. tonight.
Tell him to hook up the trailer—we've got galoshes to go.
That's right." He hung up. "There's a little town called
Belton in Texas—"

"I know Belton," said Sergeant Selz. "My wife and me

had a house there when I was at Camp Hood. That town was
so crowded they had a waiting line for Main Street."

The shelling down in the valley had begun again. Lieutenant Foley was glad the captain was ready to work. Unfolding
the overlay he had brought, he sat down near the situation
map. The storm was muffled. Within the room there were no
drafts. On the floor against one wall of the cellar were three
bedrolls. Beside them was a wooden table with two kerosene
lamps, a few dirty plates, the situation map that he was
beginning to correct, and a package from home for Lieutenant
Sallin. Sallin came in while Lieutenant Foley was working.
"Fruit cake," he announced. After a smell, "No, it's rum
cake."

"Squeeze out the rum," suggested Sergeant Selz.

"We've got rum up there in the cupboard," said Captain
McKaig, looking up from the map. "That British ration from
Holland."

"This is what my folks would like to see," said Lieutenant
Sallin, cutting the rum cake. "The receiving end."

"They'd say you were gypping 'em," commented Captain
Lunin, pouring extra glasses of rum for everybody. "Task
Force O'Hara is too comfortable."

"We had a shell right at the door last night," said Sergeant
Selz. Lieutenant Foley looked at the man. Since the first
shells in the valley had begun falling, the sergeant had moved
around the room uneasily, sitting at last in the shelter beside
the empty fireplace. The nearer bursts made the glowing tip
of his cigarette jump. The lieutenant looked away. Nobody
had a right to criticize. As a matter of fact, he was glad of
the glass of rum himself. In a little while he had to go back
over that open space in the valley where the shells were
falling.

3

"When you're ready to go, let me know," said Captain
Lunin.

The lieutenant folded up the situation map. "Right now,"
he said. "Are you coming?"

Captain Lunin was putting on his coat when Jenkins, the
supply officer, bundled slowly into the room. "That's my

ammunition dump burning over there," he said heavily. "They made a clean hit. Two hours ago."

"The ammo dump?" asked the sergeant. He stood up. "I guess . . ." He hesitated. "I guess I'd better get back over there."

"That's a good idea," Jenkins agreed.

"I want to send those galoshes out to the line tonight," shouted Captain McKaig.

"They'll be frozen stiff by morning," said Jenkins, moving over to the fire. "Better send them out with the ration truck at breakfast." He looked at Lunin. "I'd wait a while, Pappy. There's a lot of incoming stuff down there."

"Arrange a temporary truce, will you, Jenk?" said Captain Lunin. "Tell 'em the Geneva Convention is down here visiting."

"Let's go," said the lieutenant. He took a last gulp of hot coffee.

The wind had died outside the house. But the snow was coming down more heavily. The three men turned up the collars of their coats and trudged down the hill road towards the group of houses that marked the left turn towards Bastogne. No one said anything. All of them were listening to the shellfire in the valley below. Between the rolling heaviness of the incoming shells were the sharper, almost hollow "*whooms*" of the tank guns, firing counter-battery. The lieutenant remembered with a wry grimace how scared he had been the first time, unable to tell the two sounds apart. Now he could even distinguish the tank guns from the artillery.

"I don't like this," said Sergeant Selz, his voice muffled under a coat collar.

"It may let up," added Captain Lunin.

"I don't mind the small-arms stuff so much," said the sergeant. "But this artillery . . ." His voice trailed off. The lieutenant looked at him again.

"I'd go back and wait a while if I were you, Sergeant," he said. "There's no sense taking risks you don't have to."

"I have to," said the sergeant with finality.

The lieutenant felt better for having company. It was strange how soldiers disliked solitary danger. He remembered T. E. Lawrence's phrase, "Of all danger, give me the solitary sort." Something like that. But Lawrence was not an ordinary soldier. The ordinary ones preferred dying, as the lieutenant did, in a crowd. That was why so many of them shared foxholes on the front lines.

The three men paused at the open stretch on the entrance to tbe valley. Through the blizzard they could see the occasional sharp, whitish flashes of the shellbursts. The thundering was much more intense. Captain Lunin pulled his Red Cross brassard higher onto his arm. "Does anybody want to wait?" he asked. When there was no answer, "How about making a run for it?"

"I tried that coming over," said the sergeant. "The ice is too slippery"

"Let's go," said the lieutenant impatiently. He wanted to get it over. To himself he did what he always did at moments like this: he committed to God the care of his wife and child. He was not religious, but some reassurance in the words of the short prayer was always forthcoming. None of them said anything just then. Isolated by the exposure, they walked forward steadily through the swirl of storm. When a shell exploded on the end of the road they fell flat. But then they got up and continued walking forward, still silent. In the huge booming storm of the night, violence seemed manifest. The sergeant cursed when he slipped. Lunin walked as rapidly as he could. The lieutenant noticed, almost without seeing it, that the fire in the town had died down.

They had almost reached the shelter of the city gate when the shell came in. The sickening whine that it made was ended before they could move. It struck the embankment of the road and exploded. The lieutenant felt two things at once: a violent crash on his eardrums and a hot bursting upheaval that slammed him into the air. Something sliced by his ear with a whine. He heard his mind saying, "Aii!" and before he could close his eyes he was smashed blindingly into the ground. He was stunned. His ears were ringing. Struggling, he got to his feet. "Hurry up!" he shouted. "Let's get out of here." More shells would come in at the same place.

"Over here!" shouted Lunin. "Come over here!"

The lieutenant swore. "Damn it!" He floundered over to the medical man. "The sergeant," said Lunin. Hurriedly the lieutenant took the man's shoulders. Staggering, slipping, they worked their way back as fast as they could towards the road. The second shell fell a hundred yards beyond them. Climbing through the ditch, they gained the city gate.

"Hold it," said Lunin. "I'll get a stretcher." He disappeared into the storm of the city.

Dazed, the lieutenant covered the wounded man with his overcoat. He almost fell when he bent over. Sinking to his knees, he pulled off the Canadian combat jacket that he wore and made a support for the man's head. His eyes failed him for a moment, then, and he sank back against the stone. A nauseating succession of violet spirals wheeled under his eyelids. He took two or three breaths. He realized that he was shivering violently. Trying to speak to the wounded man, his shaking lips refused the words. He recognized his own symptoms: he was suffering from shock. He knew how to treat himself—or at least he knew what helped him. He got up and double-timed in place for a few moments under the shelter of the arch. Then he got slowly down on his knees again and hunted through his pockets for a flashlight. The sergeant made a shuddering noise.

"Down here," said Lunin's voice from the front. A half-track, approaching from the rear, tried to pass under the archway; the lieutenant waved it aside dizzily. He still was feeling nausea. But he swallowed hard and followed the stretcher group to the regimental aid station.

4

In the first days at Bastogne, when the airborne units had been cut off by the enemy, the regimental aid station had been set up in the chapel of the Belgian seminary. There, for almost a week, the wounded men had steadily accumulated, until they covered the whole floor, even up to the altar. It was cold in the chapel. So the command post personnel had given up their blankets to the wounded. Steady shelling and night bombing had knocked out all of the stained glass windows. Snow had drifted into the holes. When the first air resupply mission was flown to Bastogne, the recovered parachutes were added to the blankets. Then, when the armored elements opened a corridor, the wounded men were evacuated to rear hospitals and the regimental aid station moved across the street to the vaulted underground cellar of a private house.

When the lieutenant entered, the warmth struck him in the face like a blow. Holding himself, he moved as close as he could to the stove. He noticed with relief that Captain Lunin's hands were shaking too. Lunin let Captain Waldmann take charge of the wounded man.

"Let's take a look at you, fella," said Captain Waldmann. He touched the side of the man's head speculatively. The lieutenant could see, then, what had happened. . . . Like Lunin and himself, the man was trembling violently. His lips were parted; his eyes were open and staring. One of his hands kept straying up to his head. "Hold his hand," said Captain Waldmann. He bent over the wounds with a flashlight. "Now just lie quiet, fella—this isn't going to hurt. . . ." He probed the ear with a cotton-covered stick. "No ear injury apparent." Then he turned the sergeant's neck slightly and looked for a long time at the other side of the head. In the silence the lieutenant could hear the gas lamp hissing.

"You're going to be all right," said Captain Waldmann. Reaching back for the penicillin, he nodded to someone in the shadows. For the first time the lieutenant saw the chaplain.

Chaplain Engels looked at the wounded man's dog tags. "I want you to pray," he said. "Can you hear me, Al?" He paused. "If you can't speak, just think the words to yourself with me. . . ." He paused again and began. The man trembled violently. "What are his chances?" the lieutenant whispered to Captain Lunin. "He's dying," Lunin whispered back. The lieutenant took a deep breath. He looked at a magazine that lay on one of the bedrolls in the corner. It showed a picture of a flight nurse. She looked too clean and impersonal, he thought—too sure of herself. Women were out of place so close to the lines. The men were too badly hurt, too near to violence.

". . . saying," whispered Chaplain Engels, *"Our Father Who art in Heaven, Hallowed be Thy Name. . . ."* The lieutenant listened to the words. He knew Sergeant Selz very slightly. But it was hard to feel anyone's death deeply, where each life hung so narrowly, even one's own. He knew that all the soldiers felt that way. He thought again of his wife. It was odd, he reflected, how the life over here was lived on two levels. Men carried on the casual friendliness that kept them sane, and on the other level was the violence and sudden death.

Sergeant Selz closed his eyes. Sometime in the few minutes that they stood there he must have died. Two wounded armored-force men were brought in on stretchers. Neither was seriously wounded. They lay and joked with the chaplain about their home towns. The lieutenant heard the low words— "You can't be from California, Chaplain. I thought everybody out there got deferred by the shipyards. . . ." Outside the cellar, the storm and the artillery pounded like brothers on the door.

"Did ya see *The Stars and Stripes* today?" said one of the aid men. "It told how one of the Washington papers printed that 'Battered Bastards of Bastogne' business. They called it 'The Battered B's of Bastogne.'"

"Can you imagine that?" said the man who had filled the hypodermic. "They think we're a bunch of dashes."

"Things are getting rough back home," commented an armored-force man. "They've had a hell of a cold wave."

"Maybe the War Department'll send us home to lecture in the war plants," suggested the first man.

"That would cut in on my business," stated Captain Lunin. "The field is definitely closed." He buttoned his coat collar. "I think I'd better be going on. My boys may cut a finger."

5

The lieutenant and the chaplain left together. They walked in silence through the whirring snow and across the street to the convent where they both slept. "It's all very heroic, ain't it?" said the lieutenant as they entered the cloister. "What the hell *is* a hero?"

"I dunno," said the chaplain noncommittally. "Certainly not me."

Snow drifted down through the wrecked cloister onto the tables where the men were served chow. A statue of Mary looked out on the still-steaming cans where the mess kits were washed. A few fires in the grease cans were alight; some of the guards who were off duty sat there warming themselves. The lieutenant felt tired. His body had at last stopped shivering. But the weariness was overpowering. When he climbed over the coal pile in the cellar to the place where he slept, he felt a deep sense of comfort.

The coal pile had been levelled flat by the soldiers. In the next chamber, connected by vaulted arches, nuns of St. Francis, who had come to Bastogne from Aachen, spent the night sleeping upright in chairs. They had a small altar with them, and each evening at about ten o'clock, before they went to bed, they sang evening prayers. Sometimes they said the prayers in the middle of the night, if they were awakened by German bombing. They were praying as the lieutenant turned back the covers. *"Sainte Marie, Mère de Dieu . . ."* It was familiar. Somewhere upstairs in the cloister an incoming shell made a sound like a crashing door. Glass fell.

"You're not listening," objected the chaplain, who had been talking.

"I was thinking," he said sleepily. "That sergeant came from California."

"So do I," nodded Chaplain Engels. "A good place. I expect to have a home in Burbank after the war."

"You told me about that," said the lieutenant drowsily.

"I decided not to buy it ready made. Build it. Buy all the materials. Of course I'd need advice. I was wondering the other night whether we should have a cellar. Lately I've gotten tired of cellars. . . ." He paused and listened to the blizzard outside the slits in the stone. "Or maybe I can interest you in dogs?" wistfully.

"Yes," said the lieutenant. "All kinds. Especially wire-haireds. I'm going to get my kid a wire-haired."

"Now here's the trouble with wire-haireds," said the chaplain happily. "They're all right if . . . "

The lieutenant went to sleep. Much later someone in the darkness awakened him by calling his name. He raised his head. "Yes? . . ."

"The colonel wants you out at White, sir. They're having an attack."

"They want me out there now?"

"That's right, sir. They've had to commit O'Hara."

The lieutenant leaned back slowly, looking at his watch. "O.K.," he said. He pulled the blankets over him again, closed his eyes and, quietly and fluently, from four and a half years of experience in the army, he began to curse. Finished, he lay back and let the drowsy warmth of the sleeping bag climb over him. He was so damn tired. . . . The war could go to hell. He'd had enough. He was through. The hell with honor. The hell with duty. He was through. Through with the army, through with the war, through with the whole damn mess. Utterly and completely. Heroes! He laughed. He didn't even know what a hero was.

Rolling his legs out from the covers, he started passionately lacing his boots.

44

The Horrible Fiasco

Northeast of Bastogne, bounded on one side by the Liége railroad tracks, was a thickly wooded area called the Bois Jacques. This wooded area lay directly in the path of any armored advance on the Noville-Longvilly line. Before the armored units could get astride the key Noville-Bizory highway, en route to cutting the enemy salient in half, that wooded area had to be seized. The fir and pine trees were too thickly grown to permit the passage of armored vehicles, so the seizure of the Bois Jacques was assigned, as everyone had somehow expected, to the 501st Parachute Infantry.

Within the regiment the mission was reassigned to the 2nd and 3rd Battalions, with the 1st Battalion in regimental reserve.

The commander of the 2nd Battalion, Colonel Homan, had been evacuated with trench foot to a rear hospital. In his absence the battalion executive officer, Major William Pelham, was in command. Major Pelham came from Montgomery, Alabama. He was a tall, slow-speaking officer with a great jaw, a deep-lined leonine face and a caustic intelligence. His flair for sarcasm sometimes infuriated the enlisted men, who were unable to reply in kind, but like many men who employed sarcasm unconsciously, he did so because he was impatient with human weakness. If human weaknesses had been less common, he would have been a popular man.

The attack into the Bois Jacques was scheduled to begin early on the morning of January 3rd. For some reason, however, the offensive was postponed for a day. Delay of an attack was like a stay of execution, but Pelham accepted the news with as much philosophy as he had at his command. His own men and those of Griswold's battalion dug in for the day and night.

In the disastrous action that followed, Griswold's 3rd Battalion did as much as Pelham's group. Both units accomplished their missions, both found themselves in an unexpectedly perilous situation; and both prevented the enemy from taking advantage of a serious mistake. The actions of the 2nd Battalion were chosen for this chapter only because the 2nd Battalion was on the open flank where the enemy counter-attacked, and not because the 2nd Battalion had the harder job. Casualties were about equally divided between both units.

Shortly before the scheduled hour of the attack on the morning of January 3rd, the enemy concentrated every available mortar on the battalion assembly areas. The barrage was so intense that fifty to sixty rounds came down each minute—an explosion every second. This was demoralizing enough, and the 24-hour delay had made the men impatient to get the job done.

"The 3rd Battalion attacked on a 500-yard front astride the unimproved road running north and south through the Bois Jacques. The 2nd Battalion, maintaining contact with the 3rd Battalion on its left, also attacked on a 500-yard front. Each battalion was supported by a platoon of .50-caliber anti-aircraft guns."* Task Force O'Hara was in a position of mobile reserve, protecting the east flank of the regiment.

2

The morning was clouded over. A mist had hung on the land since daybreak, and even at noon it was still and heavy. When the men crossed the railroad tracks and entered the Bois Jacques, the darkness under the trees was like late evening. Mist shrouded the snow-laden pines, and men's breaths frosted in the air. Small-arms fire from the alerted enemy was audible directly ahead, but the flashes from the guns were invisible. Shortly afterwards, the opposing fire became intense—and as soon as the enemy became certain that the paratroopers were attacking, they called for artillery support.

*From the 501st "After Action" reports.

Shells striking the trees exploded over the men's heads, slicing shrapnel in all directions. Split tree trunks and branches crashed down, scattering snow from the branches like a blizzard. As the barrage increased, the noise made shouted commands inaudible. Wounded men lay on the snow, their blood incredibly red on the frozen white. So thick was the fog that the advancing men sometimes stumbled into fortified German automatic-weapons positions at a distance of a few yards.

Staff Sergeant Herschel Parks of Monticello, Maine, observed from his position in a foxhole that the company radio operator was working without cover in the open. Radio communications with battalion and regiment were vital to the success of the attack, so Sergeant Parks climbed out of his own foxhole and ordered the radio operator to take cover. A few minutes later Sergeant Parks was dead.*

Soon after the entry of the two battalions into the Bois Jacques, both units were heavily engaged. In the 3rd Battalion, Captain Stanley's company suffered fifteen casualties in as many minutes. Sergeant Frank Sciaccotti of Spokane, Washington, one of the men of his company, crawled back to Stanley to report the situation. Sciaccotti's face was a mass of torn flesh, the blood running out of the wound and down his clothes. Through two whole and articulate lips he gave Stanley his report and then said calmly, "Captain, is it all right if I get this mess in my face cleaned up?"

Another man's hand had been blown off. He squatted on his knees under the thundering tree-bursts and reported the platoon situation as calmly as if he had been in garrison.

Stanley moved forward in short dashes to the front line. When he reached the extreme forward positions, he dove into a ditch. Near him a sergeant was on his elbows, coughing up blood. A captain from another company had been shot through the lungs. Stanley raised his head and looked across the road—squarely into German foxholes ten yards away. He sent his support platoon to attack the enemy position on the flank, then pinned them down from the front with two machine guns, and presently that group of Germans surrendered.

Examining their positions, Stanley found each foxhole oc-

---

*Parks was posthumously awarded a Silver Star for this act—one of the finest examples of deliberate, premeditated bravery in the history of the regiment, by one of its best—and best loved—soldiers.

cupied by two or more soldiers. The holes were only four feet apart, and around them were more wounded and dead than he had ever seen. The total of prisoners was seventy.

But of one of the American platoons, which had begun its attack with twenty-nine men and one officer, only eight were left.

3

At just about this time a gap developed in the front lines of the 3rd Battalion, and elements of two companies lost contact with each other. Lieutenant Forney, executive officer of Company G, went forward with one of his enlisted men to repair the breach. Orders of the previous day had stipulated that company executive officers remain at their company command posts unless the commander was killed, so when Forney successfully re-established contact along the battalion line, he turned around and waded back through the deep snow. He followed a different path from the one he had taken on the way out, and he was several paces in advance of his enlisted man.

Joseph Forney came from Berkeley Springs, West Virginia. He was a self-contained and rather humorous officer who loved good food, warmth, and comfort. Well-adjusted to life, he could forego such pleasures readily enough, but all through that wintry siege at Bastogne he had dreamed of a time when he could relax again beside a warm fire, after a full meal.

Walking back to his command post, he emerged from the woods into a small clearing about seventy-five yards wide. He floundered through the snow to the other side, still followed by his enlisted man. Where the forest took up again, the pines had grown so close together that there was darkness beneath. Forney was behind his own lines, so it never occurred to him to be cautious. He pushed aside the first snow-laden boughs and stepped in.

Something exploded in his face. Simultaneously there was a crash on his helmet, a sickening snap of bullets, and a violent smash against his arm when a bullet struck his carbine. He was knocked sideward on his face. Behind him, the enlisted man dropped unhurt in the deep snow. As the man inched back to the first defilade, he saw the shadowy figures of German soldiers sieze Forney and drag him deeper into the concealment of the woods.

The blows of the bullets passing through the upper part of the helmet, and the crash of the carbine against his body, had dazed Forney momentarily. He thought that he was wounded. Nothing else occurred to him just then, not even the astonishing fact that he was a prisoner of war.

When the German soldiers had dragged him deeper into the forest, they let him lie in the snow under the trees. Forney was wearing a German pistol belt and a Luger, both of which he had picked up that morning as souvenirs. As soon as the German enlisted men noticed it, one of them grabbed the gun out of its holster and displayed it to the others. All of the group began to talk excitedly, and the man who was holding the pistol in his hand frowned several times. Forney, who decided that he was going to be shot, lay still.

Meanwhile, the battle went on.

4

At the end of the first hour Pelham's men had moved about 350 yards. The cost had been so heavy that every man not actively engaged in fighting was voluntarily evacuating the wounded. The enemy shellfire had not diminished, and the wounded men had to be dragged or carried back across the snow under the continuing shriek of high-explosives. Selflessly the cooks and clerks and staff men went out again and again to bring in the wounded.

Pelham was in the snow about a hundred yards in advance of his command post, when he received a radio message from Lieutenant Verne W. Mertz of Fairmont, Minnesota, who was with the light machine-gun platoon to Pelham's rear.

"Men are coming across this open field to our right," he radioed. "They're about a quarter of a mile away."

Pelham radioed back: "The 50th Armored is out there."

A little silence. Then the voice on the radio crackled. "I have a 50th Armored man with me here. He says his men aren't out there. They've pulled back."

This was the first indication to Pelham that anything had gone wrong. Flank protection by other units was the responsibility of higher command. If the 50th Armored had pulled back, then the flank was open.

"All right," Pelham radioed to Mertz. "Get those machine guns out to the edge of the woods and see what it is."

A few minutes later Captain Phillips, then commanding Company E, also reported men coming in on his flank. Phillips was holding Company E in reserve. He made his way to where Pelham was sitting.

"This looks like the beginning of a mess," he said. "Do you want me to do anything about it?"

Pelham told him to take the reserve company to the exposed flank. By the time Phillips had done this, and Mertz had also disposed his machine guns along the edge of the woods, the small figures on the field had opened fire. That settled the doubt.

Accompanying the Germans were several half-tracks. These drew up in defilade and poured 20mm. fire directly onto the edge of the woods. Several German tanks joined the half-tracks and began, in company with the enemy infantrymen, a gradual envelopment of the entire American position.

Languidly sarcastic, Pelham notified regiment that the unit was in danger of being wiped out. There is no record of Ewell's subsequent conversation at division. But after a while Ewell radioed to Pelham:

"Send somebody to the C.P.* We'll get you some tanks."

Pelham dispatched a battalion guide in a jeep. Meanwhile, the battalion, having reached its objective, was a thousand yards inside the Bois Jacques. By that time the entire left flank had been enveloped in fire.

At the edge of the woods, every available cook and clerk joined the infantrymen under Mertz and Phillps. As the Germans reinforced their own positions, the action became heavy. The German tanks and half-tracks had very little cover, but even from their exposed positions they were not affected by most of the small-arms fire. They were shooting point-blank into the fringe of the woods. The paratroopers who were wounded stayed where they were and went on fighting, but before long the snow beneath the trees was splattered with blood.

---

*Ewell's command post was in the forest, too, but his passion for leading from in front gave the men and the staff some uncomfortable times.

Angry at his own helplessness, Lieutenant MacGregor led several men of a bazooka team out of the concealment of the woods towards the half-tracks. Crawling forward until he was only a hundred yards away from the enemy positions, MacGregor successfully knocked out one of the armored vehicles and disabled another. An enlisted man, running forward to the disabled machine, killed the remainder of its crew and, manning the .50 caliber machine gun inside, swept the other German vehicles with their own fire.

At about the same moment, deeper in the woods to the rear, the battalion mess sergeant arrived. According to prearranged plan, he was bringing a hot turkey dinner to the 2nd Battalion troops. This comic interlude was scarcely an interruption; Pelham acridly sent the turkey back to the rear.

The battalion guide who had been sent to bring up the tanks had been gone about forty-five minutes. The situation was becoming critical. Pelham, infuriated, telephoned regiment again. The voice at the other end—it was not Colonel Ewell—said, "Your runner's here, but not the tanks."

Pelham started back himself. Half-way to the regiment, he met his guide with the armored vehicles. Turning around, he took the group to a rise of ground where they had a view of the out-flanking enemy troops. A tank was in sight a quarter of a mile away, a small black rectangle on the white snow.

"Theirs or ours?" asked the tank commander.

Pelham didn't know. So he took his jeep and drove down to get a closer look. Fired upon, he returned to the tank commander on the high ground and in five minutes saw the tank "burning beautifully" in the clear, white, frozen expanse.

By the time Pelham returned to his men, the casualties had become so heavy that many of the more recently wounded were out on the exposed snow under the desolated trees. The Germans seemed well supplied with ammunition, and even by then—four hours after the barrage had started—the heavy-caliber shells still were coming in. As the early winter darkness gathered prematurely under the trees, word came back to Pelham that his men at the flank would either have to give way or be overrun.

The engagement had become a defeat. Ewell ordered both battalions to withdraw.

5

Forney, who had not been shot, was about ten or fifteen miles behind the German lines. It was a very dark night. All he could make of his final destination was a few darkened Belgian houses. Inside of one of them was a warm room, where some Belgian civilians were feeding a group of German soldiers. Forney was taken into an adjoining office, which contained a huge bed, a hot stove, several chairs and a desk littered with papers.

Two German intelligence officers were in the room. Both spoke English, though with a British accent. They were the type that Forney had seen only in movies: one was tall, dark, heavy-set, and wore horn-rimmed glasses; the other, who was shorter, also wore glasses, though with much heavier lenses. The latter reminded Forney of Peter Lorre. Both men were arrogant and overbearing, but at the outset of the interview they were stiffly courteous.

"Empty your pockets on the table," said the one who looked like Peter Lorre.

Forney did so. His wallet, with several hundred dollars in French currency, a small black address book, and a K ration were all that he had left, his wrist watch and gloves had been taken from him along the way. Both officers looked through the wallet and book and broke open the K ration.

"You are an officer," said the tall one. "You will be treated as an officer."

Forney inclined his head.

"Now," said the man. "What division were you in?"

"I can't answer that," said Forney.

There was a little pause. "Are you a paratrooper?"

"I can't answer that," Forney repeated.

The German officer persisted. At length Forney, tired of repeating, "I can't answer that," said nothing at all. The taller officer put his face very close and, in a snarling voice, said, "If you don't want to answer our questions now, we have means of making you answer."

Forney said nothing.

"I will show you how much we know," said the man, straightening up. "You are in the 277th Quartermaster Battalion. You were captured during your attack on Noville. You are a new officer, who just came up to take command of your men, and you got lost.''

For the first time since his capture—and for the last time for half a year—Forney was slightly amused. But he made no sign.

"Were you parachuted into Bastogne?"

Silence.

"Some of the men were parachuted into the town," said the German, "and others were brought by trucks. You weren't dropped; you were trucked there."

This childish procedure went on for quite some time. At length one of the men said, "You can put your things back in your pockets now."

Forney was satisfied that neither of them knew a great deal. He was surprised to get his belongings back. As he was restoring them to his pockets, however, he noticed the tall officer studying his feet. "Take off your galoshes," the man said.

"No," said Forney loudly, "I won't take them off. You can't have them."

There was a dead silence. To his amazement the officer said nothing at all.

All three went into the outside room. There Forney saw two other American prisoners, one of whom he recognized as a sergeant of his company named Harry Plesivich. Plesivich looked at Forney and started to speak, but Forney shook his head slightly and the sergeant looked away.

The second American soldier appeared to be in great pain, so the taller intelligence officer, after asking Forney whether he knew any of the men and getting a negative reply, opened the wounded man's shirt and exposed a wide patch of crimson skin—evidently, Forney guessed, the effect of a near shellburst.

"Does it hurt?" asked the German officer.

"Yes."

"We'll fix you up," replied the German. "Our medics will take good care of you. You'll get all the medical aid you need." He paused. "You're in the 28th Division, aren't you?"

"No," said the man. "The 101st."

With all the authority at his command, Forney said, "Tell them nothing but your name, rank and serial number, soldier."

Both interrogators swung on him, shouting: "You're a prisoner of war! Keep quiet unless you're asked to talk!" Screaming a tirade of abuse, they drove him to the other side of the room, then quickly drew Plesivich into the office Forney had just left.

Forney hoped earnestly that Plesivich had been well trained.

Back in the neighborhood of Bastogne, the exhausted survivors of the 2nd and 3rd Battalions trailed into a reserve area and threw down their equipment. It was almost dawn. Their faces were streaked with blood and sweat. Their clothes were soaked from lying hour after hour in the snow. They were too tired to speak.

But at the 2nd Battalion Major Pelham's mess sergeant, who had patiently waited all night for this opportunity, triumphantly delivered for breakfast the steaming hot meal that he had saved since the previous day.

It was turkey and all the trimmings.

45
Two Down . . .

Action continued for several days. There was severe fighting as the lines pushed out toward Noville again. The Bois Jacques was finally taken, this time including its flanks. And one morning a little sign appeared on the main street of Bastogne, not far from the new civil affairs office, and when the battered airborne troops found it there, they knew that the seized Bastogne had passed forever into military history. The sign read: "OFF LIMITS TO NEW TROOPS."

Gentle snows had fallen periodically on Bastogne, and the torn ruins of the shellfire and the German bombings had been covered with a clean whiteness that made them seem older than they were. We were a little tired of Bastogne and were ready to move on. It didn't matter where. No hint of the great offensives then being planned had reached the men. To us the outlook was only a new town somewhere, a new area of

Europe, new dangers, modifications of the old discomforts.
All of us had changed greatly in our mental outlook since
the—by comparison—bright days in England when Brereton
had reviewed our assembled files.

We had become veteran troops. And in the process we had
discovered a curious truth: that veteran troops were the least
assured of them all. We had no cockiness. We pretended
nothing. We had no memories and no future; we lived wholly
and completely in the present. Prolonged exposure to immediate dangers, the repeated experience of seeing our friends'
bodies torn brutally apart, of bringing the same violence and
sudden death to other human beings, of seldom washing,
seldom really sleeping, and never waking with any hope
beyond the hour—these things had reduced our spirits to the
same bare skeleton as our bodies, awake only to peril or to
animal comforts. In features grimed with months of dirt, our
eyes were strangely luminous. We seldom smiled. The faint
light of peace had not yet begun to dispel the gloom of those
days; meanwhile, we were forever removed from inconse-
quentialities. Combat wounded all men, even those unscratched,
for it set them a little apart ever afterwards from their own
lives.

2

On the morning of January 10th, almost a month after the
occupation of Bastogne, Colonel Ewell was riding in a jeep
to the battalion positions at Recogne.

Colonel Ewell's driver was Corporal Joe A. Warner. His
bodyguard was Private Murphy. The two enlisted men knew
they were approaching the front lines, but they didn't know
that they were already under enemy observation from the high
ground around Noville. All three failed to observe a German
self-propelled artillery piece which had come up over the
crest of ground to the east.

Heavy-caliber shells from close range make a *"whisssht-
bang!"*— the explosion following almost instantly on the
shriek of the projectile. At the first explosion Warner jammed
on the brakes. He, Murphy and Ewell dove for a ditch on the
side of the road and crawled away from one another.

The shells were striking within a radius of a hundred feet.

Murphy flattened himself in the ditch. One shell exploded so close that he was shaken up.

"Murphy," called Ewell in his unexcited drawl, "I've been hit."

Murphy turned in the ditch and crawled down to him. Ewell had an ugly wound along his leg.

Somehow the two enlisted men got him into the jeep and away. Next day Ewell was evacuated to the rear, and Colonel Robert Ballard, his executive officer, became the third regimental commander of the 501st Parachute Infantry.

Colonel Julian J. Ewell had shared, with Colonel Kinnard, the greatest love of the greatest number. Johnson had been a man of color and fire, but Ewell, succeeding him, had commanded by understatement. A man of reserve, he had been one of those rare individuals whose favorable opinion was coveted by other men.

His dignity shamed officers and soldiers alike into a formality not theirs by nature. He spoke only when he had something to say, and then directly to the point—but he had a dry wit and, on occasion, could be professionally humorous.

He expected intelligence from everyone. At a staff meeting, in reply to some questions put to him by a junior officer, he once remarked: "Lieutenant, I am not interested in your questions. I want your recommendations." This insistence upon the importance of other men's judgment endeared him to the soldiers. A driver, newly assigned to him in Holland, enquired whether the colonel liked to be driven fast or slow. "I expect you know how to drive this vehicle better than I do," was the reply.

Ewell never looked worried, even when things went wrong. He never showed fear, and he remained as cool under fire as in the celler of a command post or on the stage of a lecture hall. But what set him apart from other men was the depth of his reserve. He never communicated his intentions to others to test their worth; he acted on approval or disapproval from within himself. Self-confidence does not come from making decisions; it comes from making decisions that turn out right, and if Ewell had an exceptional degree of self-confidence, this was because his decisions had an uncanny rightness.

McAuliffe had said, "He was the right man for the spot I put him in." But the soldiers and officers who had helped to make that statement true for him could say it in fewer words. "He was the right man."

Nine days later, in a furious blizzard, the division quit Bastogne. It was January 19, 1945. Though nobody knew it at the time, Bastogne had been the death rattle of the *Wehrmacht*.

PART IV

It was not peace. It was only silence.

46
Germanic France

The extraordinary German salient into Belgium had been brought to a halt four miles east of the Meuse. During the month of January, while heavy Allied air support bombed and strafed the retreating columns of troops, the Germans were pushed steadily back. Stories of a massacre of American soldiers at Malmédy reached the men, temporarily giving them that blind anger against the enemy which the information and education program of the army had never succeeded in doing. By the end of the month all the ground lost to the German divisions of von Rundstedt had been regained, and the war was almost back where it had been in December.

But not quite. The failure of the Ardennes offensive had cost the *Wehrmacht* the greater part of its reserve forces. Many of the divisions which escaped into Germany were broken and demoralized. On the snow-covered roads of the Ardennes were the tanks, half-tracks, mobile artillery and trucks which had started for Antwerp and never reached there. Thousands of German prisoners were in American hands—one of them plaintively complaining: "They didn't issue any food. They told us we'd capture your supplies in a day. I haven't eaten in a week."

And the German break-through had taught the Allies one lesson. While we gathered strength for our last great offensive, we would have to watch the quiet sectors of our own lines.

One of these quiet sectors was in the neighborhood of the Vosges Mountains near Strasbourg in Alsace-Lorraine, where French and American troops jointly shared a polite interchange of artillery fire with the Germans. Not much military confidence could be placed in the ill-equipped and ill-clad French soldiers, who seemed to be better at slap-dash than at the dull chore of holding on. So the 101st Airborne Division was sent south from Belgium, like a tired old plug horse, to an area just adjacent to the French.

Quietly, the by-then famous division disappeared from the newspapers at home.

2

The Alsatian houses were tinted pastel. In the deep snow they seemed beautiful to us. The windows were shuttered with tinted blinds, and gables overhung the doorways.

Advance parties of officers and enlisted men preceded the truck convoys to mark billets for the troops in the village homes. The regimental adjutant's experiences were typical. Captain Degenaar knocked on the door of a likely looking house. Inside there was a rattling of chains.

"Wer ist da?" said a frightened voice.

"American!" shouted Degenaar.

Dubiously, an old woman opened the door. She was small, incredibly thin and timid. *"Was willst du?"*

Degenaar looked at the officer with him. "Are these people French or German?"

"Beats me."

"Tell 'em we want to look at their house."

"How the hell am *I* going to tell them?"

Degenaar looked baffled. Then he gestured at the woman. "We want to use your house for billets," he shouted. (Americans always speak to foreigners at the top of their lungs.)

"Ja," said the woman nervously, not moving.

"BILLETS!" shouted Degenaar. "BILLETS!" When the woman made no further move, he pushed the door open and walked in.

The front hallway led to a kitchen, a dim chamber illuminated by a single bare electric lamp. Except for the adjacent barn, it was the only warm place in the house. In a front room, lamp shades with colored tassels, and furniture as poorly stuffed as it was moth-eaten, gave the place a forlornly mid-Victorian air. No fire was burning in the queer, square, porcelain-decorated and (as everyone soon found out) inadequate stove.

"*Parlez-vous français?*" queried a whiskered and red-faced old man, evidently the woman's husband.

"We'll use this front room for officers," shouted Degenaar. "Officers. Understand? Officers!"

"Ah," nodded the old man, beaming. "*Officiers!*"

"That's right."

Plucking the captain on the sleeve, the old man led him to the bedroom. The bed was pillowed in tremendous quilts; the sheets were white and clean; on the table was a lighted candle. "*Pour les officiers,*" announced the old man, bowing.

Degenaar handed around a few K-ration cigarettes. Then he pointed to his wrist watch: "Five o'clock!" he shouted. "*Officiers!* Five o'clock."

"*Ja, ja,*" the old man beamed, putting the cigarettes carefully into his shirt pocket. He and his wife followed Degenaar into the front hall, apologizing with bows and scrapes when Degenaar accidentally opened the door into the barn. They were still apologizing, still bowing, still wringing their hands when he chalked "S-1" across the front door and walked away.

That was how it went for everyone.

3

Meanwhile, the troops were on their way. Early in the morning of January 21st they scrambled into *portes*—the same huge trailer trucks which had brought them to Bastogne. This time, however, there were even fewer vehicles than before and, when the loading was completed, sixty and seventy men were crowded aboard each trailer.

The soldiers were good-humored about it at first. Dave Hart wanted to stand up so he could see the country. Sergeant Suarez found an empty oil can in the forward corner of his truck and settled himself firmly, not guessing that, before the journey ended, he would bitterly regret not having stretched out flat on the bottom layer of bodies. Other men, like Hart, stood up along the slats of the truck sides to watch the passing scenery.

By the middle of the first afternoon the interminable joggling and the below-freezing temperatures had settled everyone into a melancholy, half-humorous discontent.

"Move over, will you? That's my can you're sitting on."

"The hell it is! It's Joe's feet."

"You guys are lucky. I can't even sit down."

"Whose head is this?"

"Leave it alone, will you? It's all I got left."

"The heroes of Bastogne! Cattle—"

"Cattle! Hell, man, they don't treat cattle like this!"

"They oughta make the generals ride with us."

As evening came on, disconsolate and blue over the empty, snow-covered fields of France, we persuaded the drivers to cover the open trailers with tarpaulins. But when the tarpaulins had been roped into place, no one was able to stand up and stretch. Those who had drawn their legs up along the sides were unable to straighten out; those who, like Suarez, had found something on which to sit were unable to find room in which to lie down—and their heads struck against the flapping canvas. Someone discovered that there were not enough rations for breakfast. And to fray the edges of our tempers still more, the convoy frequently came to long and meaningless halts in open, moonlit fields or at the edges of deserted towns. A few of us were able to sleep; the remainder cursed, froze, prayed for the journey to end. And when the long columns stopped at a barn about two o'clock in the morning, while the cooks of one of the companies prepared hot coffee, at least half of us were too miserable to get out of the trucks.

Dawn came. Still the journey continued.

But a little later in the day, when the tarpaulins had been pulled aside, the convoy stopped at a small French town where there was a Red Cross clubmobile and two American girls. The natural high spirits of the American soldiers came back with a rush. And when a little old Frenchman who was ringing a bell walked down the street toward the crowds, and stopped on the sidewalk to harangue the soldiers in meaningless but eloquent French, they cheered and applauded him and shouted to the villagers:

"The Town Crier has spoken!"

The old man must have understood. For he straightened his back, gave a quick, stern nod of approval at the young Americans, and stomped off down the road in the snow, his whole attitude eloquent of the dignity of man.

4

Unknown to us at this time, the Allied forces were slowly building up along the German line. To the supreme commander and his staff, the future, which we saw through a glass darkly, was quite clear. Spring would tell the story. Supplies from America had reached their peak the year before and now were pouring into Europe in such quantities as to make the war bond posters an understatement. Tens of thousands of bomber planes and fighters were in the air. Millions of pounds of high explosives were stacked in the dumps for future use. The Germans at Cologne were fighting savagely, like animals at bay, but even animals could be flooded out.

On the maps and aerial photographs marked *"Top Secret"* at SHAEF, staff officers studied the areas surrounding the Ruhr. The 17th Airborne Division was polished up and readied. The 13th Airborne Division left the United States for France. Once again, and for the last time, there was the whisper of a distant drum. . . .

But along the front lines of Alsace-Lorraine our lives were comparatively quiet.

The regimental post office was set up a few hundred yards down the main street of Keffendorf from the command post. At that time—late January and early February—the majority of the Christmas packages from home, delayed by the Ardennes offensive, began to reach the regiment. The postal clerks were kept busy. Fruit cake was the most common gift, but a number of people at home were imaginative enough to send saltines, chopped olives, canned shrimp, caviar or mayonnaise: and if a soldier had a good many friends, and could succeed in looking hungry enough, it was not hard for him to eat well.

Hot food for the men on the lines was prepared in the rear and trucked forward in what the army calls "marmite cans." Observers on the outpost line of resistance and soldiers who were in extreme forward positions on the line were generally relieved so they could go back and eat. The men were heartily sick of chopped pork and eggs, cheese, and hash, which were the staple items of K rations. In general they were eating well, however, and all they lacked was a front-line jam factory, like the one at Driel in Holland.

A static front-line position is not what most people imagine it to be. The closer a visitor approaches to the Germans, the less can he see. Hidden in woods or in defiladed position are small dugouts, generally marking company command posts. Farther forward, individual foxholes take the place of dugouts. And if the area is under enemy surveillance, even those holes are invisible. At last, crawling forward to the outpost line of resistance—the extreme forward position of a line— nothing can be seen at all except the open ground to the front, perhaps a ridge of trees in the distance, and low hills beyond. No one is shooting at anyone else, and for the greater part of each day no artillery falls.

But a soldier has only to stand up to get killed.

47
The Sudden Spring

Spring came to Europe that year like the sudden grace of God. One morning in mid-February the air was milder than it had ever been before, even in the summertime of England. Under a bright sun the snow began to melt. Within a space of hours water ran down through all the village streets, the white blanket dissolved from the hills, and pigeons took up a contented muttering on gables and rooftops surprisingly green with moss.

It was odd how everyone's heart lifted. Perhaps we realized for the first time that we had not really left our lives behind us after all; we had just become adjusted to a need for eternal endurance. Men shouted to each other cheerily on the roads. They waited in the chow lines more patiently than before. In a few days the water from the melted snows had collected into deep pools and the roads began to bake dry. In the courtyards there was a pleasant homey odor of fertilizer. We took off our woolen underwear, discarded our scarves and

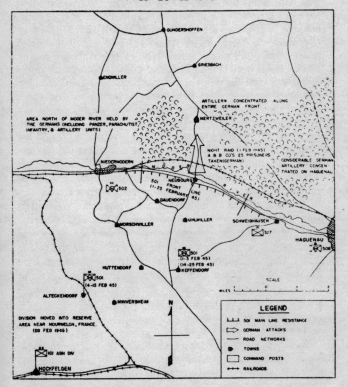

HAGUENAU, FRANCE
1 FEB- 28 FEB 1945

ARTILLERY CONCENTRATED ALONG ENTIRE GERMAN FRONT

AREA NORTH OF MODER RIVER HELD BY THE GERMANS (INCLUDING PANZER, PARACHUTIST, INFANTRY, & ARTILLERY UNITS)

MERTZWILER

NIGHT RAID (1 FEB 1945) A & B CO'S 25 PRISONERS TAKEN (GERMAN)

CONSIDERABLE GERMAN ARTILLERY CONCEN- TRATED ON HAGUENAU

GUNDERSHOFFEN

GRIESBACH

ENGWILLER

NIEDERMODERN

502

501
NEUBOURG FRONT (1-25 FEBRUARY LINE 45)

DAUENDORF

UHLWILLER

SCHWEIGHAUSEN

327

HAGUENAU

506

MORSCHWILLER

501
(1-3 FEB 45)
(14-25 FEB 45)
KEFFENDORF

HUTTENDORF

501
(4-13 FEB 45)

ALTECKENDORF

MINVERSHEIM

DIVISION MOVED INTO RESERVE AREA NEAR MOURMELON, FRANCE. (28 FEB 1945)

101 ABN DIV

MOCKFELDEN

SCALE

MILES

N

LEGEND
501 MAIN LINE RESISTANCE
GERMAN ATTACKS
ROAD NETWORKS
TOWNS
COMMAND POSTS
RAILROADS.

parachute silk and violated the standing order to carry weapons at all times.

A hurry-up call went to the graves registration crew. The melting snow in the rolling, partially wooded countryside of the front lines had uncovered German dead. And in the hot sun . . .

There was peace in the air of Lorraine that spring. Something which had not been in the world since 1931 was stealing back again, morning after morning. Perhaps it was not peace, but only weariness, the weariness of people sick to death of fighting each other. Years would have to pass before real peace came to Europe again. Yet in the sight of rolling French fields hazed with green, and villages and church spires in the soft light for miles across the countryside, and the blue mountains of the Vosges like clouds on the far horizon, there was an illusion of peace that was real and satisfying.

Spring was the signal. The division was withdrawn from Lorraine and moved by train to a new camp site outside the familiar old town of Mourmelon-le-Grand, where the sun had made the limestone roads blinding white with dust. The first week in March a gigantic bombing mission of 7,000 planes shattered the greater part of Germany. By March 7th the city of Cologne had fallen to the American soldiers. Soon afterward an adroit reconnaissance party in the vanguard of the 1st Army moved up the left bank of the Rhine through the old university town of Bonn to Remagen and seized the bridge intact. Once across the Rhine, the Americans spread out, took the *Autobahn* that ran south to Munich, and began a drive to the north. Hastily the Germans withdrew part of their strength on other sectors of the line to reinforce the path of the new threat. But it was too late.

The roll of drums was louder.

2

At the pine forest encampment outside Mourmelon-le-Grand the paratroopers felt a vague sense of foreboding. Not far away, the 17th Airborne Division had just been alerted. And General Eisenhower had addressed the 101st again.

The occasion was the award of the Presidential Unit Citation for the action at Bastogne. The ribbon, which was blue and gold, had never before been awarded to an entire division.

It was a fine, sunny day. As in England before the Holland campaign, the division was lined up on a wide field outside the camp. But this time the band was playing and the battle streamers were flying.

While the troops stood at ease, the friendly general stepped to the microphone. The only sounds on the field were the flapping of the standards and the far-off murmur of transport engines warming up. His words carried to the men drawn up before him:

It is a great personal honor for me to be here today to take part in a ceremony unique in American history. Never before has a full division been cited by the War Department, in the name of the President, for gallantry in action. This day marks the beginning of a new tradition in the American Army. With that tradition, therefore, will always be associated the name of the 101st Airborne Division and of Bastogne.

Yet you men, because you are soldiers of proved valor and of experience, would be the last to claim that you are the bravest and the best. All the way from where the Marines are fighting on Iwo Jima through the Philippines and southeast Asia, on through the Mediterranean, and along this great front and on the Russian frontiers, are going forward day-by-day those battles, sustained by the valor of you and other Allied units, that are beating this enemy to his knees. They are proving once and for all that dictatorship cannot produce better soldiers than can aroused democracy. In many of these actions are units that have performed with unexcelled brilliance. So far as I know, there may be many among you that would not rate Bastogne as your bitterest battle. Yet, it is entirely fitting and appropriate that you should be cited for that particular battle.

It happened to be one of those occasions when the position itself was of the utmost importance to the Allied forces. You in reserve were hurried forward and told to hold that position. All the elements of drama—battle drama—were there. You were cut off, surrounded. Only valor, complete self-confidence in yourselves and in your leaders, a knowledge that you were well trained, and only the determination to win could sustain soldiers under these conditions. You were given a marvellous

288 FOUR STARS OF HELL

opportunity and you met every test. You have become a
fitting symbol on which the United States, all the citizens of
the United Nations, can say to their soldiers today, "We are
proud of you" as it is my great privilege to say to you here
today, to the 101st Division and all its attached units, "I am
awfully proud of you."

With this great honor goes also a certain responsibility. Just
as you are the beginning of a new tradition, you must realize,
each of you, that from now on the spotlight will beat on you
with particular brilliance. Whenever you say you are a soldier
of the 101st Division, everybody, whether it is on the street in
the city or the front lines, will expect unusual conduct of you.
I know that you will meet every test of the future like you met
it at Bastogne.

Good luck and God be with you.

As the soldiers marched past the reviewing stand, they
could hear the echo of those last words. General Eisenhower
had said them before, they remembered. Before Normandy.
Before Holland.*

3

Meanwhile, what of Joe Forney?

Forney was at a permanent prison camp at Hammelberg,
Germany. He lived in a one-story, wood-frame barrack with
about forty other Americans. He slept on the bottom level of
a three-tiered group of wooden bunks. He had been issued
two of the blue-green German blankets. Straw stuffed in
burlap bags comprised the mattresses.

As the weeks had passed, Forney, like all the others, had
grown more starved and more haggard. Continued hunger had
worn the veneer of civilization thin. Everyone's temper was
short. In the evenings, when a ration of bread was issued, one
group at a time toasted theirs over the stove. If any man took

*Of all the citizens of a country, soldiers are usually the least patriotic. The
reason is obvious: they are the object of their country's patriotism. They have no
example higher than themselves to which they can turn—and they are not especially
impressed by themselves. It is foolish to remind them of Old Glory. If *they* are not
Old Glory, nothing is.

longer than his allotted time, all the men in the barracks grew angry. The officers' clothes and skins were filthy. The flesh had begun to recede around their cheekbones and in their eye sockets. Their eyes were a little glassy. As the days passed, more and more men fainted at roll calls. Those who were really sick were put in a sick room which the captured medical officers had devised. By deposition to the camp commandant, the medical men had secured a little extra coal for that place, and a little extra food.

The latrine was at the far end of the compound. During Allied air raids no one was allowed out of the barracks, even to go to the latrine. After a while the air raids became so frequent that the prisoners, through their own elected commander, requested permission of the commandant to go to the latrine, one at a time, during alerts. This was granted. A week later a German guard shot and killed one of the officers on his way across the compound. The man lay on the cobblestones for several hours before the all-clear sounded. The camp commander explained apologetically that the guard had been on temporary duty in the compound and was not aware of the new ruling.

The American officers organized themselves into squads and platoons, with a commander for each barrack. The officer in charge of all the barracks was a full colonel. Nobody liked him very much: he lived with a few other high-ranking officers in a separate room and was very seldom forceful in making demands of the Germans.

Despite the freezing cold of early February, most of the officers tried to shave each day. This was not so much for their own sake as for the sake of keeping up appearances before the Germans. Forney observed, however, that a few of the men didn't care. Almost without exception, they were the ones with the least education—men who had become officers because of vanity, or native energy, or simply a desire for power. Day by day they became more animal.

One other officer from the 501st was in Hammelberg. He was First Lieutenant Bob Harrison, from Arizona. He and Forney became good friends. They attended most of the lectures together. And whenever Harrison received a Red Cross package he shared it with Forney—a gesture so completely civilized that Forney never forgot it.

The lectures were organized to pass the time. An officer

who had worked on Wall Street before the war lectured on the functioning of the New York Stock Exchange. Two insurance brokers took turns explaining insurance; there were also a geologist, a county agent who knew agriculture and another officer who had been a teacher of English and who lectured on literature.

One happy day a shipment of Red Cross parcels arrived. The Germans allocated half a package to each officer. This contained a ration of cigarettes, powdered coffee, sugar, and canned meat. Heating the coffee at the stove that night, the officers talked hopefully of the progress of the war. They felt almost cheerful. If they could only resist their own slow starvation, they were sure the Allied lines would reach their camp. When a group of American prisoners of war arrived from the north, one of the newcomers had a radio which he had contrived to put together out of scraps and abandoned parts. He kept it in pieces during the day and reassembled it each night. The officers were thus enabled to hear the news broadcasts of the BBC. These brought a wild hope. The bridge at Remagen had been seized—Cologne had fallen—the Germans had begun to retreat!

In the midst of this European debacle, though before the final assault of the Rhine, the paratroopers in France were calmly going on leaves and furloughs. After five months in the combat zones they felt they deserved them. Perhaps the calmness was only apparent, but at any rate, each day before the Rhine jump, truckloads of soldiers drove hilariously out of Mourmelon in the direction of Brussels, or England, or the Riviera, or Paris.

All of us realized that we were taking these leaves and furloughs on a knife-edge. There was the unmistakable atmosphere of climax on the air; at any moment our castles of relaxation would tumble around us. But this certainty only deepened our sense of enjoyment, just as the dark moments that had ticked away audibly in the days before the invasion of Normandy had deepened our awareness of life.

Besides, it happened to be springtime. It was springtime in Brussels and in London and on the Riviera.

It was springtime in Paris, too. . . .

48

La Vie Parisienne!

A soldier who had a forty-eight-hour pass to Paris was generally billeted at Rainbow Corner on the rue Castiglione, a block or two from the Opera House. The Rainbow Corner was an old and rather shoddy hotel with French desk clerks who spoke fair English and who for the most part looked down on the soldiers. There may have been some excuse for this; soldiers on pass in Paris were not always on their best behavior. But at the Grand Hotel on the Place de l'Opéra itself, a compromise seemed to have been reached between the natural dignity of a French concierge and the natural lack of it among the American soldiers: in general, the atmosphere at the Grand was a good deal happier. In the gold dining room ordinary G.I.s could feel like officers. Fred Waring's band (less Fred Waring) played there nightly. And though it was against the rules to take girls to the rooms, a great many young women of all nationalities somehow found themselves in the lobby at the supper hour.

Of the officers' billets, the old Ritz Hotel on the Place Vendôme was restricted to field grade and general officers, plus representatives of the State Department and other civilian government officials. The Ritz was the quietest of all the leave hotels. For those who knew Paris well enough, the Ritz bar, which had no restrictions of rank, was a good place for cocktails in the old manner of the 1920s.

There were several other billets for officers. The nicest was the Hotel Crillon on the Place de la Concorde, just across the street from the (by then) very busy American Embassy. At the Crillon an officer who came to Paris from the front lines could soak in a hot bath for as long as he wished, get a haircut and shave at the barber shop, and go down to dinner in a gold dining room where the windows looked out on the lights and fountains of the Place de la Concorde. In an adjoining lounge a gypsy string orchestra played Strauss waltzes. To come to this luxury from the filth and horror of the lines (as many did) was not just a memorable experience of the war; it was an experience of a lifetime.

G.I. food was served at all of the leave-center hotels. It was food specially allocated by the army for such purpose, which meant that it should have been better than the fare at the average garrison mess. However, there was some indication that, between receipt of the rations by the French and service in the dining rooms, some mysterious process took place which probably helped to feed the waiters' families. Whatever it was, American soldiers on leave in Paris were always hungry.

As all the soldiers in Paris quickly learned, food and cigarettes were more valuable as currency than cash itself. Since food supplies in greater bulk than K rations were not portable, the standard medium of exchange was the cigarette package. Its purchase value fluctuated from week to week, depending on the supply, but in general the range lay between $12 and $15 a carton. Soldiers who were prepared for this circumstance brought an extra carton or two in their musette bags. In addition, the cooperative Seine Section post exchange issued a week's supply to each soldier on pass.

So widespread was the use of cigarettes for currency in Paris that certain groups, like the majority of bicycle-taxi men accepted nothing else. For a soldier to resolve not to deal in the black market made very little difference: the exchange rate of the franc was so unequal that, without the use of cigarettes, a forty-eight-hour pass in Paris cost as much as an officer's salary for two months. There is the record of one American who, in a slight alcoholic daze, ordered a round of oysters for eight comrades in a tiny restaurant on the rue Pigalle. The bill for the oysters alone was 5,000 francs ($100.00).

With a few surprising exceptions, prices were high everywhere in Paris. Because of the exchange rate they were higher for the Americans than the Parisians, but they were high for both. The average pair of woman's shoes cost 2,500 francs, or $50.00. Simple print dresses were usually about 6,000 francs. The fine dress designers, like Lanvin's and Madame Schiaparelli, charged lower rates, but they were not above accepting condensed milk in bulk or similar quantities of cocoa and chocolate in payment.

The carriage drivers demanded ten dollars for a twenty-minute ride. There were not many motor-driven taxis in Paris in 1945; they had been to some extent replaced by the bicycle-cabs. The latter consisted of a plastic and isinglass cylinder, very low-slung, in which the one or two passengers seemed—once they were inside—to be hermetically sealed. The cab was attached to a bicycle in a manner similar to that of a ricksha to its coolie. Though it was sometimes painful to watch the driver struggle through the hillier sections of Montmartre, progress was astonishingly swift along the boulevards—swift and expensive.

One of the unexpected exceptions to the high-price rule in Paris was the cost of fine perfume—provided the soldier bought it from its maker. Each morning at about eight o'clock, long lines of soldiers formed outside the main *parfumeries*— Chanel, Worth, Lanvin, Guerlain, Roget and Gallet, and others. The stores opened two hours later. As a rule only the first ten or twelve men in line received any perfume. Those who did, however, could buy such brands as Guerlain's *Rue de la Paix* for about six dollars. On the black market the price was closer to sixty.

The soldier who enjoyed sightseeing could, through the facilities of the Red Cross (which also managed the leave-center hotels), spend comparatively little during his forty-eight hours in Paris. He could join the organized groups which visited Notre Dame, the Eiffel Tower, the Louvre, Napoleon's tomb,* Sacré Coeur, the Bois and Versailles—the last-named being the rear headquarters of SHAEF. Or, if he was a good walker, he could visit those places alone. For special events, Gertrude Stein occasionally gave sober-minded G.I.s a good tongue-lashing, which at least brought her to the attention of *The Stars and Stripes*. For the intellectually venturesome it was possible to call on Picasso in that quarter of Paris which Daumier had made famous. And of course the bookstalls by the Ile de la Cité were open, offering among

---

*According to General Brereton, quoting General McAuliffe, two lads from the 101st were looking at the tomb and one said to the other, "That's one of the greatest soldiers who ever lived." The other asked, "When did that——ever jump?"

their trinkets an occasional Iron Cross or anonymous medallion plainly marked with the swastika.

But for the average American soldier on a forty-eight-hour furlough from the war, Paris meant the *rue Pigalle*. The soldiers called it "Pig Alley."

The Folies Bergère and the Bal Tabarin were in the neighborhood of rue Pigalle. Both offered stage shows which were an odd combination of beauty and eroticism, and neither had missed a performance during the German occupation. The performances ranged from songs in settings of extraordinary effectiveness, through comedy skits that were slightly off-color, to erotic dances by virtually naked men and women. As burlesques, however, both the Folies and the Bal Tabarin were considerably above the quality of their American counterparts.

"Pig Alley" itself was a street of many bars. By day it seemed drab and uninteresting; by night it was a little less drab and, on the surface of it, not much more interesting. It was only when a pair of soldiers chose one of the bars at random and ordered a few rounds of drinks that the fun began—and with it, the expenses. A good night on "Pig Alley," with enough liquor to get drunk, cost at least a hundred dollars. The incidents generally involved a fight or two, interesting offers from Frenchmen, the frank propositions of drabs and the more subtle insinuations of those who were only promiscuous, an additional round of a half-dozen more bars, and finally a dimly lit hotel on one of the crooked side-streets, where the *concierge* asked no questions.

2

But all this time the war was going on.

And suddenly, on the bright sunny morning of March 24th, hundreds of C-47s carrying the paratroopers of the 17th Airborne Division passed over the Reims area on their way to the Rhine jump in the north. Watching them go, the men of the 101st felt somehow as though they had been left out.

Three thousand, one hundred transports and gliders were in the airborne assault. The soldiers parachuted north of Wessel. At the same time the British 2nd Army and the American 9th

Army struck swiftly across the Rhine under cover of the greatest smoke screen of the war.

The drum-beat had become a roar.

South of the Ruhr, near Mainz, units of the 3rd Army crossed the Rhine on the same day, achieving such complete surprise that the crossing was made without a casualty.

Within a week there were five bridgeheads across the Rhine—all rapidly expanding. Before long, nine Allied armies were beyond the river. And the German resistance became the longed-for rout.

The Canadian 1st Army pushed east and north towards Emden and Wilhelmshaven.

The British 2nd Army swept out towards Bremen, Hamburg, Kiel.

The American 9th and 1st Armies drove into the heart of Germany.

The Ruhr was encircled.

And our regiment was alerted for a jump.

GERMANY

While the Wehrmacht crumbled, the regiment was readied in secret. This was a
mission to save lives.

49

The Mysterious Alert

Our "alert," which occurred at the very time when the war seemed close to an end, was surrounded by puzzling circumstances. In Phase One the 101st Airborne Division entrucked for Germany, leaving our regiment behind. All leaves, furloughs, and passes were cancelled. The group of men then on their way to England were stopped in the vicinity of Le Havre and sent back to Mourmelon. Another group on the Riviera were contacted by long-distance telephone (an extraordinary feat), but were temporarily stranded by the sudden withdrawal of all troop-carrier planes. Eventually, however, all the men on leave were recalled.

Phase Two was peculiar. Captain Raymond J. Gramont and Lieutenant Daniel M. Fry, both of regimental Headquarters Company, left Reims within a space of hours. Their orders, stamped *"Top Secret,"* contained only their destination. It was England. At the same time, several officers who were total strangers joined the regiment. They were engineers. If they knew why they had come to this new assignment, they offered no hint. To complete the mystery, written orders to the regiment from the 1st Allied Airborne Army confirmed the state of "alert," with the further provision that the unit should be prepared to load and take off within twelve hours of receipt of instructions.

What these things signified, no one knew. Anyone studying the operations map in the S-3 tent could see that, unless the Germans retreated to Bavaria, the war would be over in a few weeks. There were no obstacles ahead, no apparent need for airborne troops anywhere. Where, then, would we be sent?

The answer was, perhaps, the best-kept secret of the war.

Everyone sent his money home. Mortars and machine guns

were packed in bundles; personal equipment was consigned to barracks bags for overland shipment by truck. In a camp that was virtually bare, the puzzled soldiers settled down to wait.

2

On their arrival in England, Gramont and Fry were picked up by an English truck driver and driven a score of miles along a country road. The driver could answer no questions. At the end of the run, the two American officers were met by a second driver, who drove them another stage. After several of these changes, Gramont and Fry were picked up for the last time and brought to their destination, which seemed an ordinary military camp in the countryside.

This was an O.S.S. center. The camp was crowded with soldiers of all nationalities: French, Polish, Canadian, Belgian, British, Scandinavian, American.

Gramont and Fry had come to a camp where many of the special teams of wireless operators and interpreters, who had been parachuted behind enemy lines during the war, had received their training. As in the case of the Normandy campaign, some of them had been women. Many of them, operating with the underground before the arrival of Allied troops, had been shot as spies. But most had been successful, and by their effort supreme headquarters had been kept informed of troop dispositions and movements, weak points of fortifications, strategic reserves, and other aspects of enemy intelligence impossible to secure from aerial photographs.

The mission now was a different one. As the Allied armies pushed deeper and deeper into Germany, thousands of Allied prisoners of war were being liberated from the German prison camps—sometimes under conditions of unspeakable depravity. There had been occasions when the SS troops had shot or burned the prisoners wholesale, to prevent their recapture by the advancing American forces. But on other occasions, of which there had been a few, the German commandant of a prison camp had surrendered his personnel before the lines reached his camp.

It was in this connection that Gramont and Fry had been sent to England. As part of a team, they were to parachute down in the environs of camps where impending massacres were suspected. If the massacre seemed inevitable, the radio operator of the team would notify headquarters in England, and one or more battalions of American paratroopers would be dispatched to the spot.

Meanwhile, the American 1st and 9th Armies roared eastward across Germany towards the Elbe River. Russian forces drove relentlessly through Austria, Czechoslovakia and eastern Germany. The Ruhr was cut to pieces and 300,000 German soldiers surrendered. And the American prisoners of war at Hammelberg, including Lieutenant Forney, heard something they had been waiting to hear ever since their capture— the distant muttering of American artillery fire.

3

In a day or two the artillery fire was closer. Everyone in camp prayed that the Germans would not move them out.

On March 28th the unmistakable rattle of small-arms fire was audible. Still the Germans made no move.

With the group which had arrived from the north was a colonel by the name of Good. He outranked the officer in command of the Americans and—much to everybody's satisfaction—took charge.

By noon of March 28th bullets were whizzing through the camp. The American prisoners were ordered to stay inside their barracks. Soon the fire became so heavy that everyone had to lie down on the floor. Like the rest, Forney was wildly excited. This would be the end, he thought. And he still was alive.

About four o'clock in the afternoon, two American tanks broke into the compound. This ended the battle. There were no signs of the Germans. Word passed among the prisoners that everybody was to move out. Those who could still walk ran from the open compound as fast as they could go. At a little distance across the open fields were more tanks.

The situation, as Colonel Good explained it to the prisoners, was not as hopeful as they had expected. The tanks were a task force sent by General Patton. They had fought their way sixty miles through German territory to Hammelberg. The tanks could take only 400 men, and there were 1,200 in the camp. Those who could find no place on the vehicles could either take off across country or go back to the encampment.

This didn't look so promising. But the majority of the men who could find no room on the tanks did as Colonel Good suggested and took off across country. Forney found a place on a half-track where he squatted down in the shelter of the armor plate and ate part of a K ration which one of the men had given him. To his surprise, the tanks were delayed in getting started. At the end of four hours the vehicles still were parked in the quiet, open meadow by Hammelberg. Not until afterward did Forney learn the reason for the delay: the task force had come through without a plan of withdrawal.

Already the armored group had lost two tanks. Several of the wounded men were in Forney's half-track. The task force commander, who was a second lieutenant, wanted to avoid going back over the same route over which he and his men had come. His final choice of routes was to the northeast, and it was dark by the time the tanks at last coughed into movement. They moved across country through hilly fields until they came to a dirt road, which they followed until the column reached a small town and a paved highway. The tank commander led his group due east along this road at about twenty-five miles an hour, and in the first five minutes of such swift travel Forney began to feel light-headed.

Suddenly, heavy-caliber fire broke out directly ahead.

4

The first three tanks were put out of action at once. The bodies of the prisoners of war who had been riding on them were strewn around the road like spilled grain sacks. Without waiting to find out the strength of the German road block—a mission the prisoners would have been glad to undertake—the remainder of the American vehicles circled back the way they had come. At the first crossroad they attempted to detour. They were hit again.

After circling back twice, the column was only about five miles from Hammelberg. Casualties had been so heavy by this time that the tank commander drew his vehicles into the concealment of a wood by a deserted farmhouse on a hilltop. Colonel Good called the former prisoners of war together.

"I'm only nominally in command of you," he told them, "and from here on you're on your own. You can do one of three things. You can stay with the tanks and fight it out with them—if they can arm you. You can take off across country. Or you can go back to the camp."

Nobody said anything.

"In my opinion," said the colonel, "your chances of getting back to our lines are about a hundred to one. I think this tank group will get knocked out."

"What are you going to do?" asked somebody.

"I'm going back to Hammelberg," said Colonel Good.

Going back to Hammelberg was the last thing in the world that Forney or any of the other prisoners wanted to do. Forney was absolutely certain that if they returned they would be shot. But he had a great deal of respect for Colonel Good's judgment. He watched some of the prisoners take off through the darkness alone, or in pairs. He listened to the arguments of those who were going to stay with the tanks. And at daybreak he joined the column of men who started back to the prison camp.

From somewhere came two flags—one American, the other white. Colonel Good carried one of them, and the other was carried by a colonel named Waters, who was General Patton's brother-in-law.

The dejected Americans were bitterly critical. Scores of their comrades who had lived through months of imprisonment were dead. Scores more would certainly be dead before the apparently stupid attempt was finished. Four or five tanks had been lost already; the remainder would certainly be destroyed by nightfall. And as for themselves, they would probably be shot.

But they were not shot. Before they had left the camp, the German commandant, who thought that the American advance had reached him, had asked for and received from Colonel Good a promise of protection for his family and himself. When the prisoners marched back into the familiar and depressing compound, they were simply locked inside their barracks. That night most of the men from the armored task force were brought in as prisoners—the Germans having attacked them in the forest before they could deploy. The remainder of the men were dead; and subsequently it was learned that, of all the prisoners who had set off across country on their own, none had reached the American lines.

The time was not yet.

5

Meanwhile, the mystified paratroopers around Mourmelon remained on the alert, watching Sergeant Suarez move the red lines on the situation map deeper and deeper into Germany.

During this rather uneasy period, General Brereton and the immediate staff of the 1st Allied Airborne Army lunched at the officers' mess of the regiment with Colonel Ballard. Music was played over a loudspeaker system installed by the communications section, and, much to the amusement of everybody (except possibly Colonel Ballard), the program included one familiar piece in which the singer screamed over and over again: "I LOVE LIFE! I LOVE LIFE! I DON'T WANNA DIE!" The general ate his way through this heart-rending appeal with a poker face.

Meanwhile, General Mark Clark's spring offensive had taken his troops to Bologna. From there, 5th and 8th Army units, eager after a long winter of inaction, roared up across the Po Valley in pursuit of the rapidly disintegrating German 10th and 14th Armies. On April 29th, the first formal surrender of a German army since the Allies had landed on the shores of Europe took place at Caserta, where two enemy generals in civilian clothes, without authority from their own government, surrendered 600,000 men of the southern German forces, and 250,000 SS and security troops in northern Italy and western Austria.

Russian and American troops met on the banks of the Elbe. Huge numbers of German soldiers, denied the privilege of formal surrender to the two more generous of their three enemies—Britain and America—were achieving the same result by informal wholesale surrenders on the field of battle. The American soldiers witnessed the curious spectacle of regiments, divisions and entire corps migrating westward for the honor of becoming American prisoners. On April 30th, the day after the surrender at Caserta, Radio Hamburg, still in enemy hands, made what it termed a "grave and important announcement":

"It is reported from the Fuehrer's headquarters that our Fuehrer, Adolf Hitler, fighting to the last breath against Bolshevism, fell for Germany this afternoon in his operational headquarters in the Reich Chancellery."

Still, no one quite believed it. And doubt persisted until, on May 2nd, French troops, free to move after the surrender in Italy, pushed forward without resistance into the famed redoubt of Berchtesgaden. And Hitler wasn't there.

On the afternoon of April 29th, at a German prison camp named Musberg, Lieutenant Forney and the other American prisoners heard, once again, the sound of small-arms fire. This time there was no doubt of liberation. Within an hour two American tanks had broken into the compound. They brought the front line with them, and as they clanked to a halt in the center of the street, they were surrounded by waving, screaming, crying American prisoners, hysterical with joy.

Lieutenant Forney, trying to keep a grip on himself, accepted a K ration from one of the armored men. When he had finished it he became deathly sick. But he recovered that night, and the next day, in company with the other men, he was flown back to a hospital in Reims. What had begun in the Bois Jacques of the Ardennes on a snowy day in January, 1945, came to an end in France ten days before the close of the war.

6

Berlin had fallen. The *Wehrmacht* was in fragments. All the northern armies had surrendered to General Montgomery. All the southern armies had disintegrated. Two million German troops had given up for four days.

And one hot, sunny morning in Reims, a few soldiers on pass from our regiment noticed a crowd of military police around the entrance to the red-brick schoolhouse that was the forward headquarters of SHAEF. From across the street the paratroopers watched a pair of tight-lipped, arrogant German naval officers mount the steps swiftly and disappear inside.

That was all they could see. They turned away, winking at a pretty French girl.

But much later that night, when the lamps in the windows of the houses had blinked out, and the streets echoed back only the whispered snufflings of homeless dogs, and over the battlefields of an earlier world war lay a starry blue haze, one of the naval officers in a room at SHAEF rose to his feet.

"With this signature the German people and the German forces are, for better or worse, delivered into the victor's hands. . . ."

The distant drum was still.

EPILOGUE

From the small mountain stream at the bottom of the valley it is a climb to the main level of the town. Where the air is quiet there is a fragrance of wild flowers, and up to the very last turn of the road the climber can hear the slip and chuckle of the stream below. Set under the bushes along the way is a very old shrine to Mary and the Christ Child. Moss has grown over the wood.

At the top of the hill the road forks. One way leads past a four-story hotel of white stone and glass. If you are thirsty after the climb you can stop there for a stein of beer or a glass of cold *Liebfraumilch*. The drinks are served on a terrace, under beach umbrellas, where, in the evening, there are piano and violin concertos by starlight, and one can watch the moon rise over the snowy peak of the Vatzmann, twenty miles across the valley.

Follow the road to the right. It dips, like a slack rope, by a small park. There are scores of children. Like the young women, they are almost all blond. The girls are tanned a rich gold-brown which makes you think of wheat fields in the summertime. They wear flowered skirts and loose blouses, and if you look at them directly they will meet your eye.

There are art shops on the main street of town. Where there are no art shops, the walls themselves are painted. Above the archways on the square by the old palace is a fresco of Christ on the Cross, and around Him the heroic figures of the common people: laborers, farmers and soldiers. There is a little memorial to the war dead in the cool, sweet-smelling hallway of the church—a Christian cross supporting a helmet—and beneath it banks of wild flowers.

The houses are tinted pastel. Balconies lean over the narrow, crowded streets. Everywhere there is the clatter of life: of carts bringing families from the country, of bicycle riders, of sandals slip-slopping on the cobblestones. There is a tailor shop; there is a barber shop; there is a camera store; in another park there is a small motion-picture theater.

The hill road leads out of town, past the cemetery and the Catholic church, and overlooks the valley. Below is the other half of the town. It stands by the junction of two mountain streams. The railroad line from the north comes to an end at this point, but you can follow with your eyes where the tracks run out along the valley, adjoining the slate-colored river. The high snow mountains are all around. The clouds which make showers in the valley only make the snows deeper on those peaks. In the morning the mountains are violet and in the evening they are rose; by starlight they are as cool and remote as the firmament itself.

One of the streams that meet in the village is fed from a blue lake, about two miles away. Around the lake the snow mountains drop down in sheer stone cliffs, as they do at the *fjords* of Norway. There are boats for hire. There is also an electric launch which slips noiselessly out to the extreme end of the waterway, while the old boatman, who wears short pants and a hunting vest, blows a tin horn to demonstrate the echoes, and runs his vessel close to the waterfalls. At the far end of the lake there is a spit of land, and on it a small church dedicated to Saint Bartholomew, where the silence by the altar is so deep that one can hear the waterfalls a mile away.

This is where they thought he would be hiding.

This is Berchtesgaden.

For two months after the close of hostilities in Europe our regiment, with the 101st Airborne Division, occupied the area of Berchtesgaden, where we lived in the rich Bavarian living quarters of former SS troops. Towards the end we went to Linzen, in Austria, where we were on the border of Russian-occupied territory. In the latter part of August all the men of the division who were eligible to go home were assigned to the regiment, and, with Colonel Ballard still in command, entrained from Germany to Bar-le-Duc, France, a lonesome yellow town by a milk-white canal. Eventually, we were moved south to Marseilles and on August 8, 1945, we sailed for the United States.

The job was done.

Twice before in this story I have had to admit inability to convey a state of mind. The first of such references was during the long gloomy winter before the invasion of Normandy. The second was the state of mind, or, more strictly speaking, the state of being, of the soldier under fire. The first I attempted to suggest; the second I could only remark. But there was yet a third, of which I have made no mention at all. It was our state of mind when the firing ceased in Europe.

We had hated the war much more deeply than we had expected. Between the days of high spirits at Camp Toccoa to the sunny, quiet, mid-summer warmth of Berchtesgaden there had been, for almost all of us, experiences of horror endurable only if the heart steeled itself against kindliness, against hope, against life itself. There had been moments of bitterness so dark that, to survive, we could do nothing except go on. We had had to shut our minds against all that justified our presence here on earth and exist as the outer shells of human kind, devoid of pride, devoid of love, devoid even of faith and hope. Of modern war, nothing can be said in mitigation.

With the end of the fighting we expected these emotions to subside. And in a sense they did. But they were succeeded for a brief period by a feeling we had never known before.

Let me see if I can put it down:

During the first weeks after the end of the fighting I flew by C-47 from Salzberg to Paris. My plane was piloted by two young Americans whose names I did not ask. They were in their early twenties. Their navigation was casual—it is termed pilotage in the Air Forces—and anyone watching over their shoulders could tell that Europe had become as familiar to them, in terms of bomb-pitted fields and terra-cotta ruins, as the pleasant farmlands, the clean villages and the long white roads of home. The copilot, with a map across his knees, followed the course with his forefinger and only glanced down now and then at the silver Rhine, the shell craters slowly filling with green water, the silent, deserted gun batteries of the enemy.

It was not peace. It was only silence. And in that silence there was something strange. . . .

In Paris the great flags of the United Nations hung, unfurled, beneath the Arc de Triomphe, over the light of the Unkown—and, it sometimes seemed, eternal—Soldier. Overhead roared B-24s and B-17s, their pilots taking the ground crews on tours of the destruction in the Ruhr valley. And while I watched, one pilot, flying low over the Champs Elysées, coming straight as an arrow from the Place de la Concorde, dipped his wings in thunderous salute as he passed the arch.

But the Frenchmen on the streets below did not look up.

The crowds of men and women along the great boulevards walked slowly, silently, as though dazed and going in a dream. The American soldiers talked in subdued voices or did not talk at all. Everywhere there was a strange oppression. And in the occasional skips and hops of the little children, who had not yet recovered from the great excitement of the day of victory, and who still carried tricolors in their hands—in the sight of this childish joy there was something unmistakably obscene.

There it was. . . . That was it.

For this strange state of mind which fell upon us for a little while after the guns had been silenced was a vague sense of obscenity. It was the faint, lingering aftertaste of having achieved something monstrous. We had unleashed powers beyond our comprehension. Entire countries lay in waste beneath our hands—and, in the doing of it, our hands were forever stained. It was of no avail to tell ourselves that what we had done was what we had had to do, the only thing we could have done. It was enough to know that we had done it. We had turned the evil of our enemies back upon them a hundredfold, and, in so doing, something of our own integrity had been shattered, had been irrevocably lost.

We who had fought this war could feel no pride. Victors and vanquished, all were one. We were one with the crowds moving silently along the boulevards of Paris; the old women hunting through the still ruins of Cologne; the bodies piled like yellow cordwood at Dachau; the dreadful vacant eyes of the beaten German soldiers; the white graves and the black crosses and the haunting melancholy of our hearts. All, all, were one, all were the ghastly horror of what we had known, of what we had helped to do. . . .

Face it when you close this book.

We did.

Appendix

Casualties of the 101st Airborne Division

1,731 killed in action
5,584 wounded in action
273 missing in action

*(Preliminary figures—Report of the
Commanding General, AGF,
to the Chief of Staff,
USA, 10 Jan. 1946.)*

American and Foreign Citations
501st Parachute Infantry Regiment

United States of America

BATTLE HONORS. . . . In the name of the President of the United States as public evidence of deserved honor and distinction . . . the *501 Parachute Infantry Regiment* is cited for extraordinary heroism and outstanding performance of duty in action in the initial assault on the northern coast of Normandy, France. In the early morning of 6 June 1944, the *501st Parachute Infantry Regiment* descended by parachute in the swamps in the vicinity of Carentan, France. Widely dispersed during the descent, the regiment suffered heavy casualties from determined enemy resistance. Small groups assembled whenever possible and fought their way to the assembly area. En route, many enemy strong points and pill boxes were liquidated through acts of gallantry and disregard of self by individuals of the regiment. According to the plans the bridges and crossings of the Douve River were seized and held in the face of heavy enemy fire. This prevented the enemy from bringing up reinforcements to prevent the beach landing of the assault forces of the VII Corps. The determination and gallantry of the *501st Parachute Infantry Regiment* protected the south flank of the VII Corps, enabled a rapid inland advance of the assault troops and assured the establishment of the Allied beachhead in France.

WAR DEPARTMENT GENERAL ORDERS No. 4, 1945

BATTLE HONORS. . . . The following unit is cited by the War Department . . . in the name of the President of the United States as public evidence of deserved honor and distinction. The citation reads as follows:

101st Airborne Division . . . with the following-attached units: . . . *501st Parachute Infantry Regiment* . . .

These units distinguished themselves in combat against powerful and aggressive enemy forces composed of elements of eight German divisions during the period from 18 to 27 December 1944 by extraordinary heroism and gallantry in defense of the key communications center of Bastogne, Belgium. Essential to a large scale exploitation of his breakthrough into Belgium and northern Luxembourg, the enemy attempted to seize Bastogne by attacking constantly and savagely with the best of his armor and infantry. Without benefit of prepared defenses, facing almost overwhelming odds and with very limited and fast-dwindling supplies, these units maintained a high combat morale and an impenetrable defense despite extremely heavy bombing, intense artillery fire, and constant attack from infantry and armor on all sides of their completely cut-off and encircled position. This masterful and grimly determined defense denied the enemy even momentary success in an operation for which he paid dearly in men, matériel, and eventually morale. The outstanding courage, resourcefulness, and undaunted determination of this gallant force are in keeping with the highest traditions of the service.

WAR DEPARTMENT GENERAL ORDERS No. 17, 1945

France

Decision Number 367

The President of the Provisional Government of the French Republic
Cites to the,

ORDER OF THE ARMY

501st Parachute Infantry Regiment

A splendid airborne unit which gave proof of extraordinary heroism in the course of the Normandy landing operations on 6 to 8 June 1944. It parachuted before dawn on the assault beach on 6 June and in spite of all sorts of difficulties, succeeded in regrouping. Attacked by important forces with violent fire, it nevertheless occupied positions of strategic importance for the landing of friendly troops. This action opened the way to La Douve and the Carentan road for the assault troops. In this way it greatly contributed to the first phase of the liberation of France.

This citation includes the award of the Croix de Guerre with palm.

Paris 22 July 1946
Signed: BIDAULT

Holland

MINISTERIAL DECREE OF THE NETHERLANDS MINISTER OF WAR, dated 20 September 1945, Section A I, Secret No. P 203.

THE MINISTER OF WAR:

CONSIDERING, that the outstanding performance of duty of the

101st AIRBORNE DIVISION, UNITED STATES ARMY

during the airborne operations and the ensuing fighting action in the southern part of the NETHERLANDS in the period from 17 September to 28 November 1944, has greatly contributed to the liberation of that part of the country;

CONSIDERING also, that it is desirable for each member of the division who took part in the aforesaid operations, to possess a lasting memento of this glorious struggle;

DECREES:

That each member of the personnel of the 101st AIRBORNE DIVISION, UNITED STATES ARMY, who took part in the operations in the southern part of the Netherlands in the period of 17 September to 28 November 1944, is authorized to wear the Orange Lanyard, as laid down in article 123g of the clothing regulations 1944 of the Royal Netherlands Army.

CAPTAIN RODILAS
J.G. v.d. Glas.

Belgium

THE MINISTER OF NATIONAL DEFENSE has the honour to inform the Commanding General of the 101st Airborne Division that, by order No. 1196 of His Royal Highness The Prince Regent, dated 22 October 1945, the 101st Airborne Division and attached units comprised of:

501st PARACHUTE INFANTRY

. . . . .

are cited twice in the Order of the Day of the Belgian Army with the award of THE FOURRAGERE 1940.

The 101st Airborne Division, U. S. Army, landing by parachute, glider and assault craft on the coast of France, 6 June 1944, was one of the first units to attack the enemy in the campaign that was to liberate Europe from German domination. It was necessary for small groups to battle fiercely in many places in order that they might reach and unite at the assembly point. Many casualties were inflicted upon the enemy and many casualties were sustained by the division while it subdued enemy strongpoints, attacked and held vital communication centers, bridges and observation posts. The success with which these missions were accomplished hindered the enemy from using reinforcements which could have caused the failure of the landing of the VII U. S. Corps, which later participated in the liberation of Belgium.''

THE MINISTER OF NATIONAL DEFENSE has the honour to inform the Commanding General of the 101st Airborne Division that, by order No. 828 of His Royal Highness The Prince Regent, dated 30 July 1945, his division is cited in the Order of the Day of the Belgian Army with the award of the CROIX DE GUERRE 1940, with palm, for:

''By its splendid resistance from the 22 to the 27 of December, 1944, in the most arduous fighting in the Battle of the Ardennes, where it held, completely isolated, the key position of Bastogne, the 101st Airborne Division, U. S. Army, with attached units foiled the enemy's plans which required a complete penetration of Belgium, and served as a pivot for the Allied counter offensive which liberated the invaded territories. During these defensive operations, by their courage, their endurance, their discipline, and the knowledge of the use of their weapons, repulsing the incessant attacks led by elements of eight German divisions, in spite of the shortages of food and material, these troops and their leaders have written one of the most glorious pages of military history, and have acquired, along with the admiration of the world, the everlasting gratitude of Belgium.

The 501st parachute Infantry has a record of achievement extending from the shores of Normandy to the mountain fastness of Berchtesgaden. From the moment when the regiment first met the enemy in the early dawn of June 6, 1944, until the close of hostilities, its soldiers enjoyed an unbroken succession of victories. Twice decorated with the Presidential Unit Citation, the regiment has been honored beyond the lot which fell to most of our fighting units. It is an honor to have belonged to such a unit; it is an honor to have commanded such a unit.

> MAJOR GENERAL MAXWELL D. TAYLOR,
> *Supertintendent,*
> *United States Military Academy.*
> *Former Commander, 101st Airborne Division.*

WAR BOOKS
FROM JOVE

08578-2	AIR WAR SOUTH ATLANTIC Jeffrey Ethell and Alfred Price	$3.50
08297-X	BATAAN: THE MARCH OF DEATH Stanley L. Falk	$3.50
08477-8	THE BATTLE OF LEYTE GULF Edwin P. Hoyt	$3.95
08674-6	BLOODY WINTER John M. Waters	$3.95
07294-X	THE DEVIL'S VIRTUOSOS David Downing	$2.95
07297-4	HITLER'S WEREWOLVES Charles Whiting	$2.95
07134-X	DAS REICH Max Hastings	$3.50
08695-9	THE SECRET OF STALINGRAD Walter Kerr	$3.50
07427-6	U-BOATS OFFSHORE Edwin P. Hoyt	$2.95
08341-0	THE BATTLE OF THE HUERTGEN FOREST Charles B. MacDonald	$3.50
08236-8	WAKE ISLAND Duane Schultz	$2.95
08887-0	PATTON'S BEST Nat Frankel and Larry Smith	$3.50
07393-8	SIEGFRIED: THE NAZIS' LAST STAND Charles Whiting	$3.50
09030-1	A DISTANT CHALLENGE Edited by Infantry Magazine	$3.50
08054-3	INFANTRY IN VIETNAM Albert N. Garland, U.S.A. (ret.)	$3.50
08365-8	HITLER MUST DIE! Herbert Molloy Mason, Jr.	$3.95
08810-2	LITTLE SHIP, BIG WAR: THE SAGA OF DE343 Commander Edward P. Stafford, U.S.N. (ret.)	$3.95
08253-8	WE LED THE WAY William O. Darby and William H. Baumer	$3.50
08474-3	GUADALCANAL Edwin P. Hoyt	$3.50
08513-8	PANZER ARMY AFRICA James Lucas	$3.50
08682-7	THE END OF THE JAPANESE IMPERIAL NAVY Masanori Ito	$3.50
07737-2	48 HOURS TO HAMMELBURG Charles Whiting	$2.95
07733-X	THE INCREDIBLE 305th Wilbur Morrison	$2.95
08066-7	THE KAMIKAZES Edwin P. Hoyt	$3.50
07618-X	KASSERINE PASS Martin Blumenson	$3.50
08624-X	NIGHT DROP: THE AMERICAN AIRBORNE INVASION OF NORMANDY S.L.A. Marshall	$3.95